viva l'italia

First published in 2002 by New Holland Publishers (NZ) Ltd
Auckland • Sydney • London • Cape Town

218 Lake Road, Northcote, Auckland, New Zealand
14 Aquatic Drive, Frenchs Forest, NSW 2086, Australia
86 Edgware Road, London W2 2EA, United Kingdom
80 McKenzie Street, Cape Town 8001, South Africa

www.newhollandpublishers.com

Copyright © 2002 in text: Julie Biuso
Copyright © 2002 in photography: Ian Batchelor
Copyright © 2002 New Holland Publishers (NZ) Ltd

ISBN: 1 877246 87 5

Publishing Manager: Renée Lang
Cover and design: Christine Hansen
Editor: Barbara Nielsen

10 9 8 7 6 5 4 3 2 1

Colour reproduction by Colourscan (Singapore)
Produced by Phoenix Offset, Hong Kong

All rights reserved. No part of this publication may be reproduced, stored in a retrieval system, or transmitted in any form or by any means, electronic, mechanical, photocopying, recording or otherwise, without the prior permission of the publishers and copyright holders.
  While the publishers and author have made every effort to ensure that the information and instructions in this book are accurate and safe, they cannot accept liability for any resulting injury or loss or damage to property whether direct or consequential.

viva l'italia

Julie Biuso

photography by Ian Batchelor

NEW HOLLAND

cont

ents

INTRODUCTION	6
LET'S BEGIN THE FEAST	8
LONG, LEISURELY LUNCH DISHES	24
A FOOD FOR ALL SEASONS	48
WICKEDLY GOOD WAYS WITH FISH, FOWL & MEAT	72
VEGETABLES TO INSPIRE	100
SERIOUSLY GOOD SWEETS	118
WEIGHTS & MEASURES	140
INDEX	142

introd

When I left New Zealand in 1975 to travel on an Italian passenger liner headed for Genova, Italy, my knowledge of Italian food was limited. Yes, I'd read about polenta, but I'd never sifted it through my fingers and smelled its raw corn fragrance. I'd made risotto with short grain rice because that was all I could get. I had no idea how to procure turkey breasts without having to buy a whole bird. Rocket was a thing you sent to the moon, and parmesan, sold in canisters, smelt of old socks. Olive oil was in limited supply, mainly available from chemists, and 'extra virgin' always drew forth lewd comments.

I'd avidly read Elizabeth David's passionate accounts of travelling through Italy and I knew there was a feast for the mind and the body awaiting me. But the food on the boat did little to live up to that dream or to increase my knowledge of Italian cuisine. I was acutely aware that the smells coming out of the officers' dining room were far more tantalising than those circling the dining room where I ate the economy fare with the other second-class passengers.

It wasn't until I set foot in Italy and tasted authentic Italian food that my heart started to flutter with excitement. Every day was a journey of discovery. The markets, the way the people chose produce, the attention they gave to ripeness and freshness, the smells wafting in the streets every day around lunchtime – it was all a visual and odoriferous awakening. Watching discerning shoppers skirting their way around the stalls, looking for the freshest and best buy, and eavesdropping on their conversations with the produce sellers was an eye-opener. It was hard not to be seduced, and I didn't resist, I just surrendered with an open mouth and tried everything offered to me, searching out new food at every opportunity.

I was lucky to be welcomed into an Italian family of good cooks, and many of the recipes in this book are dishes direct from the kitchen of my late mother-in-law Mamma Rosa, or from her daughters, Margot and Marcella, and her daughter-in-law Isanna. Mamma Rosa was a great cook, there's no doubt about it, and to learn, all you had to do was turn up in the kitchen around 10am and watch the action. The kitchen, even in summer when it was as hot as a furnace, was a magnet, and everyone made their way there several times during the morning to lift lids on pots, sniff, stir and comment. Everyone had an opinion about food. Everyone talked about food, all day and all night! No sooner had lunch been finished and cleared away, than supper would be discussed and a shopping list drawn up for the second meal of the day.

This was all part of my Italian education, which went some way to forming a palette of smells, colours, tastes and textures in my senses that is so ingrained now that just a whiff of the clove-like scent of basil, a hint in the air of rosemary and garlic emitting their resinous

uction

pungent smells as they fuse, or just a faint waft of tomatoes reducing down to a sauce, transports me back to the markets, to the kitchens, and into the lives of the generous-spirited Italians I have met.

All these smells and tastes that pierce the senses are so Italian, and yet over time I have learnt that there is no such thing as 'Italian cuisine'. It remains regional, in spite of globalisation. The rich foods of Emilia-Romagna, where butter and cream are used lavishly, and fresh pasta is favoured over dried, are vastly different to the earthy simplicity of Tuscan cooking, which features grills, roasts and vegetables, flavoured with little more than a dusting of salt and a dousing of extra virgin olive oil. Yet these two regions share a border many kilometres long.

The defining characteristic of the food of Italy is the clarity of flavour and texture, whether it is a bracing sauce that stimulates the tastebuds, or one of such softness and balance that your palate feels as if it is cushioned in velvet. Every ingredient is used for a reason, forming an integral part of the flavour of the dish. Things are not thrown in willy-nilly, just for the sake of it, or to bulk up the quantity. You'll find the majority of Italian recipes have a short ingredients list. The uninitiated or the critic could find that certain dishes are too powerful, flavours too potent, and that some dishes lack subtlety. But this is the very backbone of the cuisine, giving it vibrancy and an assertive character.

Do you remember your first sight and taste of pesto? Or the first time you dug a fork into a bowl of spaghetti laced with a handful of chopped raw garlic and crushed chilli, dripping fruity, grassy-tasting extra virgin olive oil? The first furry-boned anchovy that dissolved into salty morsels on your tongue? The shock of the bitterness of radicchio? And was there a time you were made speechless and your eyes watered when a slosh of vinegar poured into a sizzling pan of food took your breath away? This is a cuisine that leaps out at you and assaults your senses. But it has a flipside, those extravagant dishes enriched with cream and mountains of parmigiano reggiano. Fearless cooking! Cooking for flavour, texture, taste and nourishment, for satisfaction, satiation, and dare I say it, greed!

'Keep it simple' is the essence of Italian cooking. The other points are obvious: fresh, seasonal food, don't skimp on the oil (it's there for a reason), season food generously with salt (yep!), and taste as you go along. Be generous in the best Italian spirit. Put on some music, whack up the volume, invite friends and family over, get stuck into the kitchen and cook up a storm. You'll be loved for it!

You'll find many classic recipes in this book – dishes which have endured and deserve their place. Some I've made dozens and dozens of times and I still love them. And then there are my more recent discoveries. I hope they all bring to you as much joy and satisfaction as they have to me and my family and friends.

let's begin

PARMIGIANO WAFERS	10
PARMIGIANO WITH ROCKET LEAVES	10
FRIED ASPARAGUS	12
MINESTRA	12
MINESTRONE	15
MUSHROOM SOUP	16
BORLOTTI AND TUNA SALAD	17
BRODETTO	18
STEAMED MUSSELS WITH BASIL DRESSING	20
MOZZARELLA AND ROASTED RED PEPPER SALAD	22

slivers of piquant parmigiano

curls of creamy sweet prosciutto

a pungent drizzle of estate olive oil

the heady whiff of basil

a coastal treat of plump mussels

the feast

wafer thin PARMIGIANO WAFERS

SERVES UP TO 10 AS NIBBLES

250g parmesan (parmigiano reggiano) cheese

Grate the cheese coarsely on a box grater. Put small mounds of cheese on a baking tray lined with a teflon baking sheet or baking paper (cook 6 at a time). Cook for 4–5 minutes in an oven preheated to 210°C, or until the cheese has melted and is lightly golden; don't overcook. Leave the cheese wafers for 30–40 seconds to settle, then lift them off with a knife, curling them over as you do so; they will go their own way to some extent, forming interesting shapes, but the idea is to make a shape into which you can put other ingredients. Cool the wafers on a rack, then store them airtight until required (they can be made several hours in advance).

Fill them with one of the following: a small cube of fresh juicy pear; a scoop of pepper jelly or quince jelly; a small curl of prosciutto.

TEFLON BAKING SHEETS

A sheet of teflon put on top of a baking tray will prevent food sticking.

Absolutely nothing sticks to it – not even meringues or caramelised roasted tomatoes. After use, the teflon sheet is washed in hot, soapy water, rinsed and dried, then stored for future use. They last for years providing you don't cut on them. If not available, use non-stick baking paper.

clever PARMIGIANO WITH ROCKET LEAVES

SERVES 4

2–3 good handfuls of rocket leaves, washed, dried and torn into bite-sized pieces
slab of parmesan (parmigiano reggiano) cheese
extra virgin olive oil

Put the rocket leaves on a serving platter. Shave the parmesan cheese into curls with a potato peeler and arrange on top of the rocket leaves. Drizzle with extra virgin olive oil and serve immediately.

A CLEVER DISH. A few snippets of peppery rocket leaves strewn on a plate, topped with curls of piquant parmesan cheese, drizzled with extra virgin olive oil (mortgage your house to buy the best available). Delicious!

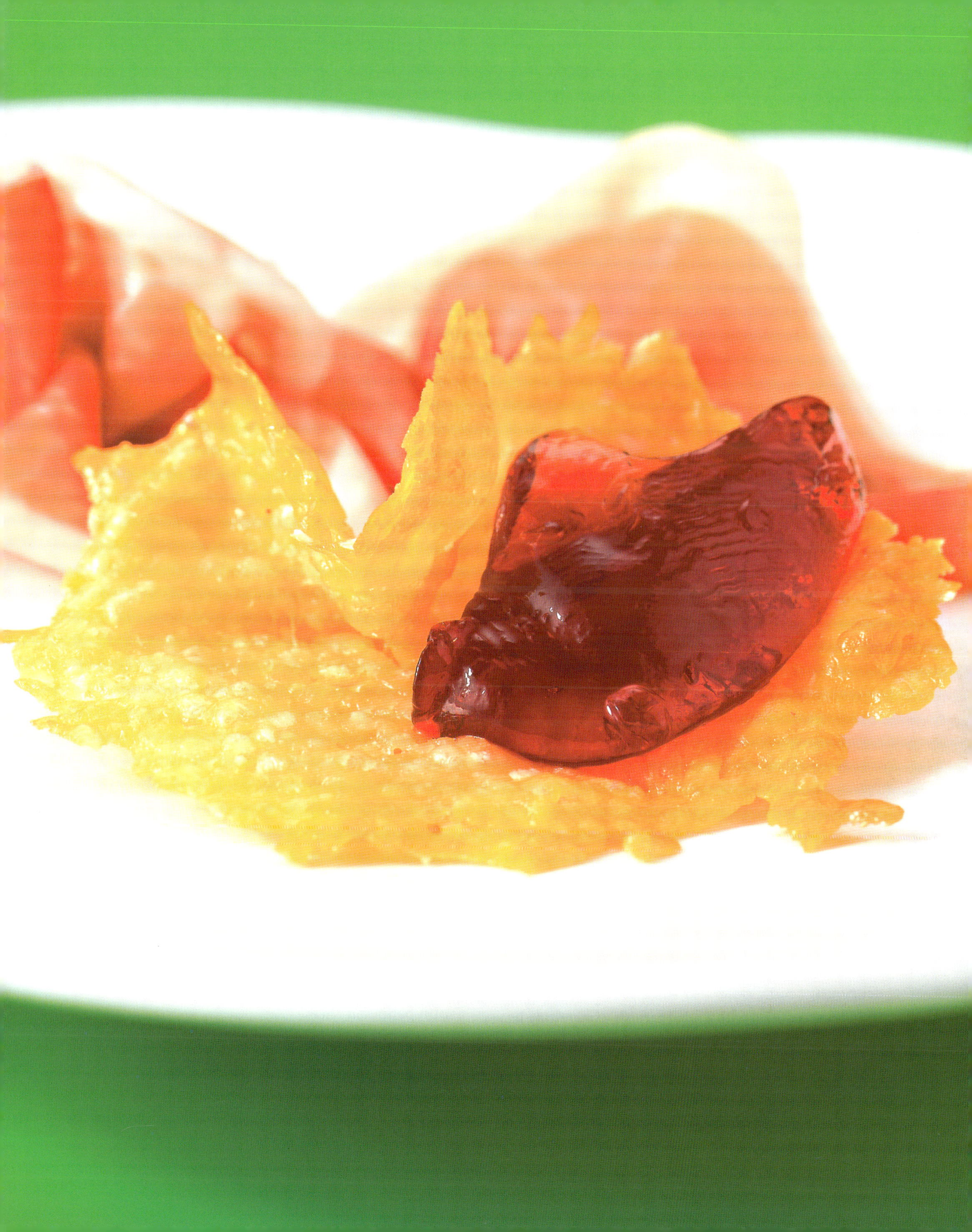

golden & crusty FRIED ASPARAGUS

SERVES 4 AS A STARTER

2 small eggs
salt
freshly ground black pepper to taste
freshly grated nutmeg
500g stubby asparagus spears, trimmed and washed
½ cup fine dry breadcrumbs, preferably homemade (see page 74)
3 tablespoons freshly grated parmesan (parmigiano reggiano) cheese, plus extra for serving
olive oil for frying

Break the eggs into a shallow dish. Whisk in ¼ teaspoon of salt, plenty of black pepper and some nutmeg. Let the egg mixture settle for 10 minutes, then beat it together again (the salt thins the eggs, making it easier to coat the asparagus). Add the asparagus and shake the dish to coat the spears with the beaten egg.

Spread the breadcrumbs on a clean piece of brown paper, or on a large plate and mix the parmesan cheese and ½ teaspoon of salt through them. Have ready a large heavy-based frying pan with olive oil to a depth of 5mm set over a medium-high heat. When the oil is hot, drain the asparagus of excess egg and transfer to the breadcrumbs. Coat each spear evenly with the crumbs (one by one) and lower them carefully into the hot oil (cook about 8 at a time).

Fry the spears until they are golden, then carefully turn and cook the second side. Transfer to a plate lined with crumpled brown paper (or absorbent kitchen paper) to drain. Transfer to a serving plate, sprinkle with a little extra parmesan cheese and serve immediately.

YOU'VE PROBABLY had asparagus every which way except coated in parmesan cheese and fried! These are so deliciously scrumptious that you'd better make plenty. If you like, serve them with a salad garnish – interesting leaves garnished with extra virgin olive oil, lemon juice, salt and pepper.

sip it MINESTRA

SERVES 6

1 tablespoon olive oil
1 onion, finely sliced
2 cloves garlic, crushed
1 tablespoon finely chopped fresh marjoram (or 1 teaspoon dried marjoram)
2 carrots, diced
2 stalks celery, finely sliced
70ml water
1 large new potato, peeled and diced
200g (1 ½ cups) peeled, chopped pumpkin, seeds removed
1 ½ teaspoons salt
3 litres water
½ small cauliflower, broken into small florets
small bunch of spinach, trimmed and chopped
1 tablespoon finely chopped parsley
freshly grated parmesan (parmigiano reggiano) cheese for serving

Put the olive oil in a large saucepan with the onion and garlic. Cover with a lid and cook gently for about 7 minutes or until soft but not coloured. Add the marjoram, carrots and celery and first measure of water. Bring to the boil, cover with a lid and cook gently for 5 minutes.

Add the potato, pumpkin, salt and second measure of water. Bring to the boil, partially cover with a lid and cook for 20 minutes.

Add the cauliflower, spinach and parsley and cook for another 15 minutes, or until the vegetables are tender. Serve with parmesan cheese.

THIS IS AN easily made vegetable soup with a clear broth. The vegetables are cooked until they are just tender and retain colour and texture. The overall effect is a tasty, uncomplicated soup.

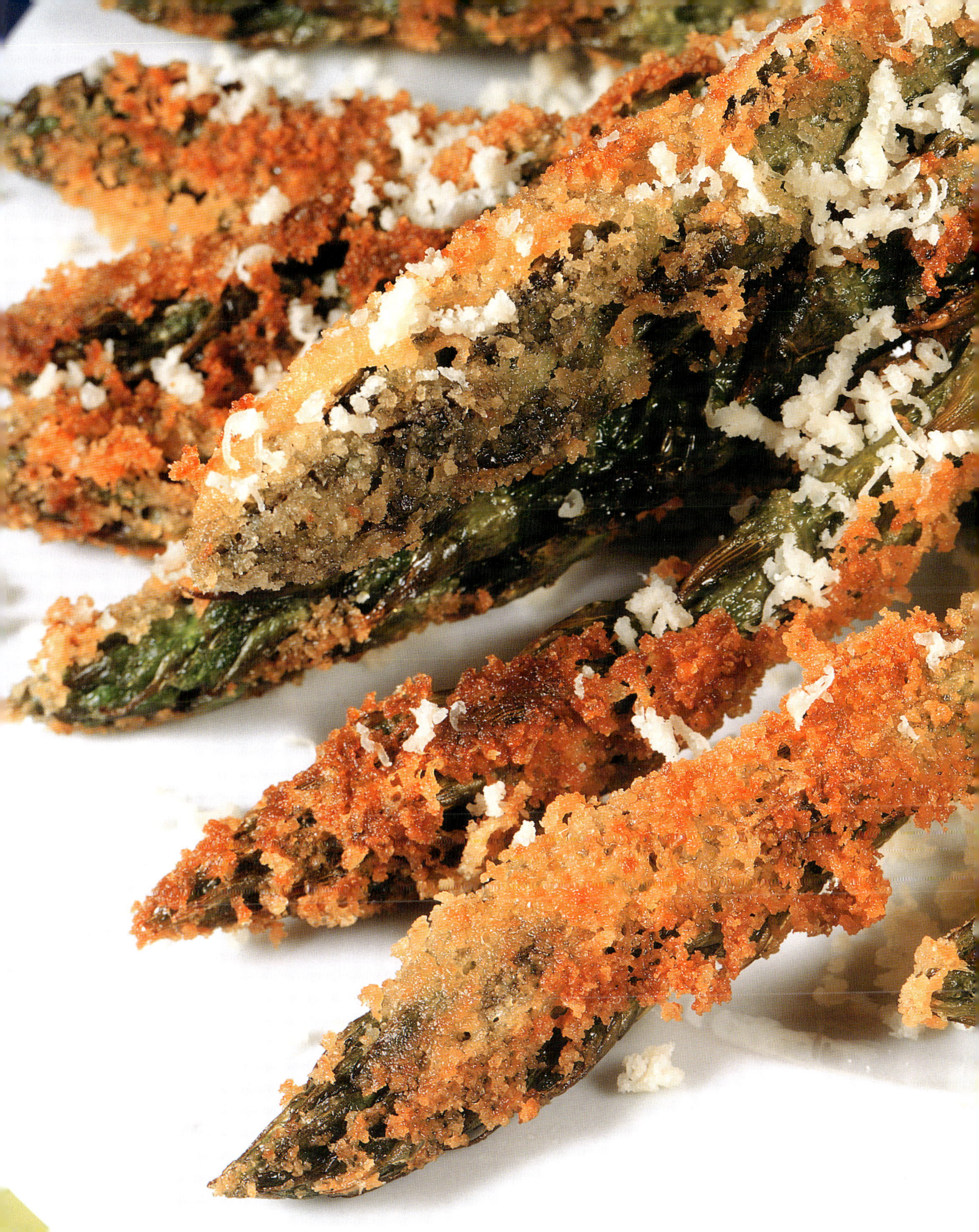

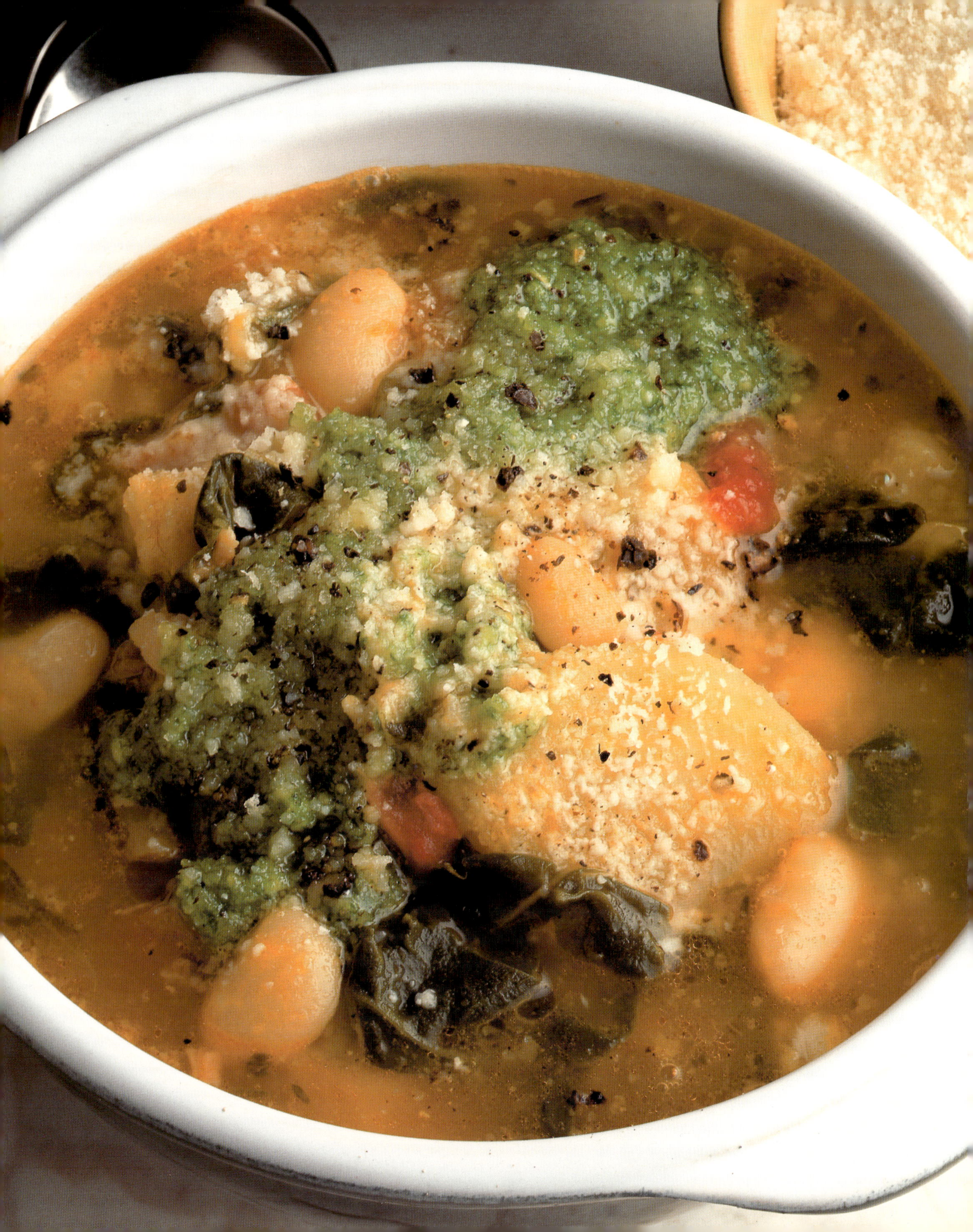

lifesaver MINESTRONE

SERVES 10

150g small, dried white beans, soaked overnight in cold water
3 tablespoons olive oil
2 medium onions, finely chopped
2 large cloves garlic, crushed
150g bacon, rind removed, finely chopped (optional)
1 tablespoon finely chopped fresh marjoram (or 1 teaspoon dried marjoram)
1 teaspoon finely chopped fresh thyme (or 1/2 teaspoon dried thyme)
400g can Italian tomatoes, mashed
3 litres stock (use light stock, or vegetable water, or 1 stock cube dissolved in water)
2 carrots, peeled and finely sliced
2 stalks celery, finely sliced
2 medium potatoes, peeled and diced
400g (3 cups) peeled, chopped pumpkin, seeds removed
250g (2 cups) cauliflower florets, chopped
2 green or yellow zucchini (courgettes), cut into thick rounds
salt
6 silverbeet leaves or a bunch of spinach (about 150g), chopped
100g (1 cup) freshly grated parmesan (parmigiano reggiano) cheese
2 tablespoons pesto (see page 56) (or 2 tablespoons finely chopped basil)

First, soak the beans.

Next day, heat the olive oil in a large saucepan and drop in the onion, garlic and bacon, if using. Cook gently for 10 minutes or until the bacon fat starts to run. Add the marjoram and thyme, cook for 1 minute more, then add the tomatoes, drained beans and stock. Bring to the boil, partially cover with a lid, and simmer gently for 1–2 hours or until the beans are tender.

Add the carrots and celery, bring back to a gentle boil and cook gently for 20 minutes. Add the potatoes, pumpkin, cauliflower and zucchini and 1 teaspoon of salt. Bring back to the boil and cook gently for about 30 minutes or until the vegetables are very tender.

Lastly, add the silverbeet or spinach and simmer for 15 minutes. Check the seasoning, adding more salt if necessary.

If not for immediate consumption, cool the pot of soup quickly in a sink filled with cold water, then refrigerate. Reheat over a gentle heat. When hot, swirl in 3 tablespoons of the parmesan cheese. Spoon the pesto on top of the soup, then ladle it into bowls and serve with the remaining cheese. (If using chopped basil leaves, swirl through the soup with the parmesan cheese.)

EVERY REGION IN ITALY has a version of minestrone, made with a selection of the locally available vegetables and herbs, thickened and enriched with rice, beans or pasta. Try to make the soup the day before you intend serving it, as the flavours will fuse together making for a tastier soup.

ADDING A GENOESE TOUCH TO MINESTRONE SOUP

Genoese minestrone is unique because a good dollop of basil pesto is stirred into the soup just before serving. The warmth of the soup draws out the heady basil perfume and pungent garlic aromas, permeating the whole kitchen.

MINESTRONE SOUP QUANTITIES

This recipe makes a huge batch of soup, enough to serve about 10, but you could serve it to a smaller group over a period of days. It will keep for 3 days providing you heat up only the amount you intend to serve; keep the rest chilled in the refrigerator or freeze it.

A SPECIAL TREAT

If you use parmigiano reggiano (genuine Italian parmesan cheese) in your cooking, you might like to indulge in a little treat.

Grate the cheese as required, but save the rinds. Wipe them clean, cut them into chunks and store in the freezer in a sealed plastic bag. When making minestrone, add several chunks to the soup along with the beans (thaw rinds for 15 minutes at room temperature before adding them to the soup). The hard rind softens into melting cheesy globs. It's divine, but just make sure you put enough in for everyone to have a piece!

funghi fest MUSHROOM SOUP

SERVES 8

30g (1 tightly packed cup) dried porcini (or cèpes) mushrooms
250ml hot water
50g butter
1 large onion, finely chopped
1 large clove garlic, crushed
5 tablespoons (about 50g) plain flour
1.25 litres chicken stock
2 teaspoons salt
freshly ground black pepper to taste
800g button mushrooms, wiped clean
125ml cream
1 tablespoon finely chopped parsley

Prepare the porcini mushrooms, using the hot water, as described opposite.

Put the butter and onion in a large saucepan, cover with a lid, and cook gently until very soft. Add the garlic and cook for 1 minute more, then remove the pan from the heat and mix in the flour. Blend in the chicken stock, salt and a little black pepper. Return to the heat and stir until boiling.

Meanwhile, process, liquidise, or finely chop the button mushrooms. If using a processor or liquidiser, use some of the strained porcini soaking liquid to prevent the machine from stalling. (I prefer three-quarters of the mushrooms puréed, to give the soup body, and the rest coarsely chopped, to give the soup texture.)

Add the button and porcini mushrooms and the strained porcini liquid to the pan. Bring to the boil, then simmer, partially covered with a lid, for 15 minutes. Blend in the cream and turn off the heat. Ladle into bowls and garnish with chopped parsley.

MAKING MUSHROOM SOUP AHEAD

If making the mushroom soup ahead of time (a day in advance is fine), don't add the cream until reheating. After making the soup, cool it very quickly, then cover and refrigerate. Reheat gently when required, then stir in the cream.

PORCINI MUSHROOM PREPARATION

Put the porcini mushrooms in a sieve and rinse under running water. Tip them into a bowl and pour on the specified amount of very hot water. Leave to soak for 30 minutes, then lift the mushrooms out of the liquid using a slotted spoon, and transfer to a sieve (reserve the soaking liquid). Rinse well under running water, then chop finely, discarding any woody bits. Strain the soaking liquid into a bowl through a sieve lined with a piece of absorbent kitchen paper. Strain again and set aside.

mean beans BORLOTTI AND TUNA SALAD

SERVES 12 AS AN ANTIPASTO DISH OR 6 AS A FIRST COURSE

200g dried borlotti beans, soaked for 3 hours in water (or use 2 cups cooked or tinned beans)
1 tablespoon olive oil
2 sage leaves
3 tablespoons extra virgin olive oil
1 tablespoon red wine vinegar
freshly ground black pepper to taste
salt
1 small red onion, finely chopped and soaked for 1 hour in cold water
185g can tuna in oil, drained
juice of 1 lemon
1 tablespoon small capers, drained
1 tablespoon coarsely chopped parsley, plus a few sprigs to garnish

Drain the beans, put them in a saucepan and cover generously with water. Add the olive oil and the sage leaves. Bring to a gentle boil, partially cover with a lid, then turn to low and cook gently until barely tender (this will take 20–60 minutes; be careful not to overcook them). Drain and cool.

In a bowl mix together the extra virgin olive oil, red wine vinegar, a good grinding of black pepper, $1/2$ teaspoon of salt and the drained onion. Add the beans and toss well.

Tip the tuna into a bowl. Pour the lemon juice over, sprinkle with salt, add the capers and the chopped parsley and toss carefully, keeping the tuna in large flakes. The beans and tuna can sit happily in their separate bowls for an hour or two at room temperature, or longer if refrigerated.

At serving time, toss the beans again, spoon them into a bowl with all the dressing and pile the tuna on top. Pour the tuna juices over, decorate with sprigs of parsley and serve.

swimming BRODETTO

SERVES 4

4 tablespoons extra virgin olive oil
3 large cloves garlic, crushed
½ cup chopped parsley
400g can Italian tomatoes, well mashed
½ large green pepper (capsicum), core and seeds removed, finely chopped
freshly ground black pepper to taste
1 teaspoon salt
250ml fish stock (see recipe opposite)
1kg assorted fish fillets, rinsed (include a few steamed mussels and small green prawns if you like)

CROÛTES

French bread or focaccia, thinly sliced
extra virgin olive oil
1 clove garlic, peeled and halved

Put the extra virgin olive oil in a wide saucepan with the garlic and parsley. Cook over a gentle heat, stirring, until the garlic just starts to change colour. Add the tomatoes and the green pepper. Cook gently for 10 minutes, then grind on some black pepper and add the salt.

Pour in the stock and bring to the boil. Cook gently for 10 minutes, then add the fish fillets. Partially cover with a lid and cook very gently for about 7 minutes or until the fish is just cooked through. If you are using mussels and prawns, add them during the last few minutes and cook until the prawns turn pink throughout (about 2 minutes).

Meanwhile, make the garlic croûtes. Brush the bread with olive oil and place on a baking tray. Toast in an oven preheated to 180°C for 7–10 minutes or until they are golden. Remove the croûtes from the oven and immediately rub each slice generously with the cut clove of garlic.

Dish the soup into hot bowls and serve with garlic croûtes.

FISH STOCK

1 fish frame, rinsed (you may need to order this from the fishmonger)
peeled rind of 1 small lemon
1 onion, sliced
1 carrot, sliced
1 bay leaf
blade of mace
a few peppercorns
2.25 litres cold water

Put all the ingredients in a saucepan. Bring to the boil, then lower the heat and simmer for 20 minutes. Strain immediately. Refrigerate when cool. Use within 24 hours or freeze for up to 4 weeks.

THIS SOUP is based on a substantial Italian fish soup, which is more of a main course than a soup. Use white fish fillets for a delicate flavour and meatier fish fillets for a more robust soup. Do go to the effort of making fish stock for the soup – it adds a layer of flavour.

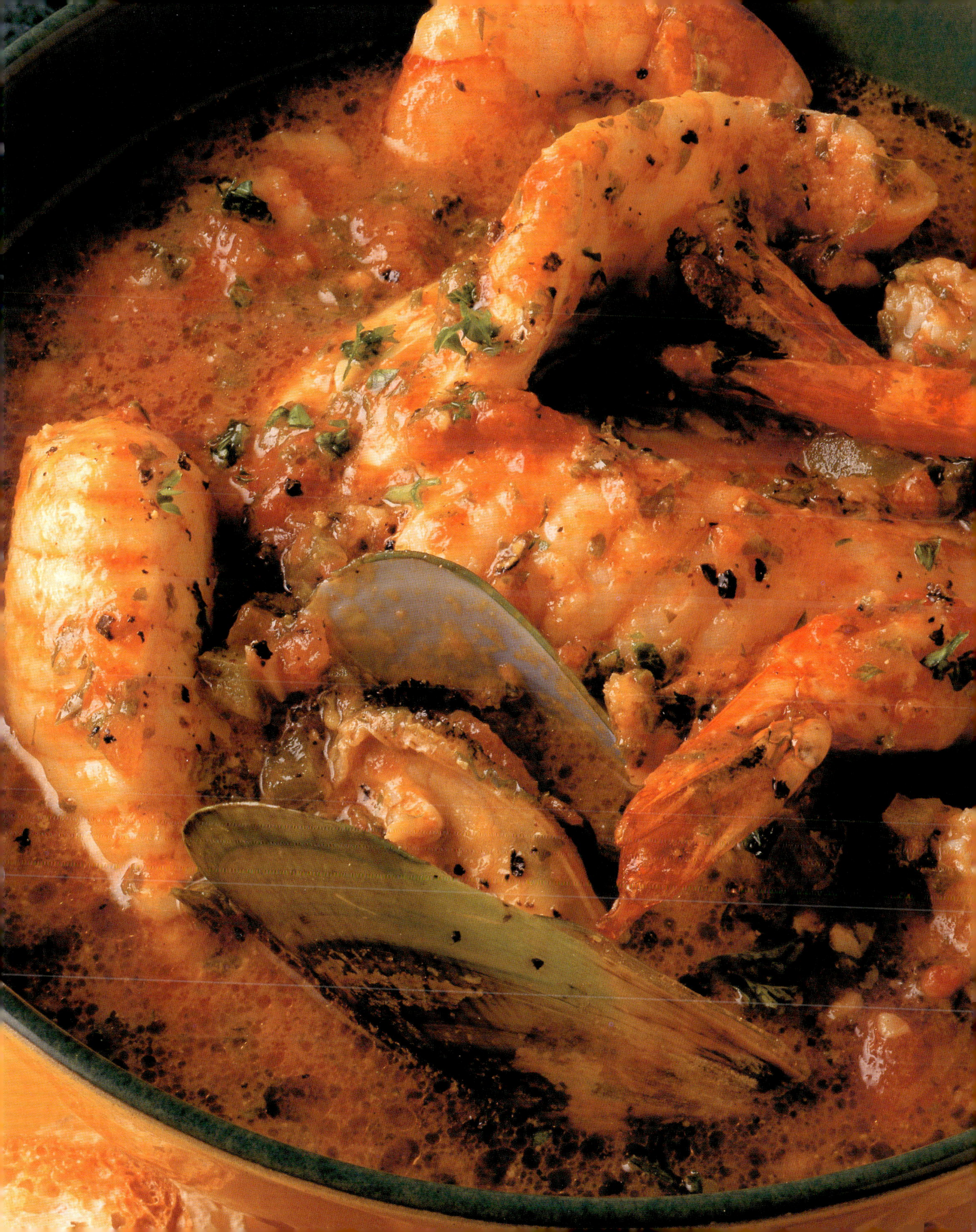

shiny shell STEAMED MUSSELS WITH BASIL DRESSING

SERVES 2–4

24 small mussels
1 clove garlic, crushed
2 tablespoons chopped parsley
2 tablespoons chopped basil
3 tablespoons olive oil
2 tablespoons white wine
3 tablespoons white wine vinegar
few pinches of salt
freshly ground black pepper

First clean the mussels (see opposite).

Put the garlic, parsley and basil in a large, shallow saucepan with the olive oil. Sauté for 2–3 minutes over a medium heat, then increase the heat to high, and add the white wine, white wine vinegar, salt and black pepper. Tip in the mussels and cover the pan with a lid. Cook for 3–5 minutes, stirring occasionally, until the mussels open. Transfer them to a dish as they are done, then pour over the juices (if the juices are gritty, strain them first). Serve hot or at room temperature.

CLEANING MUSSELS

To clean mussels, scrub them under running water with a stiff brush, then pull off the beards. Put the mussels in a large bowl and fill with cold water. Stir them around, then lift out into a clean bowl. Repeat the process until the water is clear and grit-free. Leave the mussels to soak for 15 minutes in fresh water.

STORING FRESH MUSSELS

Fresh live mussels, either personally harvested or purchased, can be stored in melting ice for several days. Put them in a clean bucket or basin, preferably one with drainage holes, or an insulated container like an esky or chillybin. Cover the mussels with a damp towel, lay a bag of ice on top, cover with a lid or damp newspaper and store in a cool place (not the refrigerator). Replenish the ice as it melts (ensure the mussels don't end up immersed in the melting ice), draining off any accumulated water.

Steamed mussels with basil dressing

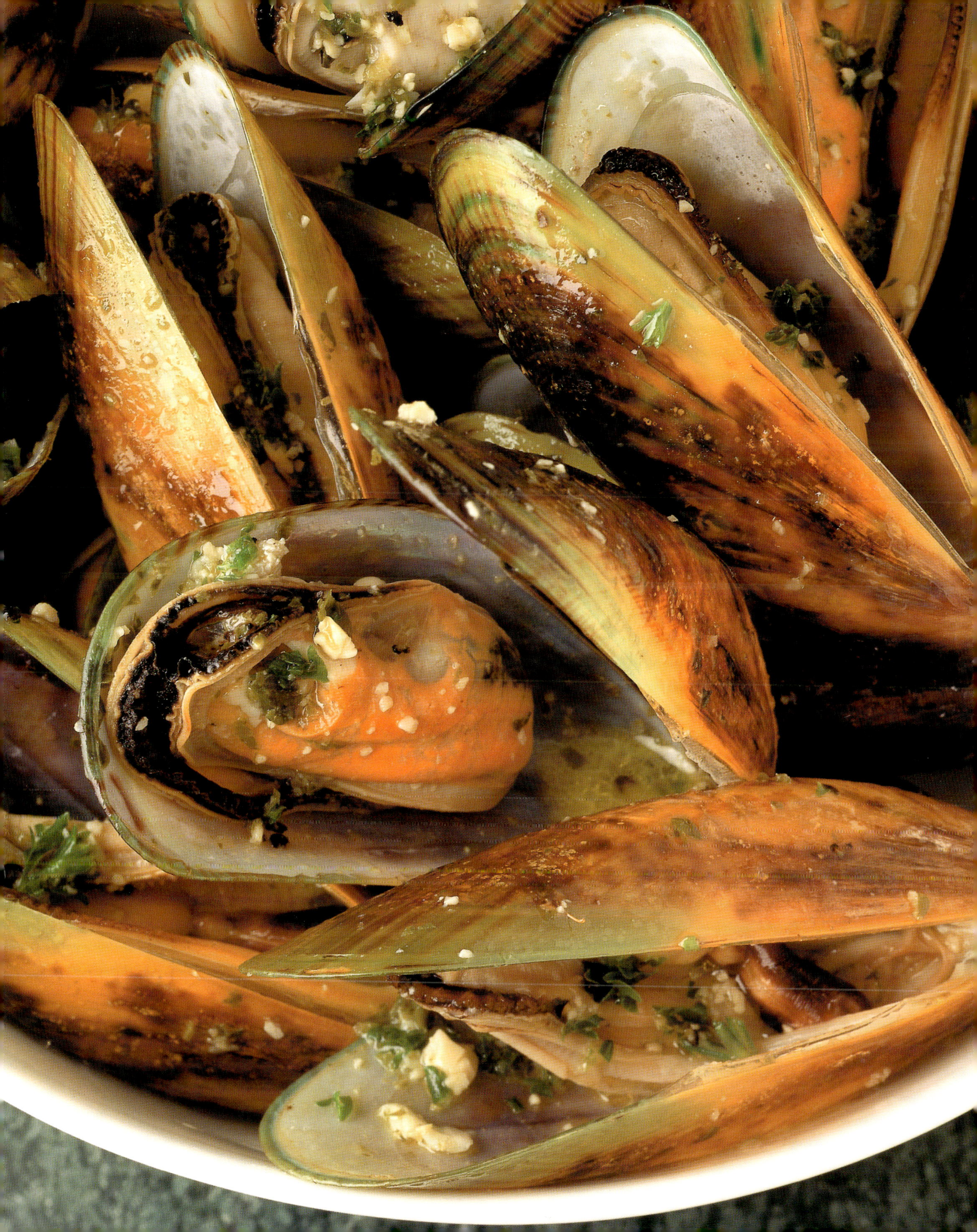

little mouthfuls MOZZARELLA AND ROASTED RED PEPPER SALAD

SERVES 4–6

3 large red peppers (capsicums)
150g mozzarella 'bocconcini' in whey, drained
a few fresh basil leaves, torn into small pieces
1 tablespoon balsamic vinegar
¼ teaspoon salt
freshly ground black pepper to taste
1 clove garlic, crushed
2 tablespoons capers, drained
4 tablespoons extra virgin olive oil

Prepare the red peppers first. Roast them as described below, then slice thinly and set aside with the juices.

Pat the mozzarella balls dry with absorbent kitchen paper, then slice them thinly with a sharp knife and arrange on a serving platter with the prepared peppers. Scatter the torn basil leaves over the top.

In a bowl, blend the balsamic vinegar, salt, black pepper, garlic, capers and extra virgin olive oil. Mix in any reserved pepper juices. Pour over the mozzarella and peppers, toss gently, and serve immediately.

ROASTING PEPPERS

There's no need to make roasting peppers (capsicums) into a complicated affair. If you have barbecuing facilities, the peppers can be roasted on the barbecue grill-rack and will take on a wonderfully smoky flavour. Alternatively, put the peppers on a rack in an oven preheated to 200°C and cook, turning occasionally with tongs, for about 20 minutes, or until they are blistered and charred. (They will be softer prepared this way). Transfer to a board and, when cool, peel off the skins and slip out the cores and seeds. Putting a sheet of aluminium foil underneath the peppers to catch the drips will save messing up the oven. My favourite way is to roast them over a gas flame because they char quickly, taking on a wonderful flavour, but retain a good texture. Put two or three peppers in the gas flame on a hob. Cook until charred all over, turning with tongs. Cool, then peel. Some recipes call for the pepper juices to be saved for use in the recipe.

LITTLE MOUTHFUL

Bocconcini means little mouthful and it is used to describe small balls of fresh mozzarella sold in whey. The bland, milky taste of fresh mozzarella cheese is a perfect foil for the sweetness of roasted red peppers. Serve this with olives and bread as an antipasto dish.

Mozzarella and roasted red pepper salad

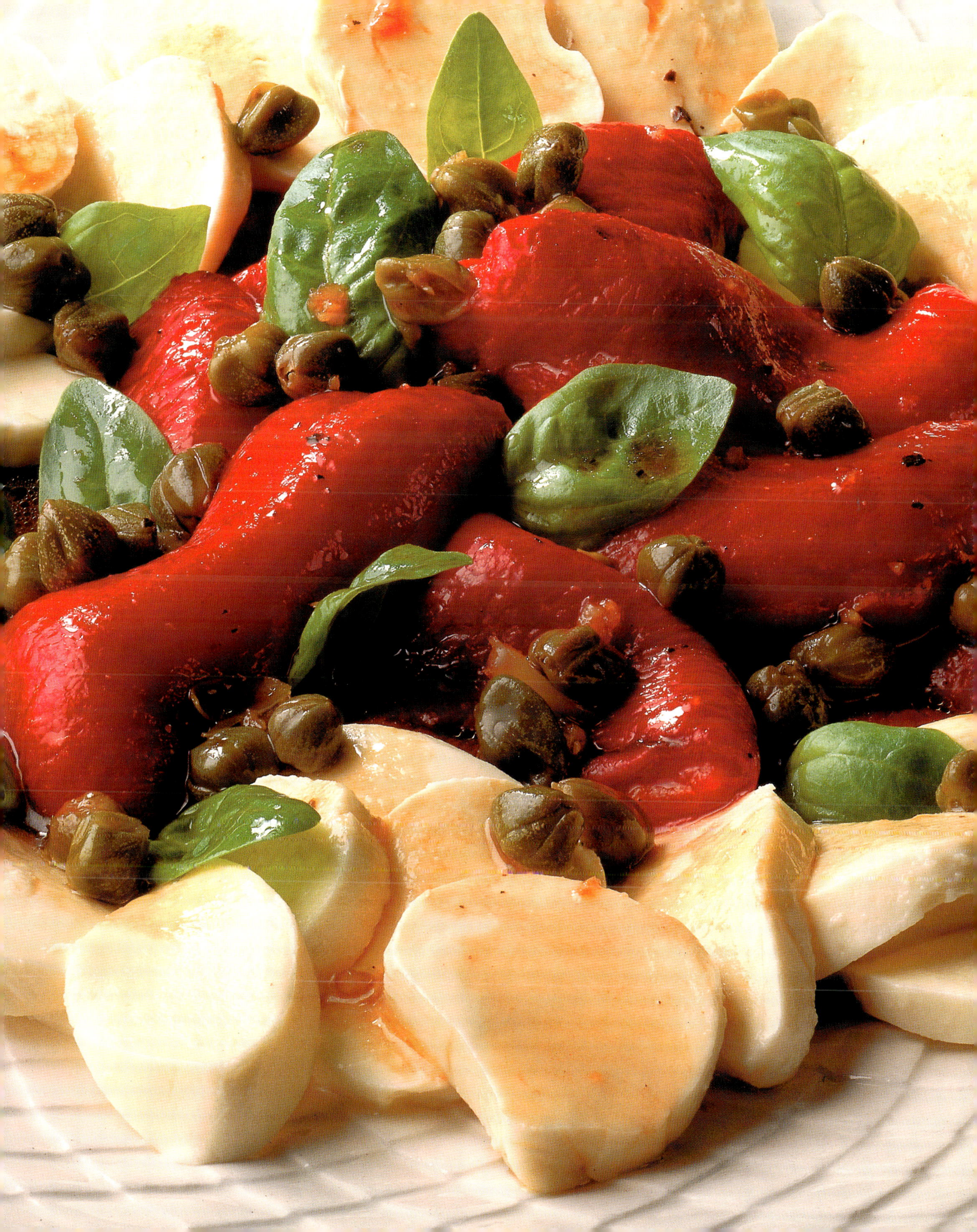

long, leisurely

EASTER PIE	26
EGGPLANT PIE	28
POTATO PIE	28
THREE CHEESE PIE	30
ARTICHOKE AND HAM PIE	31
SPINACH TORTE	32
SPINACH FRITTATA	32
FOCACCIA	34
BASIC RISOTTO	35
OVEN-BAKED EGGPLANT RISOTTO	36
OVEN-BAKED MUSHROOM RISOTTO	39
SPRING RISOTTO WITH ROASTED FENNEL AND SCALLOPS	40
RISOTTO MILANESE	41
BASIC FERRON NO-STIR RISOTTO	41
BASIC POLENTA	42
POLENTA AND MUSHROOM PIE	42
POLENTA PIE WITH PUTTANESCA SAUCE	43
GRILLED PARMESAN POLENTA WITH OLIVES, PINE NUTS AND ROSEMARY	44
SCACCIATA	47

wedges of crisp-crust pie

bubbling cauldrons of grainy polenta

pots of steaming, fragrant rice

melting golden globs of cheese

porcini with scents of the forest floor

lunch dishes

flaky layers EASTER PIE

SERVES 8

2 tablespoons olive oil
1 large onion, finely chopped
2 x 400g cans artichoke hearts, well drained
freshly ground black pepper to taste
350g ricotta cheese
175ml milk
pinch of salt
about 100g butter
350g packet filo pastry
8 eggs
freshly ground black pepper to taste
1 tablespoon finely chopped marjoram (or ½ tablespoon dried marjoram)
75g (¾ cup) freshly grated parmesan (parmigiano reggiano) cheese

Heat the olive oil in a frying pan over a medium heat and add the onion. Cook until lightly golden, stirring occasionally.

Squeeze all the brine from the artichokes, chop them roughly and add to the onion. Cook for 3–4 minutes, stirring, until any moisture is driven off. Grind over plenty of black pepper, then cool.

Put the ricotta cheese in a bowl and beat until smooth, then blend in the milk by degrees. Add a pinch of salt and the artichoke mixture. Mix well.

Melt most of the butter. Lay the first sheet of filo pastry on a clean, dry surface and brush lightly with the butter, then lay a second sheet on top and brush it with butter, too. Continue layering buttered sheets of filo in this way until 11 sheets of pastry are stacked up. Mould the buttered sheets into a buttered rectangular dish, about 32cm x 21cm x 5cm, and trim off any overhanging pastry.

Spoon in the ricotta mixture and use a large metal spoon to make eight hollows in it. Crack the eggs, one by one, into a small dish and drop them into the hollows. Put 2–3 small dots of butter on each egg, grind some black pepper over and sprinkle with the marjoram and parmesan cheese.

Prepare another 11 sheets of filo in the way described and place these on top of the pie. Gently press in place, then trim off any overhanging pastry.

Brush the top lightly with butter and bake in an oven preheated to 200°C for about 40 minutes or until the filo is a rich golden colour on top (lower the top heat, if necessary, to prevent over-browning, or drape a piece of aluminium foil over the top of the pie). Allow it to cool slightly before cutting into wedges.

TORTA PASQUALINA

Torta Pasqualina (Easter Pie), an Easter specialty, was originally made with 33 layers of pastry, representing Christ's age at the time of his crucifixion. I use filo pastry in place of olive oil dough, as it not only saves time but also produces an appetisingly crisp result.

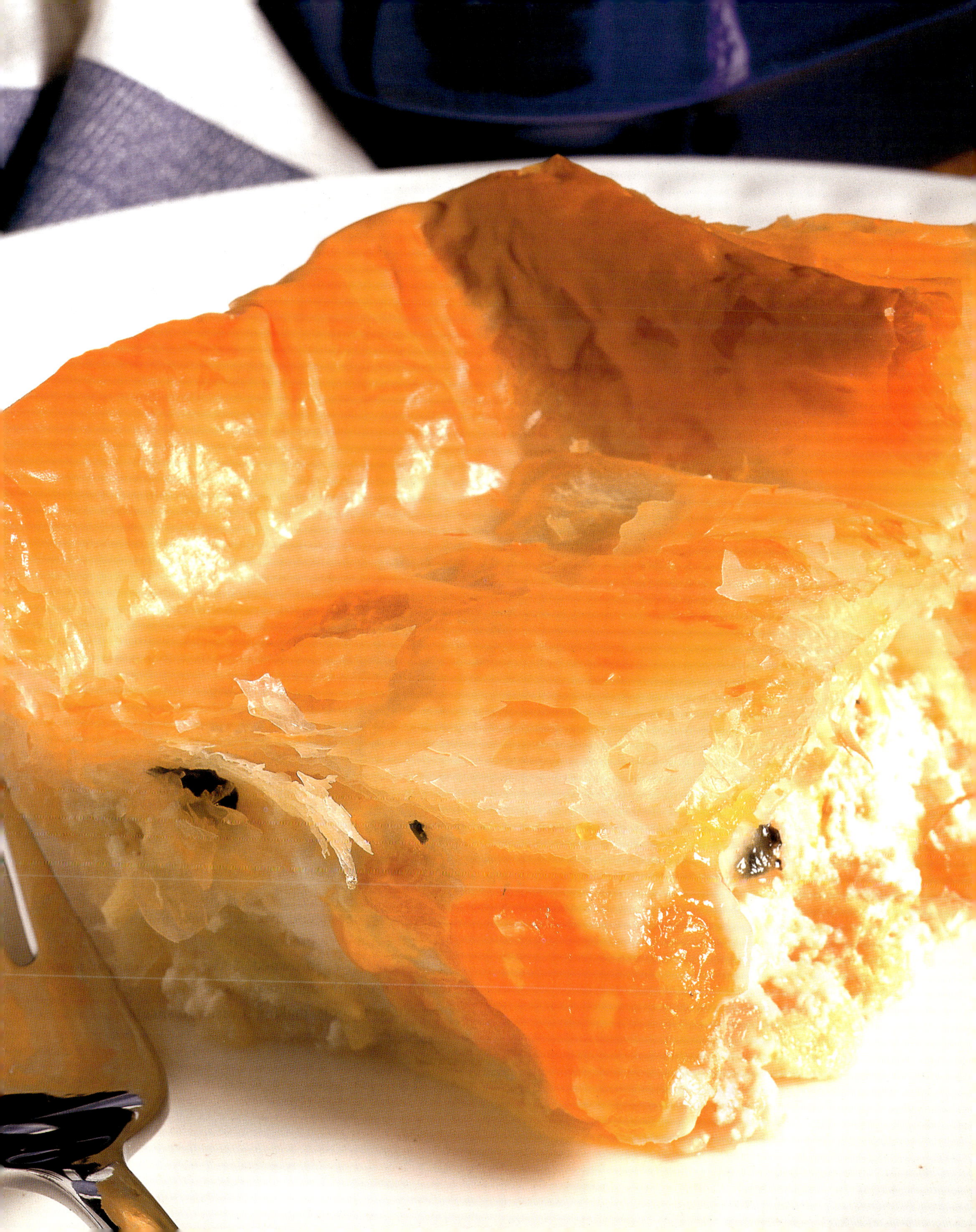

drool EGGPLANT PIE

SERVES 6–8

2–3 medium eggplants (aubergines) (about 600g total)
plain flour
olive oil for frying
250ml Quick Tomato Sauce (see page 30)
small handful of basil leaves
salt
150g mozzarella 'bocconcini' in whey, drained and sliced
50g (½ cup) freshly grated parmesan (parmigiano reggiano) cheese

Cut the eggplants into thin slices and dust about a third of them with flour. Heat ½ cup of olive oil in a frying pan over a medium-high heat. When the oil is very hot, put in a single layer of eggplant slices. Fry on both sides to a rich golden brown, lift out and drain on a plate lined with crumpled absorbent kitchen paper. Continue cooking the rest of the eggplant slices, dusting them with flour first, and adding more oil when necessary. Alternatively, oven-bake the eggplant slices, according to the instructions on page 36.

Lightly grease a medium-sized ovenproof dish and put in a layer of eggplant slices. Top each eggplant slice with a teaspoonful of tomato sauce, ½ a basil leaf, a light sprinkling of salt and a slice of mozzarella. Sprinkle some parmesan cheese over. Continue layering the pie in this way, ending with a layer of eggplant slices and a generous sprinkling of parmesan cheese.

Bake the pie in an oven preheated to 180°C for 30–40 minutes, or until it is a rich golden colour on top. Cool for 10 minutes in the dish before serving. (If the juices appear watery, pour them off; they should be dark and richly flavoured.) Serve with crusty bread.

SERVE THIS RICH and filling classic Neapolitan dish with a salad of mixed leaves.

If making the Eggplant Pie or Stuffed Baby Zucchini (page 110), there will be tomato sauce left over. Store it refrigerated and use within 3 days, or freeze it for later use.

soft crust POTATO PIE

SERVES 6–8

1kg even-sized potatoes (choose a variety which mashes well)
salt
2 tablespoons freshly grated parmesan (parmigiano reggiano) cheese
50ml extra virgin olive oil
400g can Italian tomatoes
225g mozzarella 'bocconcini' in whey, drained and sliced
100g bacon, rind removed, finely chopped
1 teaspoon dried oregano
freshly ground black pepper to taste

Wash the potatoes, then put them in a metal colander or steaming basket over a saucepan of boiling water (the colander or steaming basket should nearly fill the inside of the pan). Sprinkle generously with salt and cover tightly with a lid or double thickness of aluminium foil. Steam over vigorously boiling water until tender.

As soon as the potatoes are cool enough to handle, peel off the skins, then pass them through a mouli-légumes (or mash them with a potato masher). Beat in 1 tablespoon of the parmesan cheese, ½ teaspoon of salt and 2 tablespoons of the olive oil. Spread the potato mixture over the base of a large, non-stick 'pizza' tray (about 28cm in diameter).

While the potatoes are cooking, prepare the tomatoes. Drain them in a sieve, split each tomato, remove the core and flick out the seeds. Chop the tomatoes finely, then drain the chopped pulp for 10 minutes.

Distribute the sliced mozzarella over the potato, then spoon the tomato on and top with the bacon, oregano and plenty of black pepper. Sprinkle the last of the parmesan cheese over the top and drizzle on the remaining olive oil.

Bake in an oven preheated to 200°C for 25–30 minutes, or until it is well browned. Serve warmish or at room temperature (although the pie is delicious hot, the potato base sets as it cools, making it easier to slice).

Eggplant pie

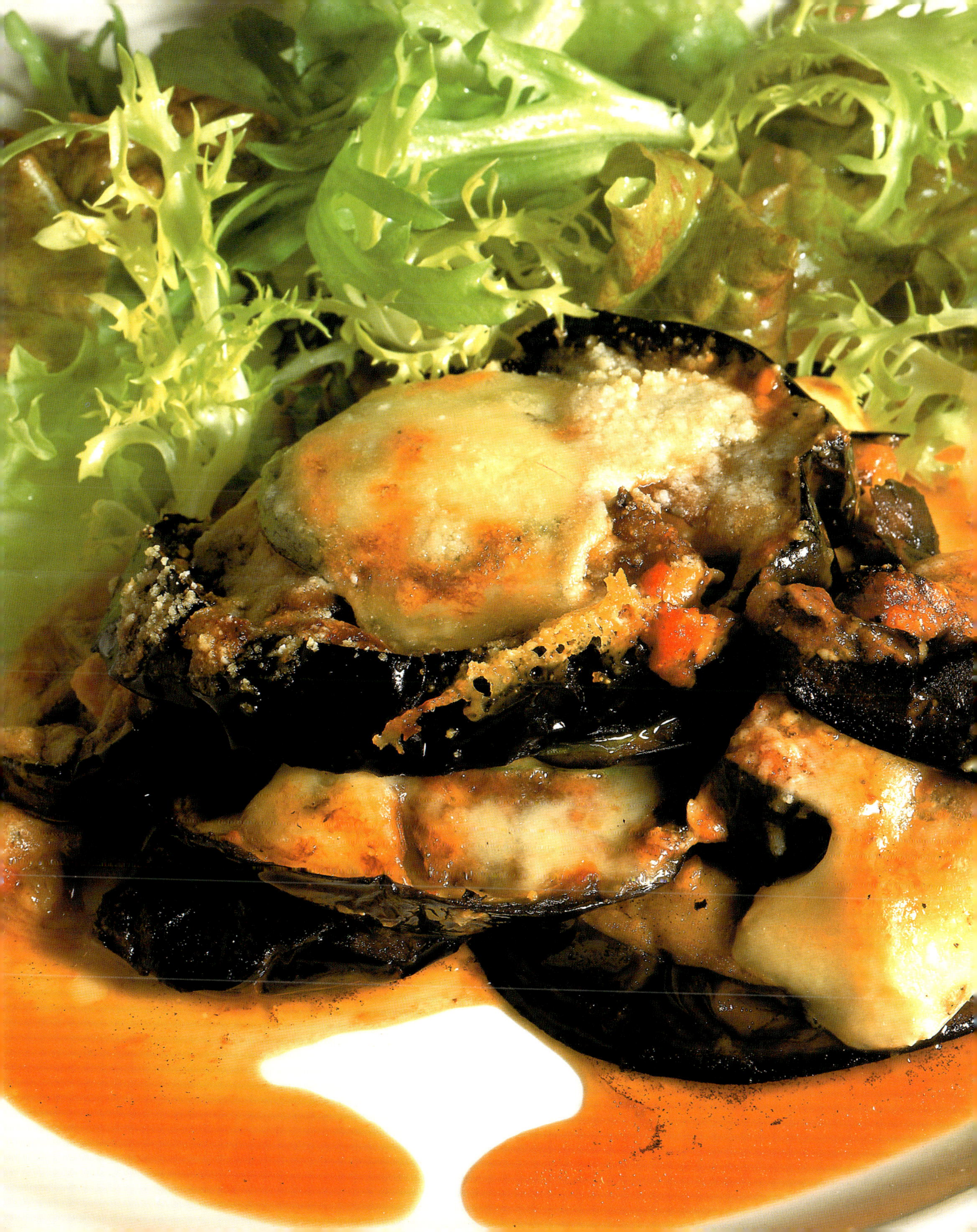

trio of cheeses THREE CHEESE PIE

SERVES 8

PASTRY
330g plain flour
pinch of salt
250g butter, softened until pliable
2 small egg yolks
about 4 tablespoons ice-cold water

FILLING
knob of butter
200g piece ham off the bone, trimmed of fat and cut into small cubes
freshly ground black pepper to taste
salt
good grating of fresh nutmeg
2 eggs
250g ricotta cheese
250g mozzarella 'bocconcini' in whey, drained and sliced
2 tablespoons freshly grated parmesan (parmigiano reggiano) cheese

Sift the flour and salt into a large mixing bowl. Cut the butter into large lumps, then drop into the flour. Using two flat-bladed knives, cut the butter through the flour until the pieces are like small marbles. Use your fingertips to rub the butter into the flour until the mixture resembles coarse breadcrumbs.

In a small bowl, mix the egg yolks and water together, then tip into the flour mixture. Stir with a knife to combine, then knead lightly with your hands until the mixture forms a ball.

Turn onto a lightly floured surface and knead briefly until smooth. Cover with plastic food wrap and chill for about 40 minutes or until firm (but not hard). Roll out on a lightly floured surface, then line a fluted 23–25cm flan ring with the pastry. Reroll the scraps into a long rectangle, cut into strips and place on a tray. Chill the lined flan ring and pastry strips for 30 minutes.

To make the filling, put the knob of butter in a small frying pan and set over a medium heat. Add the ham and fry for about 5 minutes until lightly browned. Transfer to a bowl and grind on black pepper, add a pinch or two of salt and a good grating of fresh nutmeg. Cool for 5 minutes.

Break in the eggs, mix with a fork, then blend in the ricotta, mozzarella and parmesan cheese. Tip into the chilled pastry case. Dampen the rim of the pastry and lay strips of pastry over the top to form a lattice, pressing them gently onto the rim of the pastry.

Bake the pie in an oven preheated to 190°C for 30 minutes or until crisp and golden. Cool for 5 minutes, then slide onto a cooling rack. The pie can be served hot or warmish.

QUICK TOMATO SAUCE

2 tablespoons olive oil
1 smallish onion, finely chopped
2 cloves garlic, finely chopped
2 x 400g cans Italian tomatoes, mashed
1 tablespoon tomato paste
1 teaspoon sugar
¼ teaspoon salt
freshly ground black pepper to taste

Put the olive oil in a saucepan, set over a medium heat and add the onion. Cook for 2–3 minutes, stirring occasionally, then add the garlic. Cover, lower the heat and cook gently until soft.

Add the tomatoes, stir well, then mix in the tomato paste, sugar, salt and black pepper. Bring to the boil, then turn the heat down and simmer gently for 30 minutes, stirring occasionally. Pass the sauce through a mouli-légumes or a sieve.

tart art ARTICHOKE AND HAM PIE

SERVES 6–8

1 batch focaccia dough, made to the end of Stage 2 (see page 34)
plain flour for rolling out dough
400g can artichoke bottoms or artichoke hearts
2 tablespoons sun-dried tomato paste
4 shallots (eschallots), finely chopped (or 3 spring onions without greenery)
150g ham, cut into short strips
1 tablespoon capers, drained
freshly ground black pepper to taste
salt
1 tablespoon chopped parsley
1 teaspoon dried oregano
150g emmenthal cheese, thinly sliced
olive oil for brushing the top of the pie

First, make the dough, then cut it in half. Lightly flour one half and set it aside. Roll out the other half on a floured surface, dusting it with more flour to prevent sticking. If the dough is difficult to roll – if it keeps shrinking back after rolling – leave it to rest for 2–3 minutes. Roll out to about 32cm in diameter. Wrap the dough around a rolling pin and transfer it to a baking tray lined with a teflon baking sheet or greased aluminium foil.

Next, make the filling. Drain the artichoke bottoms or hearts very well, then slice them. Spread the tomato paste over the rolled dough, scatter the shallots over, then add the artichokes, ham and capers, keeping the mixture slightly in from the edges. Grind on some black pepper, sprinkle lightly with salt, sprinkle on the parsley and oregano, then cover with the sliced emmenthal cheese.

Roll out the second half of the dough, wrap it around the rolling pin and lay it on top of the pie. Press the edges of the dough together to seal them, then 'crimp' the edges with your fingers. Prick the surface all over with a fork, then brush with olive oil. Leave uncovered in a warm spot for 15 minutes.

Bake the pie in an oven preheated to 200°C for 40–45 minutes until it is golden brown. Leave on the tray for 2–3 minutes, then carefully slide it off onto a cooling rack. Cool for 5–10 minutes, then transfer to a large plate and serve cut into large wedges. Best eaten warmish.

portable feast SPINACH TORTE

SERVES 6–8

500g (large bunch) spinach, trimmed and washed well
250g (1 well-packed cup) Italian rice – arborio, vialone nano, carnaroli
salt
butter
3 tablespoons olive oil
1 large onion, finely chopped
1 large clove garlic, crushed
freshly ground black pepper to taste
freshly grated nutmeg
4 eggs, lightly beaten
1 teaspoon finely chopped sage (or a few pinches of dried sage)
75g (¾ cup) freshly grated parmesan (parmigiano reggiano) cheese
extra butter, melted

Bring 3 cups of water to the boil in a large saucepan. Plunge in the spinach, pushing it under the water with a wooden spoon, and cook until wilted. Drain and refresh with cold water, then drain again. Press out as much moisture as possible, then chop with a knife.

Tip the rice into a saucepan of salted water. Bring to the boil, then cook gently, uncovered, for 10 minutes. Drain, then return to the rinsed and dried saucepan. Stir in a large knob of butter.

Meanwhile, put the olive oil in a frying pan with the onion. Cook over a gentle heat until lightly golden. Add the garlic and cook for another minute, then tip the mixture into the rice. Grind over plenty of black pepper and nutmeg and add ½ teaspoon of salt. Pour in the eggs and add the spinach, sage and most of the parmesan cheese.

With a large fork blend the mixture together, then turn it into a buttered, loose-bottomed 20cm-diameter cake tin (line the base with buttered baking paper or blanched spinach leaves). Drizzle the surface with a little melted butter. Sprinkle the rest of the cheese over the top.

Bake in an oven preheated to 200°C for about 25 minutes or until the top is crisp. Rest for 5 minutes, then loosen from the sides of the tin, invert and lift off the base of the tin (peel off the paper, if using). Serve hot or warm.

flip it SPINACH FRITTATA

SERVES 4–6

100g fresh spinach, trimmed and washed well
5 eggs
½ teaspoon salt
freshly ground black pepper to taste
freshly grated nutmeg to taste
100g (1 cup) freshly grated parmesan (parmigiano reggiano) cheese
2 tablespoons extra virgin olive oil

Blanch the spinach leaves in a saucepan of boiling water for 10 seconds. Drain, refresh with cold water, then squeeze out the excess water. Chop finely.

Break the eggs into a bowl and beat lightly with a fork. Mix in the salt, black pepper, nutmeg, parmesan cheese and spinach.

Heat the olive oil in a non-stick frying pan over a medium heat (choose a pan with a 23cm diameter). When it is hot, pour in the egg mixture and cook until it is golden brown on the underside. Have the grill preheated. Cook the top of the frittata under the grill until lightly browned. Loosen the frittata from the frying pan and turn it onto a plate. Serve warm or at room temperature.

FRITTATA

Describing a frittata as an Italian omelette does little justice to this versatile egg dish. For a start, a frittata is cooked on both sides in a regular frying pan and is more substantial than a French omelette. It does not need to be eaten piping hot – in fact, most are better warmish or at room temperature. This makes them an ideal prepare-ahead dish. They are usually enriched with cheese and can incorporate ingredients such as onions, garlic, herbs, peppers (capsicums), eggplant (aubergine), artichokes, zucchini (courgettes), asparagus, potatoes, mushrooms, spinach, tomatoes, ham, bacon and spicy sausage. The trick lies in using a well-oiled pan, cooking the vegetables first, and not making the frittata too thick.

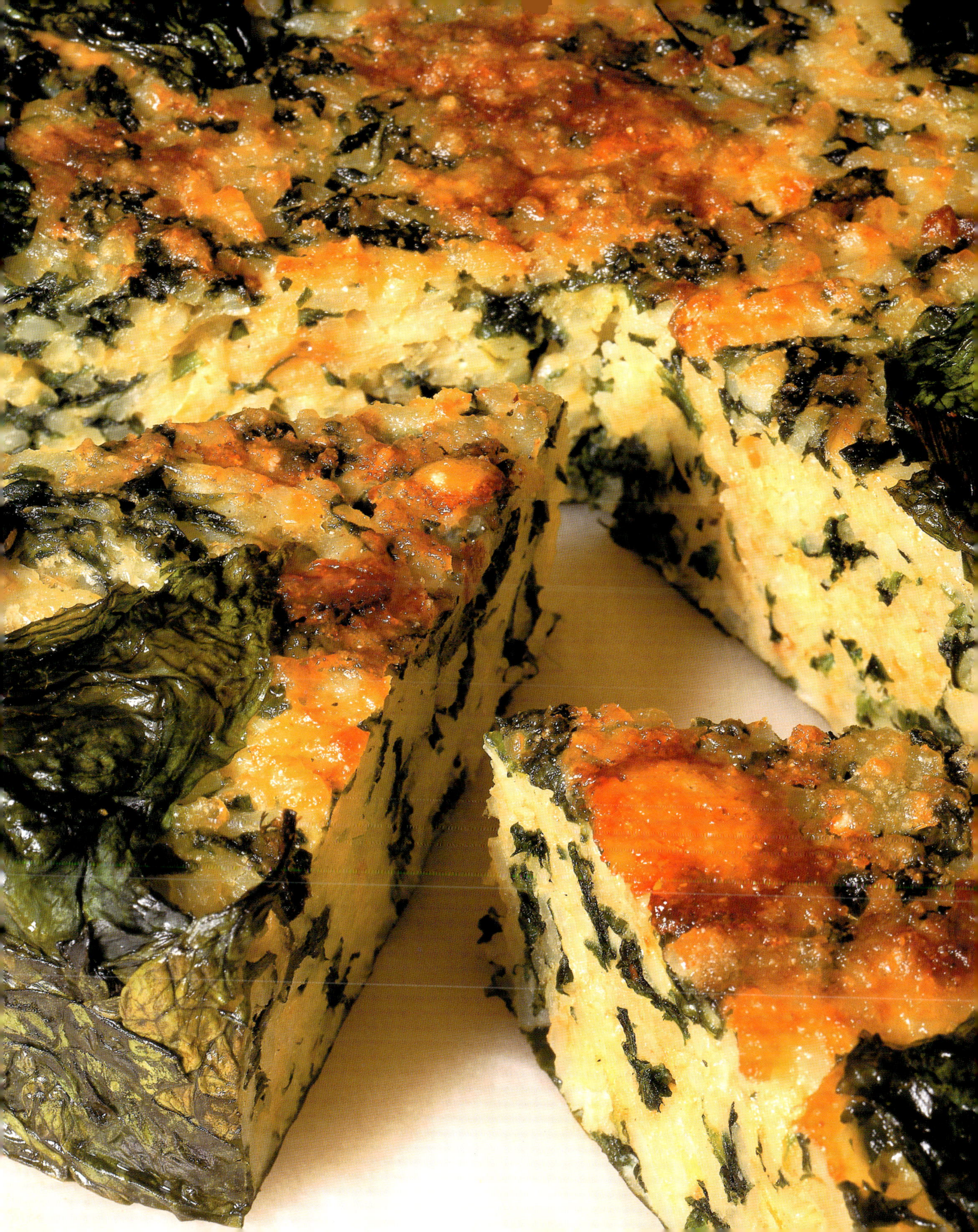

dimpled dough FOCACCIA

15g (about 2 level tablespoons) dried yeast
100ml lukewarm water
450g high-grade flour, plus about 50g extra for kneading
2 teaspoons salt
250ml of lukewarm water
50ml olive oil for the dough, plus extra for brushing over the surface
salt mill

STAGE 1

Put the yeast granules in a bowl and pour the first measure of lukewarm water over them. Leave for about 10 minutes or until dissolved and fluffy, then stir well. Sift the flour and 1 teaspoon of the salt into a large warmed bowl. Make a well in the centre and pour in the dissolved yeast. Sprinkle a little of the flour over the yeast – just enough to cover it – then cover with a damp cloth and leave in a warm place for 20 minutes, or until the yeast breaks through the flour.

STAGE 2

Blend in the second measure of lukewarm water, first using a fork, then your hands. Turn onto the work surface and knead for 8–10 minutes, using the extra flour to prevent sticking. (This can be done in a bread-mixing machine, or in a food processor, or with a food mixer fitted with a dough hook; follow the manufacturer's instructions.) Clean and dry the bowl, then smear it with a little oil. Put the ball of dough in the bowl, turn it over to coat it with oil, then cover with a damp cloth. Leave in a warm place for about 1–1 1/2 hours, or until it has doubled in bulk.

STAGE 3

Punch down the dough and turn it onto a floured work surface. Pat the dough flat, then sprinkle it with the remaining teaspoon of salt. Pour one-third of the olive oil into the centre, bundle up the dough, keeping the oil enclosed, then squash and squelch it until the oil is worked into the dough. Knead until smooth like putty. Repeat this step twice more, adding the rest of the oil (but no more salt), then finish off with 3–4 minutes' kneading.

Put the dough in an oiled bowl, turn it to coat all sides, cover with a damp cloth and leave in a warm place for 1–1 1/2 hours, or until it has doubled in bulk.

STAGE 4

Punch down the dough, then turn it onto a well-used baking tray (scone tray) or a baking tray lined with a teflon baking sheet. Pat it down and spread into a large oval or rectangle nearly as big as the tray. Leave in a warm spot for 15–20 minutes to prove, or until it has slightly risen and feels puffy. Make dimples all over the surface with your fingertips, brush generously with oil and grind over a little salt.

Bake for 25–35 minutes in an oven preheated to 210°C. Remove the tray from the oven halfway through cooking, brush the focaccia with oil, then return the tray to the oven, positioning it so that the side of the tray that was near the back of the oven is now near the oven door. Finish baking, remove from the oven and cool on a wire rack.

COMMERCIALLY made focaccia is not always what it should be. If you like working with yeast, you'll find focaccia is easy enough to make, and you can flavour it according to your taste.

FOCACCIA WITH SAGE OR ROSEMARY

Add 1 tablespoon of finely chopped fresh sage or rosemary along with the salt in Stage 3. Proceed as described. (Both these herbs are potent, so don't be tempted to add any more than the stated amount.)

FOCACCIA WITH OLIVES

If the olives are put on top of the focaccia, they will fall off (there's nothing worse than buying a loaf of olive bread which is devoid of olives!). Mixed into the dough, the olives give the focaccia a 'shorter' texture and a fuller olive taste.

Use 100g (about 20) black olives, drained, and pat them dry with absorbent kitchen paper. Remove the stones with an olive pitter, or cut them in half through the middle, twist apart and extract the stones. Chop the olives roughly.

Prepare the dough to the end of Stage 3. Punch it down and turn it onto a lightly floured surface. Scatter the olives and 1 teaspoon of dried marjoram or oregano (optional) over the dough. Knead briefly until well amalgamated. Proceed as for the basic focaccia dough.

plump grains BASIC RISOTTO

SERVES 4–6

1.3 litres chicken stock
2 tablespoons olive oil
75g butter
1 small onion, finely chopped
1 clove garlic, crushed
125ml dry white wine
400g (about 1¾ cups) Italian rice – arborio, vialone nano, carnaroli
¼ teaspoon salt
freshly ground black pepper to taste
freshly grated nutmeg
50g (½ cup) freshly grated parmesan (parmigiano reggiano) cheese, plus extra for serving

Bring the chicken stock to simmering point, then set the heat so that it is kept very hot, but does not boil and evaporate.

Choose a 2.5–3 litre heavy-based saucepan. Set it over a medium heat, put in the olive oil and half the butter, and add the onion and garlic. Sauté until a pale golden colour, then pour in the wine and cook until it has nearly evaporated.

Tip in the unwashed rice, sauté for 2 minutes, stirring often with a wooden spoon, then stir in a ladleful of hot stock. This will evaporate quickly. Add a second ladleful of stock and stir, gently but continuously, until the stock has evaporated. Continue cooking in this way, stirring every few seconds (if you don't stir, the rice will stick to the pan), adding more stock once the rice is no longer sloppy. The rice is ready when, like pasta, the grains are al dente (still firm and only just cooked through, but no longer chalky inside). It requires a certain amount of judgment to arrive at the finishing point with the last ladleful of stock absorbed so that the rice is creamy, but not dry.

Remove the pan from the heat, add salt, black pepper, nutmeg, the rest of the butter and the parmesan cheese. Beat well for 1 minute, cover with a lid and leave for another minute to allow the flavours to fuse. Dish into hot plates and serve immediately.

RISOTTO

Do not attempt these recipes with any rice other than the types suggested. It's worth reading these notes about risotto before making one of the recipes.

The rice should not be washed as the clinging starch provides creaminess. Typically, the rice and any additional ingredients and flavourings are cooked together in a small amount of reducing liquid. This encourages the rice to release the starch while allowing the grains to absorb the flavoursome liquid. The result is (or should be) a mixture that is bound together creamily, yet it should be possible to separate each individual grain of rice from the mass. It should not be gummy or gluggy.

To prepare a risotto, the unwashed rice is usually sautéed briefly in butter and/or oil, along with onion, and often garlic. Once the grains of rice are coated with the oil or butter, the rice is cooked by adding a small quantity of liquid at a time. The liquid, usually stock, is added hot to prevent the cooking process from slowing down (keep the liquid just under simmering point in a saucepan). As the liquid evaporates, more is added, so the rice cooks and softens while absorbing the flavoursome liquid and releasing the starch.

Be careful not to flood the rice with liquid because it will stew and not retain its structure when cooked. The risotto must be stirred constantly during cooking to prevent it sticking. Before serving, further seasonings (such as butter, cheese and herbs) are whipped in, which helps lighten the risotto.

A NOTE ON STOCK

By all means use homemade stock, but be aware that any defects in the stock (saltiness, strong herbal or vegetal flavours, or sharpness) will be emphasised through reduction. If necessary, dilute the stock with water. A light vegetable water, or meat or chicken stock is my preference, but a chicken stock cube, reconstituted in plenty of water, can be used. You can also include soaking, poaching or blanching water conserved during preparation of the risotto ingredients.

melting mozzarella OVEN-BAKED EGGPLANT RISOTTO

SERVES 4

2 medium-large eggplants (aubergines) (about 250g each)
250ml (1 cup) olive oil for frying
750ml (3 cups) light stock
2 tablespoons olive oil
30g butter, plus a little extra
1 small onion, finely chopped
2 cloves garlic, crushed
400g can Italian tomatoes, mashed
2 tablespoons finely chopped basil (or 1 tablespoon finely chopped parsley and $1/2$ teaspoon dried oregano)
salt
freshly ground black pepper to taste
250g (1 well-packed cup) Italian rice – arborio, vialone nano, carnaroli
125ml ($1/2$ cup) dry white wine
50g ($1/2$ cup) freshly grated parmesan (parmigiano reggiano) cheese
150g mozzarella 'bocconcini' in whey, drained and cubed

Slice the eggplants into large rounds about 5mm thick. Heat the frying oil in a large frying pan until it is hot and lightly smoking. Put in several slices of eggplant and cook until they are golden brown. Turn with tongs and cook the other side. Drain on absorbent kitchen paper. Repeat with the remaining eggplant slices. Alternatively, oven-bake the eggplant slices (see opposite).

Make the risotto next. Bring the stock to a simmer, then set the heat so that it is kept very hot, but does not boil and evaporate. Put the olive oil and half the butter in a heavy-based saucepan over a medium heat, add the onion and garlic and sauté until a pale golden colour. Tip in the tomatoes and add the basil, $1/2$ teaspoon of salt and some black pepper. Cook gently, uncovered, for 10 minutes, then pour all but $1/2$ cup of the mixture into a bowl and set aside.

Add the rice to the tomato mixture in the pan. Increase the temperature to medium-high and stir for 2–3 minutes. Pour in the wine and cook, stirring, until it has nearly evaporated. Start adding the stock as described in the recipe for Basic Risotto (see page 35) and cook until the rice is three-quarters cooked.

Layer the ingredients in a greased ovenproof dish (about 16–18cm diameter and 8–9cm deep) in this order: rice, parmesan cheese, eggplant slices, tomato mixture and mozzarella. Finish with a top layer of rice, then parmesan cheese. (The dish can be prepared ahead to this point, refrigerated, then cooked when required, but it must be brought to room temperature before cooking.)

Dot the top with butter and bake in an oven preheated to 200°C for about 15 minutes until it is crisp on top and heated through. Allow to stand for 5 minutes before serving.

TIME-SAVERS

Making risotto is easy but time-consuming, because the best result is achieved by stirring the rice continuously while adding small amounts of hot stock. If time is short, but you like the idea of serving an Italian rice dish, consider making a rice mould (such as Spinach Torte, see page 32) or a layered gratin rice dish (such as Oven-baked Eggplant Risotto, see this page) both of which are quicker to make and can be prepared in advance, or check out the Ferron method on page 41. The oven-baked eggplant risotto is rich and satisfying. It can be prepared ahead and requires only a quick reheat in the oven to meld the flavours together. Serve as a main course with a good salad.

OVEN-BAKED EGGPLANT

Fried eggplant (aubergine) is rich and delicious, but it has a bad habit of soaking up too much oil. If the eggplant is to be incorporated into other dishes (e.g. the eggplant risotto on this page), it can be brushed with olive oil and oven-baked. This uses much less oil than frying and ensures the dish it is incorporated into does not become excessively rich and oily.

Slice the eggplant into rounds and brush both sides with olive oil. Lay the slices flat in one layer on a baking tray (line the tray with a teflon baking sheet if you have one). Bake for about 20 minutes, or until tender and brown, in an oven preheated to 180°C. Use immediately, or cool, refrigerate and use within 24 hours.

Oven-baked eggplant risotto

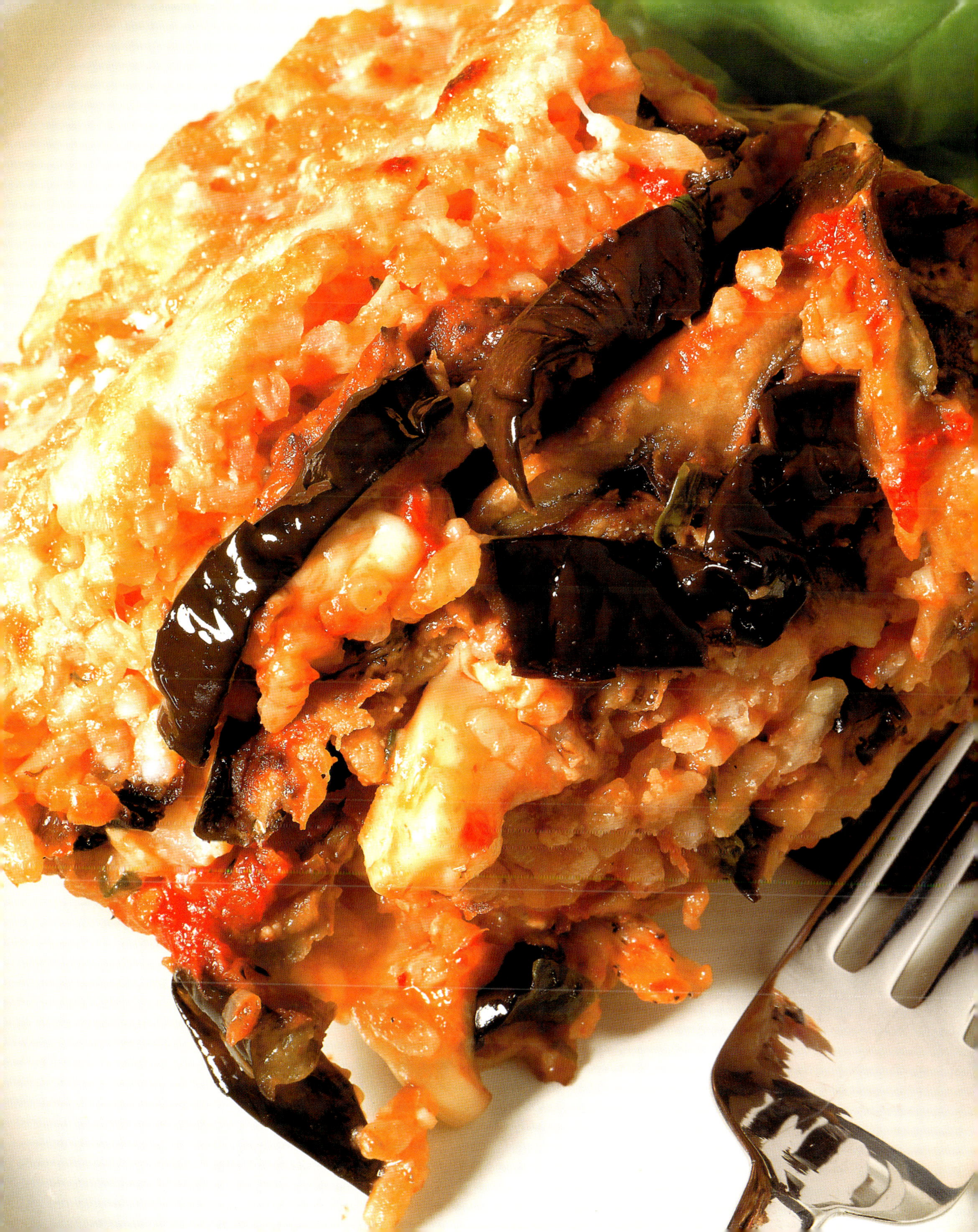

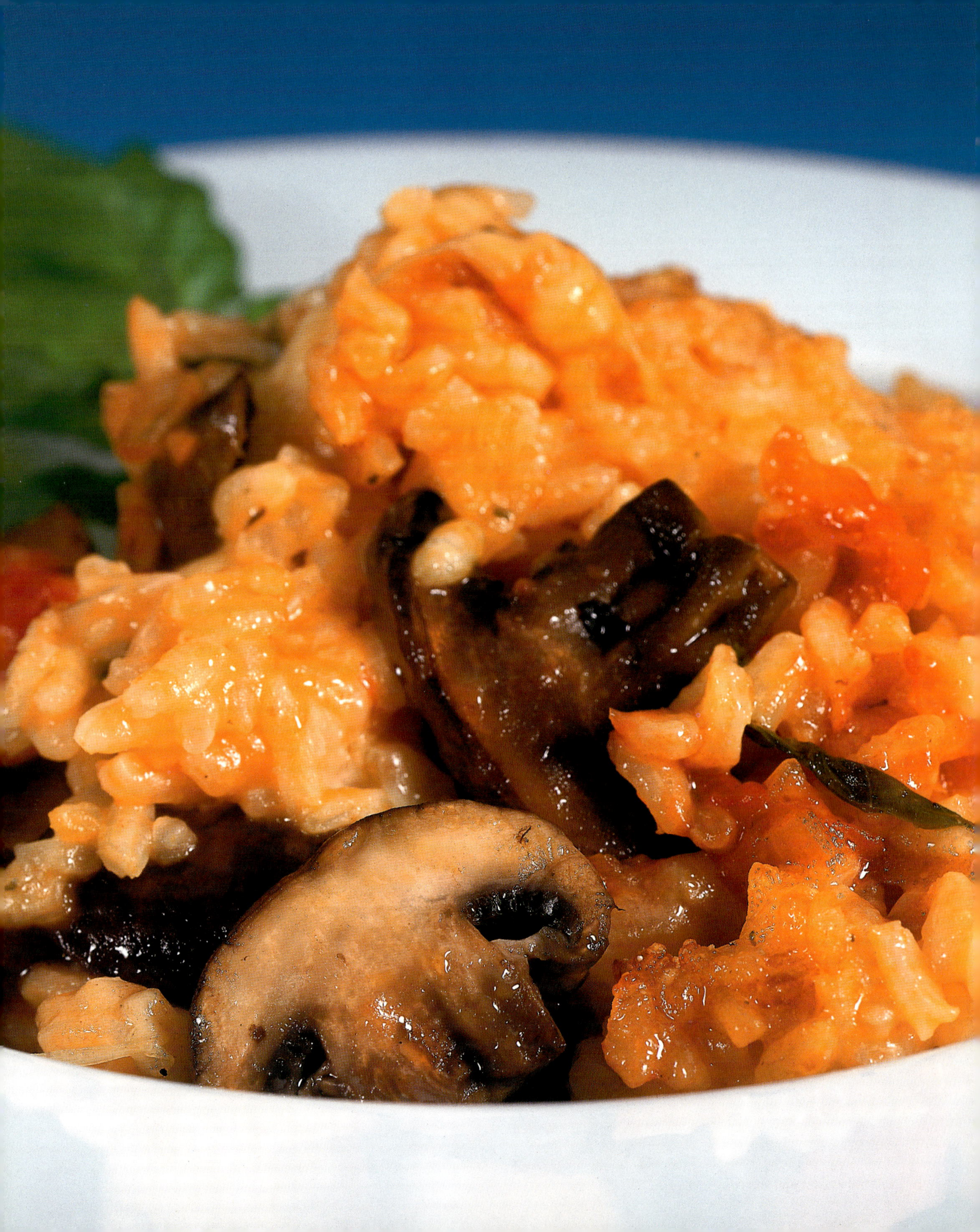

bello riso OVEN-BAKED MUSHROOM RISOTTO

SERVES 4

4 tablespoons butter
500g open-cup portabello mushrooms, wiped with a damp cloth and cut into thick slices
salt
freshly ground black pepper to taste
2 tablespoons olive oil
1 small onion, finely chopped
2 cloves garlic, crushed
400g can Italian tomatoes, mashed
2 tablespoons finely chopped basil
1 litre (4 cups) light vegetable stock
350g Italian rice – arborio, vialone nano, carnaroli
100ml dry white wine
50g ($\frac{1}{2}$ cup) freshly grated parmesan (parmigiano reggiano) cheese
150g mozzarella 'bocconcini' in whey, drained and sliced

Heat a large frying pan over a high heat. Add 2 tablespoons of butter and let it sizzle. Put in the mushrooms and cook, stirring, for 2–3 minutes; the butter will be absorbed and the pan will look dry. Season with salt and pepper, lower the heat and continue stirring until the juices start to run from the mushrooms. Increase the heat again and cook until most of the juice has evaporated.

Put the olive oil and 1 tablespoon of the butter in a heavy-based saucepan over a medium heat. Add the onion and garlic and sauté until a pale golden colour. Add the tomatoes, basil, $\frac{1}{2}$ teaspoon of salt and some black pepper. Cook gently, uncovered, for 10 minutes, then pour all but $\frac{1}{2}$ cup of the mixture into a bowl and set aside.

Meanwhile, bring the stock to a simmer, then set the heat so that it is kept very hot, but does not boil and evaporate.

Add rice to the tomato sauce in the pan. Increase the temperature to medium-high and stir for 2–3 minutes. Pour in the wine and cook, stirring, until it has nearly evaporated. Start adding stock a ladleful at a time. Continue cooking and adding stock as described in the recipe for Basic Risotto (see page 35), until the rice is about three-quarters cooked. If you run out of stock, use hot water. Aim to finish with the rice sloppy but not soupy (it will take 15–18 minutes).

Layer the ingredients in a buttered ovenproof dish in this order: rice, parmesan cheese, mushrooms, tomato sauce and mozzarella. Finish with a top layer of rice and parmesan cheese. (The dish can be prepared ahead to this point, refrigerated, then cooked when required, but it must be brought up to room temperature before cooking.)

Dot the top with butter and bake in an oven preheated to 200°C for about 15 minutes, until it is crisp on top and heated through. Allow the risotto to stand for 5 minutes before serving. Accompany with a green salad.

Oven-baked mushroom risotto

sea fresh SPRING RISOTTO WITH ROASTED FENNEL AND SCALLOPS

SERVES 6

2 medium bulbs of fennel, cooked as described in the recipe for Roasted Fennel (see page 114)
1.2 litres stock
3 tablespoons olive oil
50g fresh unsalted butter
½ small onion, finely chopped
1 large clove garlic, crushed
400g Italian rice – arborio, vialone nano, carnaroli
125ml (½ cup) dry white wine
salt
freshly ground black pepper to taste
grated zest of 1 lemon
300g scallops, cleaned, rinsed and patted dry
2 tablespoons capers, drained, rinsed and chopped

Roughly chop the roasted fennel, discarding any fibrous pieces.

Bring the stock to a simmer, then set the heat so that it is kept very hot, but does not boil and evaporate.

Choose a 2.5–3 litre cast-iron casserole or heavy-based saucepan. Set it over a medium heat, pour in 2 tablespoons of the olive oil and three-quarters of the butter. Add the onion and garlic and sauté until a pale golden colour, then tip in the rice and stir thoroughly. Cook the rice for a minute, stirring. Add the white wine and cook for 3–4 minutes. Start adding stock (2 ladlefuls to begin with). Stir gently but continuously until the stock has nearly evaporated. Continue cooking in this way, adding more stock once the rice is no longer sloppy, for 10–12 minutes, stirring continuously to stop the rice sticking.

The rice is ready when the grains are al dente – still firm and only just cooked through, but no longer chalky inside. This will take around 20 minutes. Season with ¾ teaspoon of salt and plenty of black pepper, then whip in the rest of the butter and the lemon zest. Stir the prepared fennel through. Cover with a lid and leave to infuse for 2 minutes.

While the risotto is infusing, cook the scallops. Have ready a large heavy-based frying pan, or a ridged cast-iron steak pan, heating over a medium-high heat. Put the scallops in a bowl, drizzle the last tablespoon of oil over and toss the scallops to coat them in the oil. When the pan is hot, put in some of the scallops (do not crowd the pan – cook in 2–3 batches if necessary) and cook them on both sides for 1–2 minutes until nearly cooked through. Transfer them to a dish as they are done. Season with black pepper and add the capers.

Serve the risotto immediately in hot bowls, topped with the seared scallops.

PASTA AND RISOTTO dishes that feature seafood are traditionally served without parmesan cheese in Italy. However, in your kitchen you can make your own rules. If you decide to whip some grated parmesan into the risotto along with the butter, cut the salt back to ½ teaspoon or less. The risotto can be made with Ferron rice using the no-

golden filaments RISOTTO MILANESE

SERVES 4–6

1.2 litres light chicken stock
2 tablespoons olive oil
75g butter
1 large knob of beef or veal marrow, chopped (optional)
1 small onion, finely chopped
125ml (½ cup) dry white wine
400g (about 1¾ cups) Italian rice – arborio, vialone nano, carnaroli
¼ teaspoon saffron strands, dissolved in 150ml hot water
½ teaspoon salt
freshly ground black pepper to taste
5 tablespoons freshly grated parmesan (parmigiano reggiano) cheese, plus extra for serving

Bring the stock to simmering point, then set the heat so that the stock is kept very hot, but does not boil and evaporate.

Choose a 2.5–3 litre heavy-based saucepan. Set it over a medium heat, put in the olive oil, half the butter and the chopped bone marrow if using. Add the onion and sauté until a pale golden colour, then pour in the wine and cook until evaporated.

Tip in the unwashed rice, sauté for 2 minutes, stirring often with a wooden spoon, then stir in a ladleful of hot stock. Continue cooking and adding stock as described in the recipe for Basic Risotto (see page 35), but after 15 minutes cooking time, stir in the dissolved saffron.

Continue cooking until the rice is al dente, then remove the casserole from the heat, add salt and black pepper, the remaining butter and the parmesan cheese. Beat well for 2 minutes, cover with a lid, and leave for another minute to allow the flavours to fuse. Serve hot.

This is a traditional accompaniment to Ossobuco (see page 94).

organic grains BASIC FERRON NO-STIR RISOTTO

SERVES 4–6

2 tablespoons extra virgin olive oil
1 small onion, finely chopped
2 cloves garlic, finely chopped
2 cups Ferron risotto rice, vialone nano or carnaroli
150ml dry wine (optional)
4 cups light vegetable stock, brought to boiling point just before adding to the rice
salt
freshly ground black pepper to taste
extra virgin olive oil or butter
freshly grated parmesan cheese

Heat 2 tablespoons of oil in a wide but shallow saucepan and add the onion and garlic. Cook gently until softened but not coloured. Add the rice and cook for 2–3 minutes, stirring, until the rice feels hot. Add the wine, if using, and let it evaporate. Add the boiling stock all at once, season with salt and black pepper, stir and bring back to the boil. Stir again, cover with a lid and immediately reduce the heat to a simmer. Cook gently for 14–16 minutes. Take off the heat. Add a little extra virgin olive oil or butter and a few tablespoons of parmesan cheese. Beat for 30 seconds, cover with the lid for 1 minute, then serve immediately.

OTHER FLAVOURINGS can be added at the end, before the risotto is creamed.

If using porcini mushrooms, soak them first in hot water for 30 minutes, strain, reserving the liquid, rinse and chop (Full instructions for the preparation of porcini mushrooms are given on page 16.) Add to the risotto about halfway through cooking. Use some of the strained soaking liquid in the risotto.

For pumpkin risotto, use red wine in the cooking. Add the rice, then the boiling stock, and cook for 15 minutes as described. Add 1 small cooked, cubed pumpkin and a large knob of butter, some chopped parsley and parmesan.

BASIC POLENTA

Polenta (ground maize) is a versatile, nutritionally rich ingredient that can easily form the cornerstone of a meal. To make half the quantity (as specified in several of the following recipes), simply halve the ingredients, i.e. 1.25 litres of water, 1 teaspoon of salt and 250g of polenta.

2.5 litres water
2 teaspoons salt
500g polenta

Bring the water to the boil in a large, wide (not tall and narrow) saucepan. Add the salt, then sprinkle in the polenta a handful at a time, letting it fall through your fingers from a height. Stir continuously, using a wooden spoon. If you add the polenta too fast, it will form lumps (if this happens, fish them out because they will not break down during cooking). Once all the polenta is added, turn the heat to low and cook, giving 3–4 good stirs every 20 seconds or so, for 25 minutes.

When the polenta is cooked, it can be served immediately as a first course, like pasta. Beat in a large knob of butter and 1 cup of freshly grated parmesan cheese. Serve with extra cheese and butter at the table.

INSTANT POLENTA

Regular polenta gives off a more pronounced corn aroma as it cooks and has a richer corn taste and gruntier texture than instant polenta, but most people will find these differences hard to detect. If you're a purist, use regular polenta, which will take about 25 minutes to cook. But if you like speedy cooking, opt for the instant variety that will cook in about 5 minutes.

THE WOODEN SPOON TEST

The best way to check if slow-cooking polenta is done is to insert a wooden spoon in the centre of the pot. In the early stages of cooking, the spoon will flop to the sides. As the polenta cooks and firms, it will support the spoon. When it will stay upright in the middle of the polenta, it is cooked.

bubbling layers POLENTA AND MUSHROOM PIE

SERVES 6 AS A MAIN COURSE

1 batch polenta made with half quantities (see this page)
70g butter
6 level tablespoons plain flour
450ml milk
100ml cream
salt
good grinding of black pepper
freshly grated nutmeg
75g (3/4 cup) freshly grated parmesan (parmigiano reggiano) cheese
large knob of butter
400g button mushrooms, sliced

Cook the polenta as described in the recipe for Basic Polenta. Pour half of it into a shallow, buttered ovenproof dish (25cm x 18cm). Put the other half on a board or tray and spread it out with a damp knife to the same size as the dish. Smooth the top then leave it to cool.

Gently melt the first measure of butter in a small saucepan, take it off the heat and stir in the flour. Blend in the milk and cream, put the pan over a medium heat and stir constantly until boiling. Turn the heat to low and cook for 1–2 minutes more, stirring. Add 3/4 teaspoon of salt, black pepper, nutmeg and 3 tablespoons of the parmesan cheese. Cover with a lid and set aside.

Heat a large frying pan over a medium-high heat and add the second measure of butter. When it is sizzling, add the mushrooms, increase the heat to high and cook, tossing often, until the butter is absorbed and the mushrooms are glistening. Add 1/2 teaspoon of salt and some black pepper. Keep the pan over a high heat and cook until all the liquid evaporates.

Scatter half the cooked mushrooms over the polenta in the dish and spoon half the béchamel sauce over, then lay the second slab of polenta on top, trimming it to fit if necessary. Cover with the remaining mushrooms and sauce, then scatter the remaining parmesan cheese over the top.

Bake in an oven preheated to 220°C for 25–30 minutes, or until it is golden and bubbling on top. Serve hot, cut into squares with a spinach salad.

sauce it up POLENTA PIE WITH PUTTANESCA SAUCE

SERVES 6

1 batch polenta made with half quantities (see page 42)
1 batch Puttanesca Sauce (see page 54)
75g (¾ cup) freshly grated parmesan (parmigiano reggiano) cheese, plus extra for serving
50g butter

Cook the polenta as described in the recipe for Basic Polenta or Instant Polenta (see page 42). Spread it out 1cm thick on a plastic tray and leave to cool. Make the Puttanesca Sauce.

Cut the polenta into large diamond shapes. Lightly butter a shallow ovenproof dish, about 23cm in diameter, and put in a layer of slightly overlapping polenta shapes. Pour the sauce over and sprinkle with half of the parmesan cheese. Form another layer of polenta shapes on top, again slightly overlapping, and sprinkle with the rest of the cheese. Melt the butter and drizzle a little over each piece of polenta. (The polenta pie can be prepared several hours ahead to this point; cover with plastic food wrap and refrigerate, but bring to room temperature before baking.)

Bake in an oven preheated to 220°C and allow the pie to heat through and brown on top (about 30 minutes). Serve hot, with extra grated parmesan cheese.

OTHER WAYS TO SERVE POLENTA
Polenta can be topped with a ragù, tomato sauce or porcini mushroom sauce (or sauce of your choice) to make it more interesting, or used as a pillow for sausages (see the recipe for Sausage Coil with Hot Polenta and Sautéed Mushrooms, page 96), poultry or game.

If it is to be served with a main course in place of potatoes or rice, mix in a little butter and cheese as described earlier, and mound the polenta in a heated serving dish (a large, scrubbed wooden board is traditional; the wood absorbs a little of the liquid, preventing it from spilling out). Form a hollow in the centre and pour in the saucy part of a stew, braise or casserole (serve the meaty parts separately).

Alternatively, spread it out on trays, leave to cool and continue with the chosen recipe when desired. The polenta can be prepared to this point 48 hours in advance; cover in plastic food wrap and refrigerate. The polenta can be grilled, fried, barbecued, or layered in a pie dish with a sauce and cheese, then oven-baked.

a good grilling GRILLED PARMESAN POLENTA WITH OLIVES, PINE NUTS AND ROSEMARY

SERVES 8 AS A STARTER OR 6 AS A MAIN COURSE WITH SALAD

1.2 litres water
1 teaspoon salt
250g polenta (use the instant variety, which cooks in 5 minutes)
30g fresh butter
50g (½ cup) freshly grated parmesan (parmigiano reggiano) cheese
3 red peppers (capsicums)
1 yellow pepper (capsicum)
extra virgin olive oil
2 cloves garlic, chopped
1 tablespoon chopped rosemary
½ cup stoned and chopped black olives
3 anchovy fillets (buy anchovy fillets in oil), drained and squished (optional)
¼ cup fresh pine nuts (old ones can be rancid)
sea salt (optional)
olive oil

Bring the water to the boil in a large, wide (not tall and narrow) saucepan. Add the salt, then shake in the polenta from a height. Stir continuously, using a wooden spoon. When the polenta is cooked, 5 minutes for instant polenta (or about 20 minutes if you use regular polenta), stir in the butter and parmesan cheese. Tip it onto a shallow tray and spread out to 1cm thick. Smooth the surface and leave to cool. The cooked polenta can be stored for several hours at room temperature, or it can be made a day in advance, but keep it covered and refrigerated until you are ready to use it.

Cook the peppers in hot coals, or roast them in a very hot oven for about 20 minutes, until blackened and charred (see page 22). When cool, peel off the skins and slip out the cores and seeds, reserving any juices. Chop the peppers into fine strips. Heat 1 tablespoon of extra virgin olive oil over a low heat in a small pan and add the garlic and rosemary. Cook gently until aromatic, but don't let the garlic colour. Add the black olives, take the pan off the heat then stir in the peppers and any juice. If using anchovies, blend them into the mixture. This can be prepared a few hours ahead; cover and keep it at room temperature.

Toast the pine nuts in a small dry pan, or fry them in a little hot oil. (I prefer them fried in hot oil; move them around in the pan as they colour, turn them onto a plate lined with absorbent kitchen paper and sprinkle with sea salt.)

When ready to finish off the polenta, cut it into squares and brush it on both sides with olive oil. Barbecue the pieces of polenta on a very hot barbecue grill, until lightly browned and crispy. Transfer to a serving platter. Spoon on the pepper topping and scatter pine nuts on top. Serve immediately with a good, interesting green salad.

THIS IS NOT WHAT they do with polenta in Italy, but who cares! It's a fantastic recipe for a vegetarian barbecue – it's got everything (you can prepare it ahead, it's got loads of flavour, it's filling and it's good for you). Serve it as a vegetarian starter (omit the anchovies) or as a main course.

Grilled parmesan polenta with olives, pine nuts and rosemary

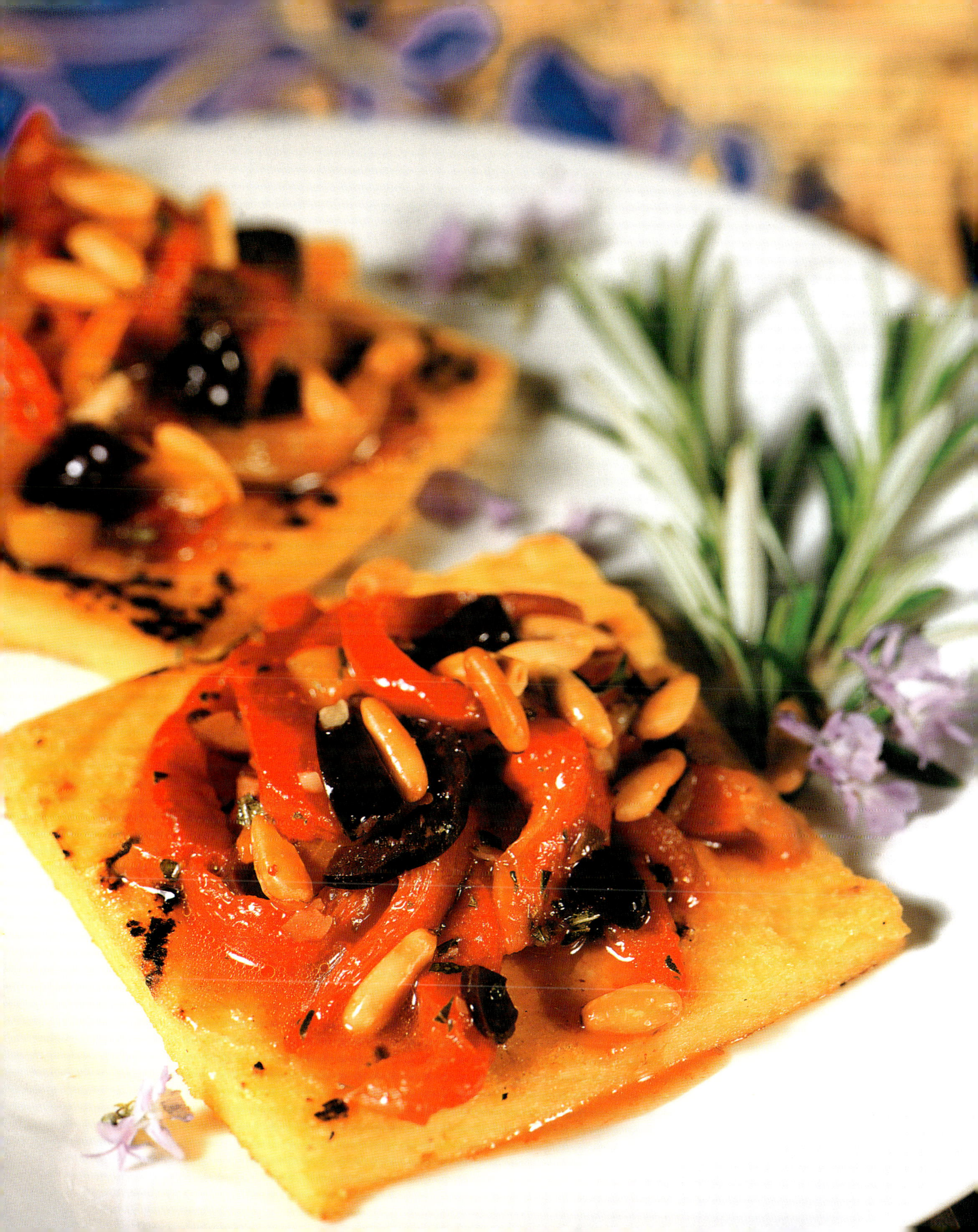

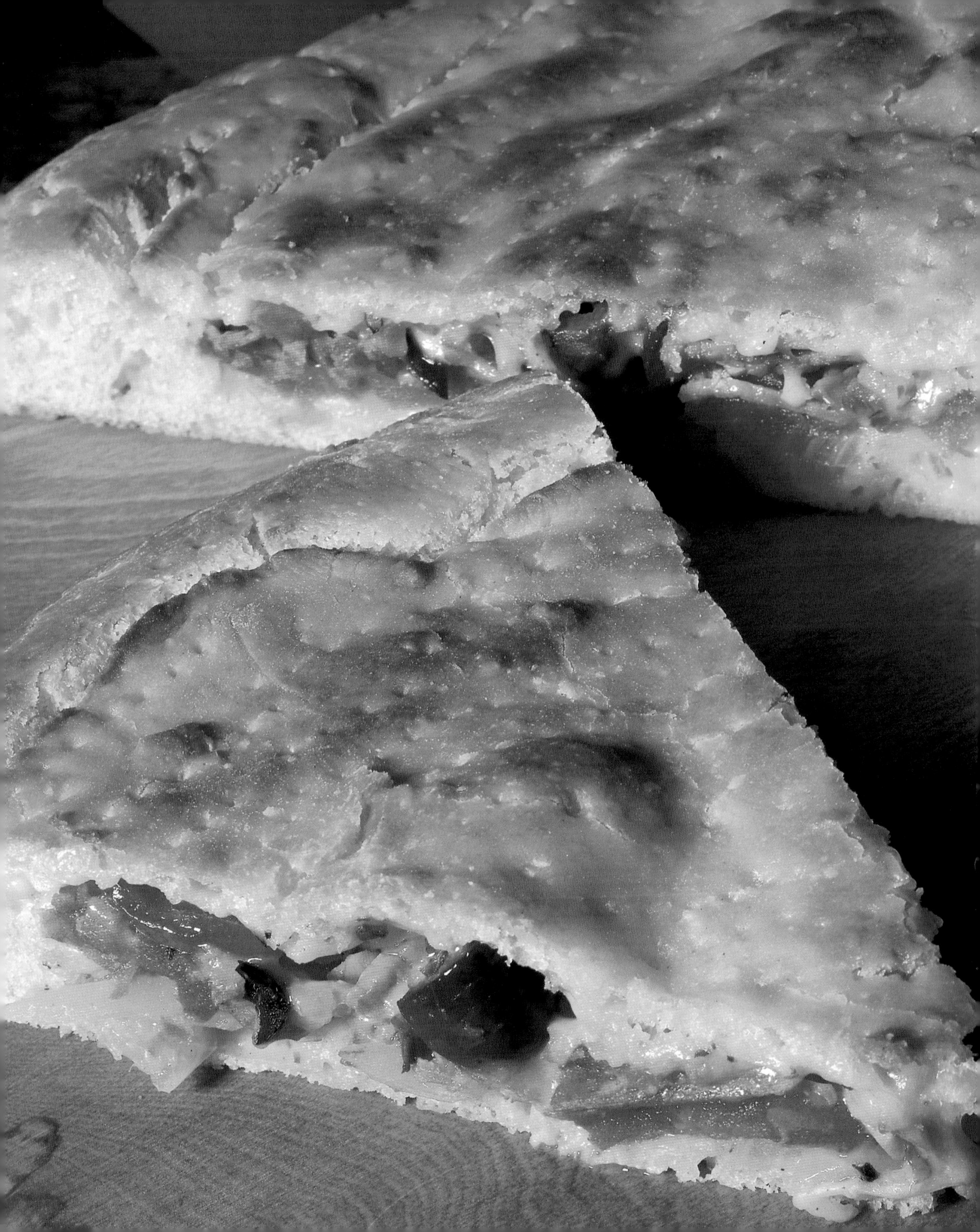

golden flakes SCACCIATA

SERVES 8

1 batch focaccia dough, made to end of Stage 2 (see page 34)
a little extra plain flour and olive oil

FILLING
2 fleshy tomatoes, preferably plum tomatoes
1 medium onion, sliced into rings
150g ham off the bone, cut into thin, short strips
100g (about 20) black olives, stoned and chopped
1 teaspoon dried oregano
freshly ground black pepper to taste
125g emmenthal cheese, thinly sliced

First make the dough. Cut the dough in half. Lightly flour one half and set it aside. Roll out the other half on a floured surface, dusting it with more flour to prevent sticking. If the dough is difficult to roll – if it keeps shrinking back after rolling – leave it to rest for 2–3 minutes. Roll out to about 32cm in diameter. Wrap the dough around a rolling pin and transfer it to a baking tray lined with a teflon baking sheet or greased aluminium foil.

Next, make the filling. Cut a slice off the flower end of the tomatoes (the opposite end to the stalk or core end). Squeeze out most of the seeds and juice, then slice the tomatoes thinly. Scatter the onion rings over the dough, then add the tomatoes, ham and olives, keeping the mixture in slightly from the edges. Sprinkle the oregano over, grind on some black pepper and cover with emmenthal cheese.

Roll out the second half of the dough, wrap it around the rolling pin and unroll it gently on top of the pie. Press the edges of the dough together to seal, then crimp the edges with your fingers. Prick the surface all over with a fork, then brush with olive oil. Leave uncovered in a warm spot for 15 minutes.

Bake in an oven preheated to 200°C for 40–45 minutes, or until it is golden brown on the top and bottom. Leave on the tray for 2–3 minutes, then carefully slide off onto a cooling rack. Cool for 5–10 minutes. Serve cut into large wedges.

Scacciata

a food for all

CRAB AND LEMON PASTA	50
FETTUCCINE WITH GORGONZOLA SAUCE	50
SPAGHETTI SALTATI	53
FUSILLI WITH TOMATO AND ROSEMARY SAUCE	53
SPAGHETTI PUTTANESCA	54
ZITI WITH EGGS FRIED IN CHILLI OIL	54
TAGLIATELLE WITH PESTO	56
FUSILLI WITH EGGPLANT AND GREEN PEPPER	57
RIGATONI WITH TOMATO SAUCE	58
PENNE WITH QUICK CHILLIED TOMATO SAUCE AND FRIED ZUCCHINI	60
LINGUINE WITH CASHEW NUT AND GARLIC SAUCE	61
LINGUINE WITH ZUCCHINI AND MARJORAM	61
SPAGHETTINI WITH FRESH TOMATO SAUCE, CHILLI AND SAFFRON PRAWNS	62
CONCHIGLIE WITH BUTTON MUSHROOMS	62
FETTUCCINE WITH ZUCCHINI	64
SUMMER PASTA SALAD	67
LASAGNETTE WITH ITALIAN SAUSAGE AND MUSHROOM RAGÙ	67
MACCHERONI WITH CAULIFLOWER SAUCE	68
TAGLIATELLE WITH PROSCIUTTO	68
BAKED RIGATONI WITH RICOTTA	69
SPAGHETTI WITH GARLIC AND OIL	69
FETTUCCINE ALLA CARBONARA	70
FETTUCCINE WITH ROMAN-STYLE MEAT SAUCE	70

silken sheets shaped to suit

dancing on fire with chilli-laced oil, or

bathed in sauce as smooth as velvet

pasta pleases and teases the palate

food to nourish and nurture the soul

seasons

light and lemony CRAB AND LEMON PASTA

SERVES 4 AS A STARTER

250g dried Italian egg pasta (or fresh pasta such as fettuccine)
salt
300ml cream
zest of 2 lemons
freshly ground black pepper to taste
1 tablespoon green peppercorns, drained
sea salt
250g fresh crabmeat (if frozen, thaw, then squeeze out excess moisture by hand)
2 tablespoons chopped flat leaf parsley
sautéed crab claws (optional)

Cook the pasta in plenty of gently boiling, well-salted water until al dente; this will take only a few minutes and you should have everything co-ordinated before putting the pasta on to cook.

Meanwhile, put the cream, lemon zest, black pepper, green peppercorns and a good pinch of sea salt in a small pan and heat gently. Reduce by a quarter. When the pasta is nearly ready, add the crabmeat to the cream sauce. Cook for a few minutes more, add the parsley and check the seasoning.

Drain the pasta, turn it into a heated serving bowl and pour the crab sauce over. Toss well and serve immediately in hot pasta bowls. Garnish with crab claws if you like.

THIS IS LIGHT and lemony, despite it being a rich cream sauce, and belongs on delicate pasta. The green peppercorns burst on the palate and lift the flavour.

creamy and dreamy FETTUCCINE WITH GORGONZOLA SAUCE

SERVES 4 AS A STARTER

40g butter
125g creamy gorgonzola cheese
170ml cream
salt
300g fresh fettuccine (or tagliatelle)
50g (1/2 cup) freshly grated parmesan (parmigiano reggiano) cheese, plus extra for serving

Choose a large saucepan or casserole which is big enough to hold all the pasta once it is cooked. Put the butter, gorgonzola cheese, 100ml of the cream and a good pinch of salt in the saucepan. Mash the ingredients, using a potato masher or strong wooden spoon, and warm through over a medium heat.

Meanwhile, bring a large saucepan of water to the boil. Salt well, then put in the pasta. Cook gently for 2–3 minutes or until al dente.

Drain the pasta and add to the warmed sauce. Pour in the rest of the cream and toss gently. Sprinkle with the parmesan cheese. Toss gently and serve immediately from the pan.

A RICH, SEDUCTIVE sauce that takes less than 5 minutes to make. Use a mild creamy blue cheese in place of gorgonzola if you prefer.

CO-ORDINATING PASTA AND CREAMY SAUCES

It might be easy for the Italians, but for the rest of us co-ordinating perfectly cooked pasta and a perfectly cooked creamy sauce is tricky. Until you feel confident enough to whip up the sauce while the pasta cooks (the way Italians do it, making for some very quick dishes), it is safer to partly prepare the sauce before putting the pasta on to cook. Remember not to over-reduce cream sauces; it is better to keep the sauce on the thin side so it will flow over the pasta. If it is too thick, it will stick and quickly turn tacky and heavy. Reduce the sauce until it just coats the back of a wooden spoon. See Pesto Tips (page 56).

Crab and lemon pasta

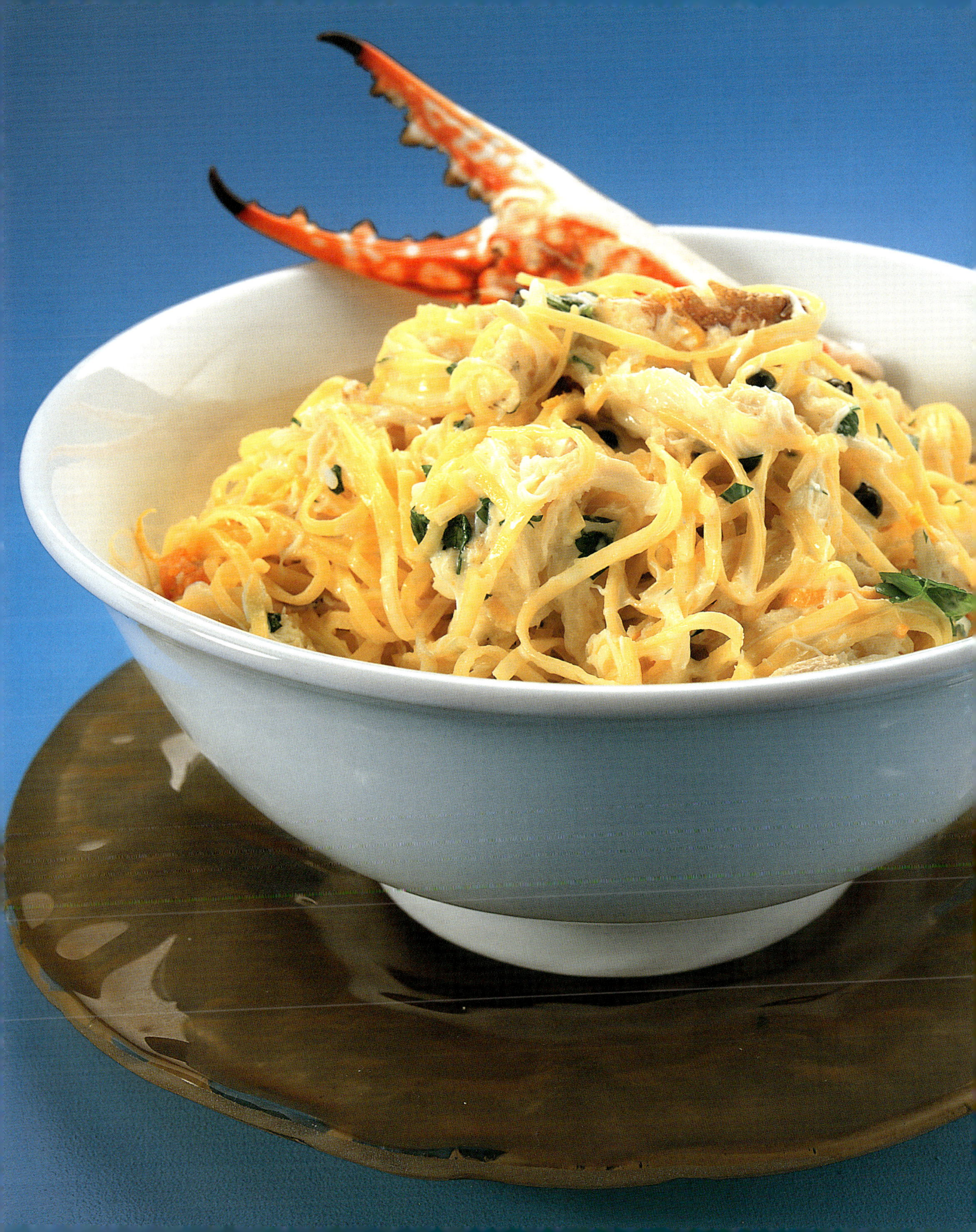

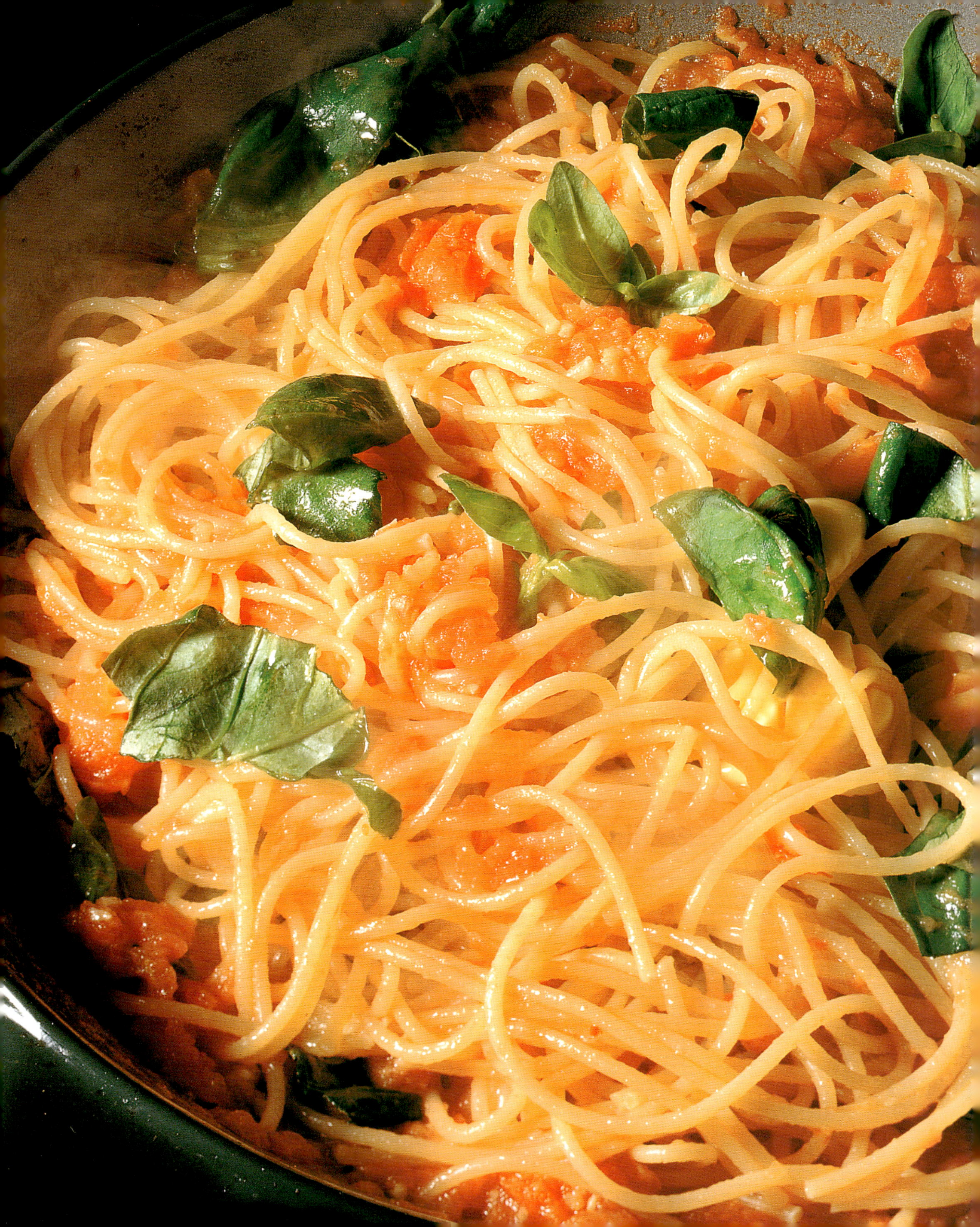

jumping pasta SPAGHETTI SALTATI

SERVES 4 AS A STARTER

4 large vine-ripened tomatoes, skinned
3 tablespoons extra virgin olive oil
4 cloves garlic, halved
salt
3 tablespoons chopped basil
350g spaghetti
knob of butter
2–3 small dried 'bird's eye' chillies, crushed (optional)
freshly grated parmesan (parmigiano reggiano) cheese
   for serving

Halve the tomatoes, remove the cores and flick out the seeds. Chop the flesh very finely until pulpy. Put the extra virgin olive oil in a large heavy-based frying pan and add the garlic. Cook gently until golden, then remove with a slotted spoon and discard. Take the pan off the heat, carefully tip in the tomatoes and stir well. Return the pan to the heat and cook the tomatoes gently, uncovered, for 20 minutes, or until sauce-like. Add $1/4$ teaspoon of salt and the basil and turn off the heat.

Cook the pasta in plenty of gently boiling, well-salted water until nearly al dente. Drain. Set the frying pan back over a medium-high heat and add the butter and the chillies, if using. Mix well, then tip the spaghetti into the pan. Heat through for 1 minute, tossing, then transfer to hot pasta bowls. Serve immediately with plenty of parmesan cheese.

evocative scents FUSILLI WITH TOMATO AND ROSEMARY SAUCE

SERVES 4 AS A STARTER

75ml olive oil
3 cloves garlic, crushed
2 sprigs fresh rosemary
600g ($1 1/2$ cans) Italian tomatoes, mashed
salt
freshly ground black pepper to taste
400g fusilli (pasta spirals)
freshly grated parmesan cheese for serving

Put the olive oil in a heavy-based saucepan, set it over a gentle heat, and add the garlic and rosemary. Cook gently, stirring occasionally, until the garlic turns a pale biscuit colour. Remove and discard the rosemary sprigs, then carefully pour in the tomatoes. Add $1/4$ teaspoon of salt and a little black pepper.

Bring the sauce to the boil, then lower the heat and simmer, uncovered, for 25 minutes, or until the sauce is nice and pulpy.

Meanwhile, cook the pasta in plenty of gently boiling, well-salted water until al dente. Drain briefly and turn the pasta into a heated serving bowl. Quickly toss three-quarters of the sauce through the pasta, then pour the rest of the sauce on top. Serve immediately with grated parmesan cheese.

Spaghetti saltati

sustaining SPAGHETTI PUTTANESCA

SERVES 6 AS A STARTER OR 4 AS A MAIN COURSE

PUTTANESCA SAUCE
75ml extra virgin olive oil
2 cloves garlic, crushed
75g can anchovies, drained and mashed (optional)
2 small dried 'bird's eye' chillies, crushed (optional)
600g (1 ½ cans) canned Italian tomatoes, mashed
2 tablespoons Italian tomato paste
1 tablespoon capers, drained (if large, chop them)
1 tablespoon finely chopped fresh oregano (or 1 teaspoon dried oregano)
salt
freshly ground black pepper to taste
50g (approximately 10) black olives, pitted and chopped

500g spaghetti (or use spaghettini, penne, penne rigati, or rigatoni)
freshly grated parmesan (parmigiano reggiano) cheese for serving

Put the extra virgin olive oil in a heavy-based saucepan, set it over a medium heat and drop in the garlic. Sauté the garlic until it turns a pale biscuit colour, then stir in the anchovies and chillies, if using. Carefully tip in the tomatoes, the tomato paste, capers, oregano, a few large pinches of salt and some black pepper (omit the salt if you are adding the anchovies; check the seasoning once the sauce is cooked).

Bring the sauce to the boil, lower the heat and cook gently, stirring occasionally, for 25–30 minutes or until the tomatoes are pulpy. Add the olives.

Meanwhile, cook the pasta in plenty of gently boiling, well-salted water until al dente. Drain briefly and turn it into a heated serving dish. Pour three-quarters of the sauce over the pasta, quickly toss together, then top with the rest of the sauce. Serve immediately with parmesan cheese.

PROSTITUTE'S SPAGHETTI

Without a doubt, this is the most loved pasta dish I've ever put in print. People rave about it and I often return to it myself, because it's got everything a good pasta dish should have: the ingredients are usually close at hand, it's quick to cook, it fills the kitchen with hunger-inducing odours, and it tastes so good, I can't live without it!

The translation of Spaghetti Puttanesca is 'as a prostitute would prepare spaghetti'. Supposedly, ladies of the night whip up a bowl of this when they need a bit of sustenance, as they can shop in advance and have the ingredients ready in the store cupboard. Interestingly, this dish has turned many olive-haters into olive-lovers! A star dish.

sizzling ZITI WITH EGGS FRIED IN CHILLI OIL

SERVES 4 AS A LIGHT MEAL

350g ziti (long tubular pasta)
salt
75ml extra virgin olive oil
3 cloves garlic, peeled and flattened with a mallet
3 (or to taste) small dried 'bird's eye' chillies, crushed
4 eggs, cracked into a jug (try not to break the yolks)
50g (½ cup) freshly grated parmesan (parmigiano reggiano) cheese
2 tablespoons finely chopped parsley

Cook the pasta in plenty of gently boiling, well-salted water until al dente.

Meanwhile, heat 3 tablespoons of the extra virgin olive oil with the garlic and chillies in a large frying pan. Sauté until the garlic is lightly browned; remove and discard the garlic. Pour the eggs carefully into the pan and cook gently until the whites are set.

When the pasta is al dente, drain and shake it very well, then tip it into a heated bowl. Pour the rest of the extra virgin olive oil over, toss well, then add the cheese and parsley. Toss lightly, then dish into individual hot pasta bowls. Top each with a fried egg and pour any flavoured oil from the pan over the top. Serve immediately.

Spaghetti puttanesca

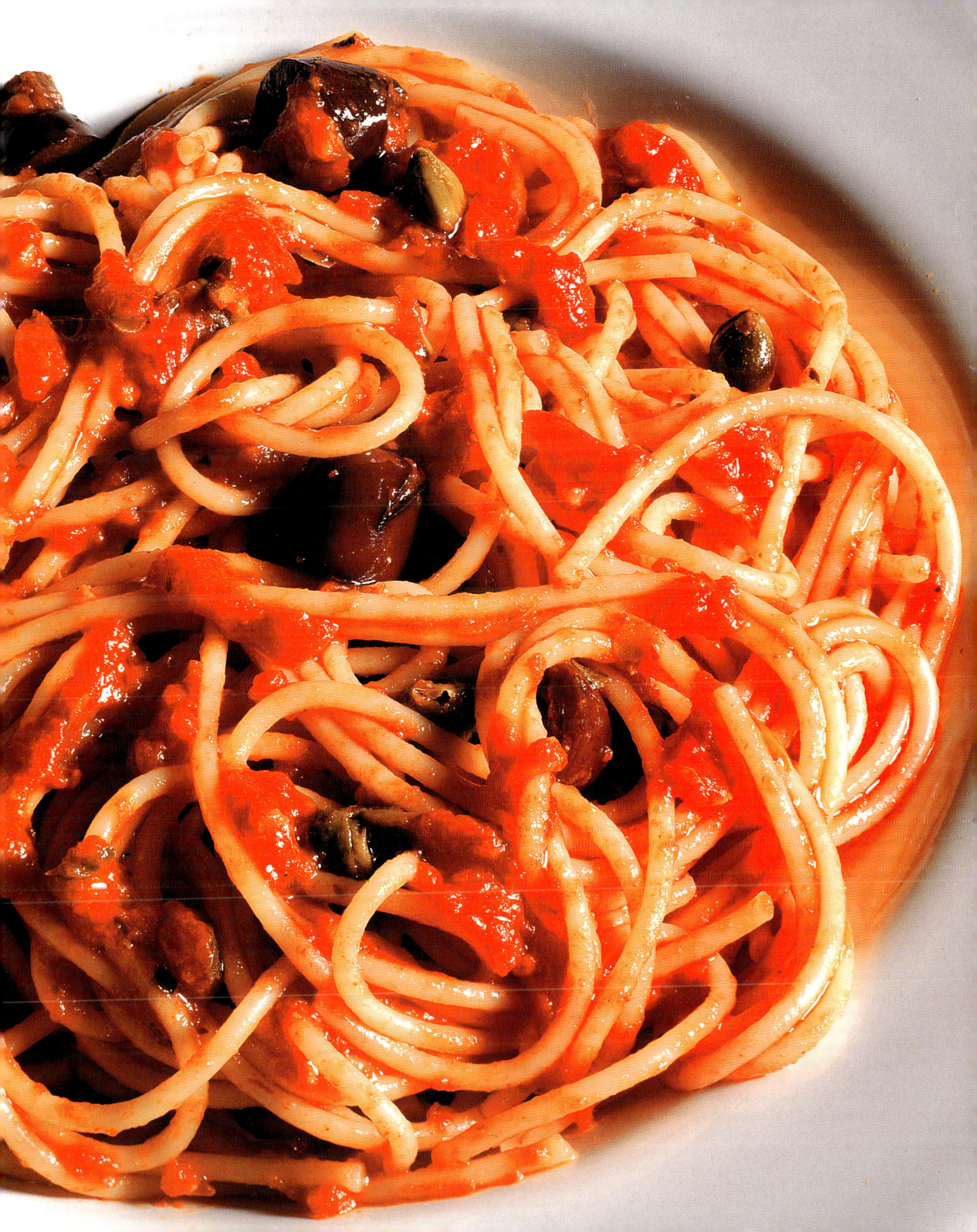

heady scents TAGLIATELLE WITH PESTO

SERVES 6

2 cups tightly packed fresh basil leaves
pinch of salt
2 cloves garlic, chopped
3 tablespoons pine nuts
3 tablespoons extra virgin olive oil
4 tablespoons freshly grated parmesan (parmigiano reggiano) cheese
2 tablespoons freshly grated pecorino Romano cheese (if not available, use 6 tablespoons parmesan cheese)
500g tagliatelle (or spaghetti, spaghettini or trenette)
salt
50g butter

Make the pesto in a food processor. Put the basil leaves, salt, garlic, pine nuts and extra virgin olive oil in the processor bowl fitted with the steel chopping blade and process the mixture until blended. Transfer to a bowl, then mix in the cheeses by hand. Cover the surface with plastic food wrap and set aside until required.

Cook the pasta in plenty of gently boiling, well-salted water until al dente. Drain briefly, reserving a cup of the cooking water, then tip the pasta into a heated serving bowl and quickly toss the butter through. Have ready about half the pesto in a bowl and mix in 2 tablespoons of the reserved pasta water. Toss it through the pasta, adding about 1/4 cup more of the water or enough to give the sauce a light consistency. Toss and serve immediately.

PESTO TIPS

Have you ever eaten a bowl of pasta dressed with an oil-based sauce that starts out tasting delicious, but halfway through you find it's gone sort of heavy and oily – and the more cheese you put on, the tackier it becomes? This happens frequently with a pasta and pesto combination, and strange though it may sound, adding a little of the hot pasta cooking water to the pesto and then to the finished dish will produce a deliciously light result. Here are some more tips.

- *Don't over-drain the pasta – leave a fair amount of moisture clinging to it. If you over-drain it, the heat dries the surface of the pasta and the sauce sinks in instead of sliding over and coating it.*
- *Toss the pasta with a little butter to flavour it and to help the sauce flow over.*
- *Dilute the pesto with a little of the hot pasta water rather than oil (extra oil would make it too rich). The hot water brings up the colour, too.*
- *When you toss the pesto and pasta together, add enough hot pasta water to enable the pesto to flow easily over the pasta.*

PECORINO

Pecorino is the name given to Italian cheeses made from sheep's milk. It is the second word of the name that indicates where the cheese is from, or the style in which it is made. The flavour of the cheese varies according to the pastures the sheep graze on and, as is the case with pecorino Romano, on whether the curd is cooked. Most pecorino cheeses can be eaten young and fresh, or aged and used as a table or a grating cheese.

The recipe for pecorino Romano, the most well known of the pecorino cheeses, has remained unchanged for centuries. The flavour is salty, slightly fruity and tangy once it matures.

Pecorino Sardo (from Sardinia) and pecorino Siciliano (from Sicily) are the most pungent varieties and differ from other pecorinos because the curds are not cooked, the cheese has a higher fat content and it has a shorter ripening time. Peppercorns are added to pecorino Siciliano to make pecorino pepato, a pungent, spicy table cheese.

Pecorino Toscano is eaten as a table cheese when it is young and has a delicate lactic taste and semi-creamy texture. As it ages it becomes more pungent in flavour, firmer and dryer and is used like parmesan as a grating cheese. The same cheese is also sold as pecorino canestrato, the name of which comes from the basket (canestro) the cheese is drained in and which leaves its tell-tale weave on the outside of the cheese.

Pecorino Toscano is my favourite. I love its rich, fruity taste. It's not as pungent as the other pecorinos but it has plenty of fresh vigour in the mouth. Try it as table cheese, drizzled with extra virgin olive oil and accompanied by crusty bread.

savoury spirals FUSILLI WITH EGGPLANT AND GREEN PEPPER

SERVES 4 AS A MAIN COURSE OR 6 AS A STARTER

1 large eggplant (aubergine)
salt
1 large green pepper (capsicum)
100ml olive oil
3 cloves garlic, crushed
2 tablespoons coarsely chopped parsley
freshly ground black pepper to taste
600g (1½ cans) canned Italian tomatoes, mashed
100g (approximately 20) black olives, pitted and chopped
1 tablespoon capers, drained
3 anchovy fillets, mashed (optional)
500g fusilli (pasta spirals)
freshly grated parmesan (parmigiano reggiano) cheese for serving

Cut the eggplant into small cubes, transfer to a sieve and sprinkle with salt. Put a plate underneath to catch the drips, then leave to drain for 30 minutes.

Preheat the oven to 200°C. Put the pepper on the middle rack and place a piece of aluminium foil on the rack below to catch any drips. Roast the pepper for 20–30 minutes or until evenly charred, turning occasionally with tongs. (Consider cooking more peppers at the same time, to use in other dishes, since you already have the oven on.) Transfer the pepper to a plate and allow it to cool. Peel off the blackened skin, slip out the core and seeds, then cut into strips. Set aside with any juices. If preferred, cook the pepper by the alternative methods described in Roasting Peppers (see page 22).

Pat the eggplant cubes dry with absorbent kitchen paper. Heat the olive oil in a heavy-based saucepan and drop in the eggplant cubes. Cook for several minutes until lightly browned, stirring often, then add the garlic and parsley. Grind over plenty of black pepper and cook for 3–4 minutes or until the garlic starts to colour. Don't worry if the cubes of eggplant start to break apart.

Carefully pour the tomatoes in, stir well, then lower the heat. Partially cover with a lid and cook gently for 20 minutes. Lightly mash the sauce with a potato masher, then add the olives, capers, pepper strips and anchovy fillets, if using (if you are not using anchovy fillets, add a pinch or two of salt).

Cook for 5 minutes more, stirring occasionally. The sauce is now ready to use. It can be prepared 24 hours before required if necessary; cool quickly, cover and refrigerate and reheat gently before using.

Cook the pasta in plenty of gently boiling, well-salted water until al dente. Drain briefly and turn the pasta into a heated serving bowl. Quickly toss three-quarters of the sauce through the pasta, then top with the rest. Serve immediately with parmesan cheese.

rich and red RIGATONI WITH TOMATO SAUCE

SERVES 4 AS A MAIN COURSE OR 6 AS A STARTER

75ml extra virgin olive oil
3 large cloves garlic, crushed
2 x 400g cans Italian tomatoes, mashed
2 tablespoons Italian tomato paste
freshly ground black pepper to taste
salt
2 large eggplants (aubergines)
olive oil
500g rigatoni (or elicoidali, penne or penne ziti)
freshly grated parmesan (parmigiano reggiano) cheese
   for serving

Put the extra virgin olive oil and garlic in a heavy-based saucepan and cook gently until it turns a pale biscuit colour.

Carefully pour the tomatoes in. Add the tomato paste, some black pepper and $1/2$ teaspoon of salt. Rinse the tomato cans with a little water (a frugal Italian trick, making sure nothing is wasted!), using about $3/4$ cup of water in total, and add the water to the pan of sauce.

Bring the sauce to the boil, then cook, uncovered, for 30–35 minutes or until reduced and pulpy.

Meanwhile, slice the eggplants into rounds about 5mm thick. Pat dry with absorbent kitchen paper. Heat a good depth of oil (about 1cm deep) in a large heavy-based frying pan over a high heat until it gives off a haze.

Carefully slide in as many slices of eggplant as will fit in one layer and cook until they are a rich golden brown on both sides. Transfer to a plate lined with absorbent kitchen paper and sprinkle lightly with salt. Repeat the process with the rest of the eggplant slices.

When the sauce and eggplant are ready (both can be prepared in advance), cook the pasta in plenty of gently boiling, well-salted water until al dente. Drain briefly then turn the pasta into a heated serving dish. Toss three-quarters of the sauce through the pasta. Spoon the rest of the sauce on top and serve immediately with the eggplant slices (which are best served hottish) and plenty of parmesan cheese.

TOMATO SAUCE is the quintessential pasta sauce served throughout Italy. Other ingredients can be added to break the tedium, but this idea – culled from my Italian family – is one of my favourites.

EGGPLANT AND ZUCCHINI TOPPINGS

Other pasta dishes dressed with tomato-based sauces can be topped with fried eggplant (aubergine) or fried zucchini (courgettes). Adding the vegetables makes the pasta dish visually more enticing and provides contrasts in flavour and texture. It also gives the dish more substance, making it suitable for a main course.

TOMATO SAUCE TIPS

Tomato sauce should be cooked until it is pulpy and no longer watery. Depending on the amount of oil used in the recipe, the oil will either separate from the tomato base or give an oily sheen to the surface of the sauce (both results are correct). It should pour easily off a spoon. If it is over-reduced, it will stick to the pasta instead of flowing over it. If insufficient oil is used, the sauce will be dull in colour and dense in consistency. It will also stick to the pasta.

Most homemade tomato sauces will keep for 3 days in the refrigerator and most can be frozen. If you want to prepare the sauce ahead, reheat it gently in a saucepan while the pasta cooks, or thaw it in a microwave.

Rigatoni with tomato sauce

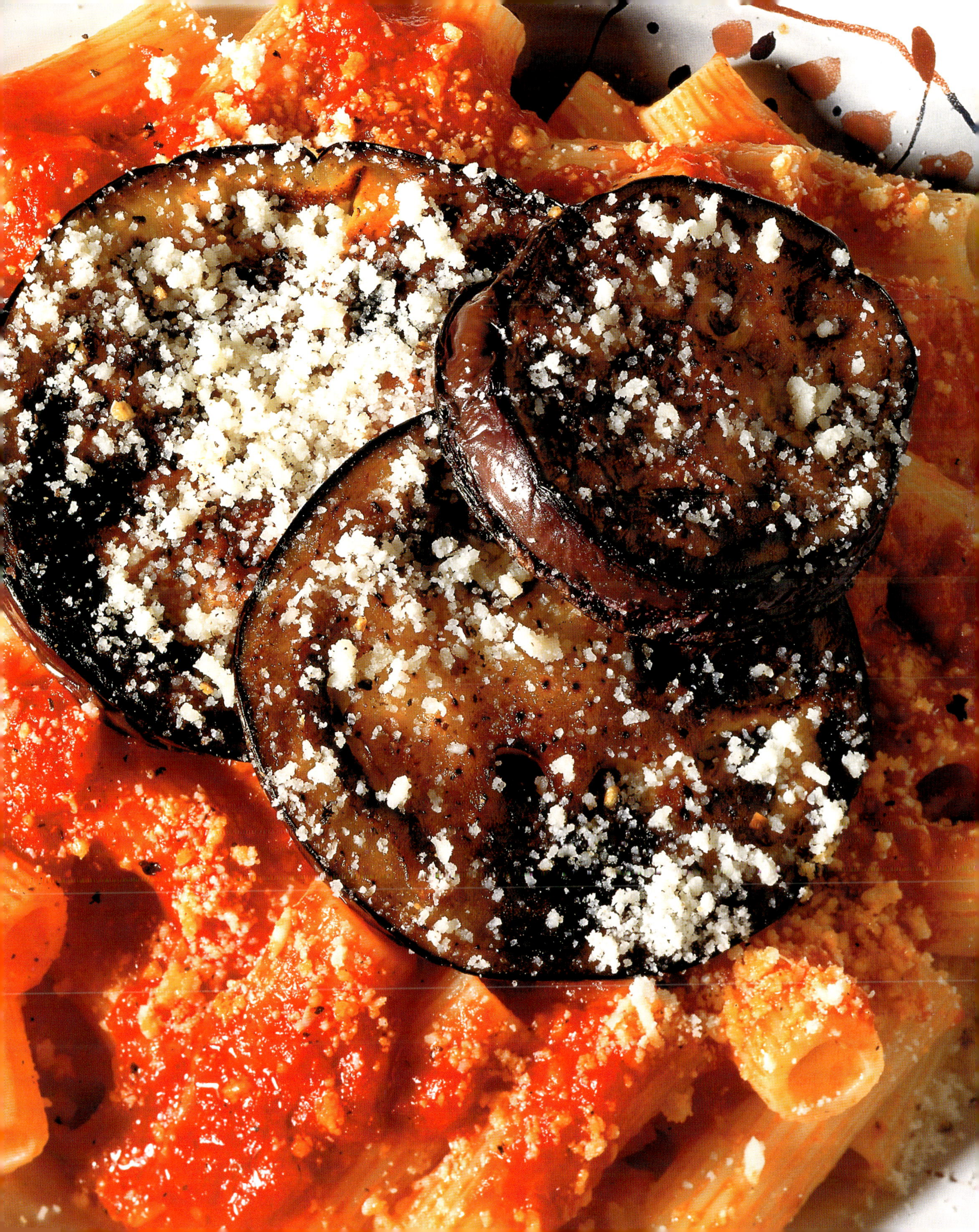

rapid pomodoro PENNE WITH QUICK CHILLIED TOMATO SAUCE AND FRIED ZUCCHINI

SERVES 4 AS A STARTER

2 yellow or green zucchini (courgettes)
1 medium onion, very finely chopped
75ml olive oil
4 small dried 'bird's eye' chillies, crushed (or 2 tablespoons finely chopped fresh basil or parsley)
700g jar pre-sieved Italian tomatoes
salt
500g penne (or penne rigate)
oil for frying
freshly grated parmesan (parmigiano reggiano) cheese for serving

Slice the zucchini thinly and spread the slices on a tray lined with absorbent kitchen paper. Cover with another layer of kitchen paper and leave to dry for 10–15 minutes.

Put the onion in a saucepan with the olive oil and set over a low-to-medium heat. Cook until pale gold in colour, then add the chillies, or the basil or parsley if you prefer this. Cook for 3–4 minutes, then tip in the tomatoes and add $1/4$ teaspoon of salt. Bring to a gentle boil, lower the heat and partially cover with a lid. Cook gently for 15 minutes.

Once the sauce is ready, cook the pasta in plenty of gently boiling, well-salted water until al dente and fry the zucchini.

While the pasta cooks, heat a little oil in a frying pan set over a medium heat and put in a layer of zucchini slices. Fry until the zucchini is lightly golden, turn with tongs and cook the other side until golden. Transfer to a plate lined with absorbent kitchen paper and sprinkle with a little salt. Cook the rest of the zucchini in the same way.

When the pasta is ready, drain it briefly and turn it into a heated serving dish (or individual bowls). Mix three-quarters of the sauce through the pasta, pour the rest over, top with fried zucchini and sprinkle generously with parmesan cheese. Serve immediately.

PRE-SIEVED ITALIAN TOMATOES FOR QUICK SAUCES

Pre-sieved Italian tomatoes (sold under various names such as passata) make a quick tomato sauce even faster. The advantage is not only a quicker sauce, but a sweeter one, as the seeds have been removed (tomato seeds, especially if crushed, are bitter). Cook pre-sieved tomatoes in oil with a few seasonings and, in less than 15 minutes, a rich red sauce is yours.

'BIRD'S EYE' CHILLIES

The minuscule dried hot chilli pepper, often referred to as the 'bird's eye' chilli, is the nearest equivalent to the tongue-hot, small dried chillies (not to be confused with lip-burning or throat-burning varieties) used in various ways in Italy. These chillies can transform a very simple dish into one of notable character. Use them whole and discard before serving for a mild flavour, or crush or chop finely for a hotter, more powerful impact. They are an optional ingredient in many recipes in this book. If you don't like chilli – simply leave them out.

nutty and pungent LINGUINE WITH CASHEW NUT AND GARLIC SAUCE

SERVES 4

400g linguine
salt
½ cup plus 1 tablespoon extra virgin olive oil
150g salted cashew nuts, finely chopped
freshly ground black pepper to taste
6 cloves garlic, crushed
1 cup basil leaves, chopped
freshly grated parmesan (parmigiano reggiano) cheese
  for serving

Cook the pasta in plenty of gently boiling, well-salted water until al dente.

Put the ½ cup of extra virgin olive oil, the cashews, ¼ teaspoon of salt, black pepper and garlic in a large frying pan. Heat gently.

Drain the linguine and turn it into a heated serving bowl. Toss the tablespoon of extra virgin olive oil and the basil through the pasta then tip the cashew sauce on top. Toss and serve immediately with parmesan cheese.

musky perfume LINGUINE WITH ZUCCHINI AND MARJORAM

SERVES 4–6

6 smallish zucchini (courgettes), washed, dried and trimmed
½ cup extra virgin olive oil
2 large cloves garlic, crushed
¼ cup white wine
salt
freshly ground black pepper to taste
400g linguine (or spaghetti)
2 tablespoons chopped parsley
1 tablespoon chopped marjoram
½ cup freshly grated parmesan (parmigiano reggiano) cheese

Slice the zucchini thinly and spread the slices on a tray lined with absorbent kitchen paper. Cover with another layer of kitchen paper and leave to dry for 10–15 minutes.

Put the extra virgin olive oil and garlic in a large frying pan. Cook the garlic over a medium heat until it is a pale golden colour. Drop in the zucchini and fry for 3–5 minutes, stirring often. Pour the wine in, season with salt and black pepper, then cook gently, stirring often, for about 20 minutes, or until the zucchini are very tender.

Cook the pasta in plenty of gently boiling, well-salted water until al dente, then drain and tip into a heated bowl for serving.

While the pasta is cooking, reheat the zucchini mixture and add the parsley and marjoram.

Pour the sauce, including all the pan scrapings, over the pasta, toss well and sprinkle with the parmesan cheese. Toss briefly and serve immediately.

strands of gold SPAGHETTINI WITH FRESH TOMATO SAUCE, CHILLI AND SAFFRON PRAWNS

SERVES 4

500g vine-ripened tomatoes (or flavoursome outdoor tomatoes)
1 large clove garlic, crushed
2 tablespoons coarsely chopped flat leaf parsley
2 tablespoons small basil leaves
salt
4 small dried 'bird's eye' chillies, crushed
12 black olives, pitted and chopped
3 tablespoons estate bottled extra virgin olive oil plus a little regular extra virgin olive oil for frying the prawns
24 medium prawns
pinch saffron strands
400g spaghettini (or use spaghetti)

Skin the tomatoes, and cut them in half. Remove the cores and flick out the seeds. Chop the flesh into tiny dice, then put the tomatoes in a sieve set over a bowl. Leave to drain for one hour. Transfer the tomatoes to a bowl and mix in the garlic, parsley, basil leaves, 1/2 teaspoon of salt, 2 of the crushed chillies, the olives and extra virgin olive oil. Set aside while preparing the prawns and pasta.

Heat a drizzle of extra virgin oil in a small frying pan over a medium heat. Add the prawns and cook until pink. Turn them, crumble the saffron and last 2 chillies on top, and cook until pink on the other side. Transfer to a small bowl with any scrapings from the pan.

Meanwhile, cook the pasta in plenty of gently boiling, well-salted water until al dente. Drain and tip into a heated serving dish. Pour the sauce over and quickly toss together. Tip the prawns on top and serve hottish or at room temperature. This is even good the next day, chilled!

little shells CONCHIGLIE WITH BUTTON MUSHROOMS

SERVES 4 AS A LIGHT COURSE

75ml olive oil
3 cloves garlic, crushed
300g tiny button mushrooms, wiped clean (if not available, use larger mushrooms, quartered)
salt
freshly ground black pepper to taste
1 teaspoon chopped fresh marjoram (or 1/2 teaspoon dried marjoram)
50ml dry white wine
600g (1 1/2 cans) canned Italian tomatoes, mashed (or 600g vine-ripened tomatoes, skinned, cored and diced)
400g conchiglie pasta shells
freshly grated parmesan (parmigiano reggiano) cheese for serving

Put the olive oil and garlic in a heavy-based saucepan and set over a low-to-medium heat. Cook until the garlic turns a pale biscuit colour, then add the mushrooms. Increase the heat to medium and fry for about 5 minutes, stirring often. Add 1/2 teaspoon of salt, some black pepper and the marjoram, then pour in the wine. Increase the heat to medium-high and allow the liquid to evaporate until syrupy, stirring occasionally.

Tip the tomatoes in, bring to the boil, then turn the heat to low and simmer gently, partially covered with a lid, for 20–30 minutes or until thick and sauce-like.

Meanwhile, cook the pasta in plenty of gently boiling, well-salted water until al dente. Drain briefly and turn the pasta into a heated serving dish. Quickly toss the sauce through the pasta. Serve immediately with parmesan cheese.

Spaghettini with fresh tomato sauce, chilli and saffron prawns

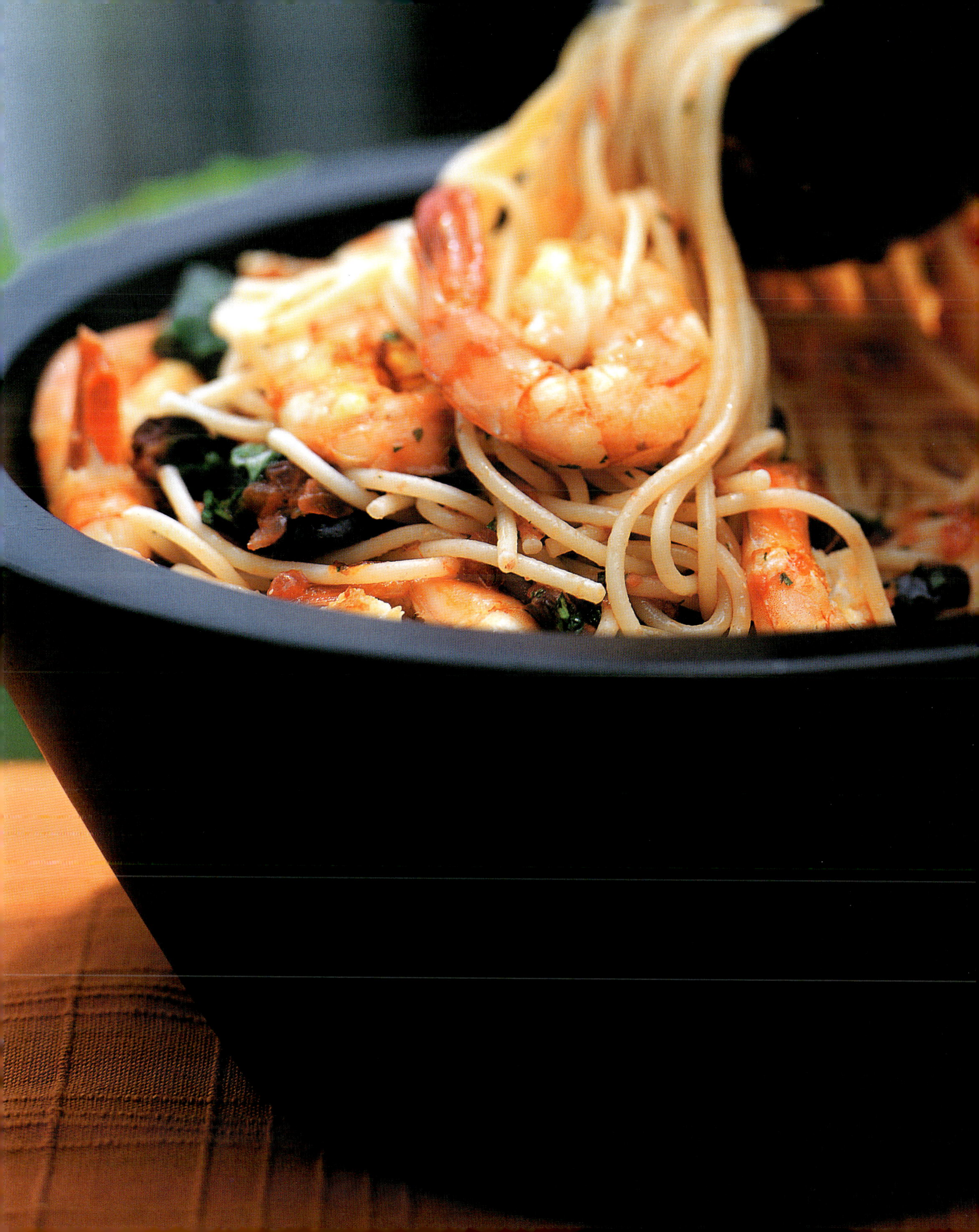

crispy batons FETTUCCINE WITH ZUCCHINI

SERVES 4

750g small, firm zucchini (courgettes)
salt
½ cup flour
olive oil
freshly ground black pepper to taste
2 large cloves garlic, chopped (use mild new season garlic, organic if you can find it)
1 tablespoon chopped marjoram
500g dried egg pasta such as fettuccine
50g butter
handful of basil leaves, torn into small pieces
½ cup freshly grated parmesan (parmigiano reggiano) cheese, plus extra for serving

THE CONTRAST of delicate pasta with crispy batons of fried zucchini is sensational. This is not a difficult dish to make, just ensure you start with small zucchini, not big watery ones full of seeds.

Cut the zucchini into fat matchsticks. Put in a colander and toss with a teaspoon of salt. Leave to drain for 1 hour, then gently squeeze to push out as much water as possible. Wrap the zucchini sticks in absorbent kitchen paper and get them as dry as possible.

Put half the flour on a double thickness of kitchen paper and add half the zucchini sticks. Toss them in the flour until they are coated.

Have ready a pan with hot olive oil to a depth of 5mm set over a medium-high heat. When the oil is nice and hot, drop in the zucchini. Cook quickly until golden brown on both sides, then transfer them to a colander to drain. Sprinkle with a little salt and grind on some black pepper. Repeat the process with the rest of the zucchini. Add the garlic to the pan for the last 2–3 minutes of cooking, until it is a pale golden colour, then scatter the marjoram over. Transfer to the colander with the first batch of zucchini.

Meanwhile, cook the pasta until al dente; if using dried pasta, put it into the water once you've cooked the first batch of zucchini but, if using fresh pasta, which cooks more quickly, put it in the water when the second half of the zucchini is nearly cooked.

Drain the pasta, then turn it into a very hot bowl. Mix the butter, basil, some black pepper and the parmesan cheese through the pasta. Toss quickly, then top with the zucchini. Toss briefly and serve immediately in hot bowls.

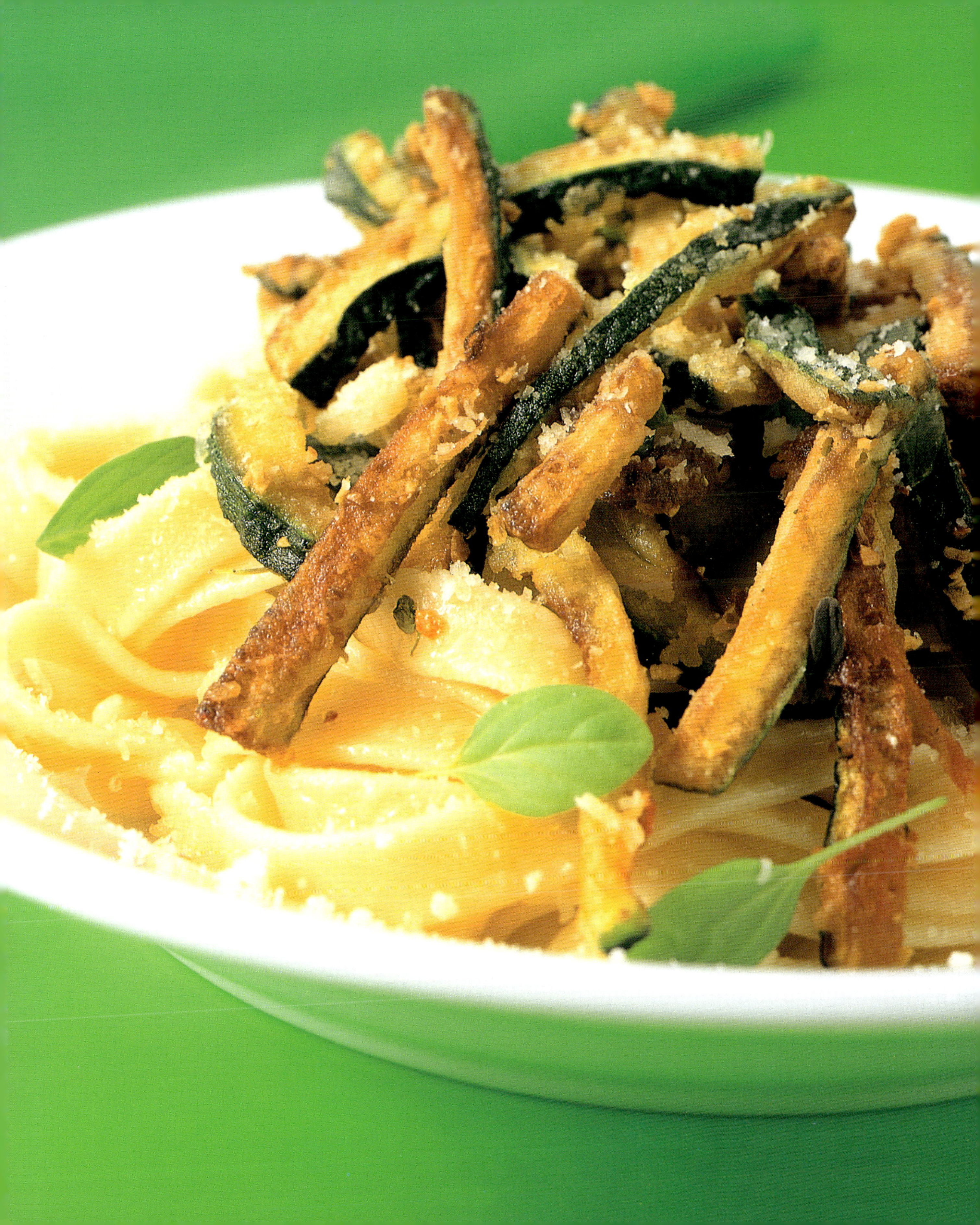

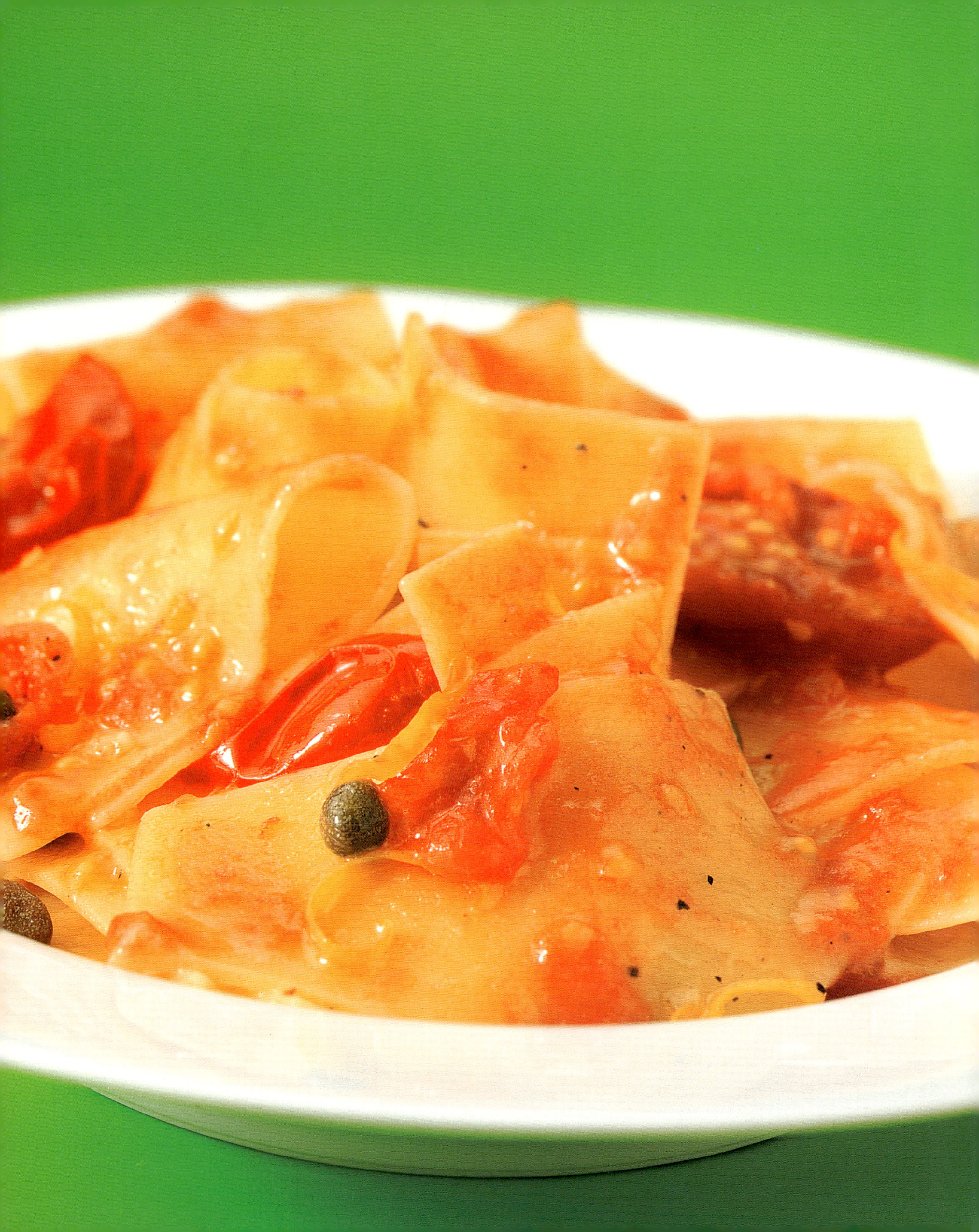

bits and pieces SUMMER PASTA SALAD

SERVES 6

300g maltagliati Emilian egg pasta
salt
4 tablespoons extra virgin olive oil
12 small vine-ripened tomatoes, halved
1 large clove garlic, crushed
2 tablespoons salted capers, rinsed, soaked for 15 minutes, rinsed again and drained
zest of ½ a lemon
freshly ground black pepper to taste

Cook the pasta in plenty of gently boiling, well-salted water until al dente.

While the pasta is cooking, put 1 tablespoon of the extra virgin olive oil in a frying pan and add the tomatoes. Cook very gently for about 10 minutes, to encourage the juices to run; don't let them fry. This can be done ahead.

Mix the remaining extra virgin olive oil, garlic, capers, lemon zest, black pepper and a few pinches of salt in a small bowl.

When the pasta is ready, drain it and tip into a large bowl. Pour the dressing over and toss well, then tip the tomatoes on, with all their juices. Toss carefully.

The pasta can be served hottish, or at room temperature.

PASTA SALADS when well made are light and delicious. This one is particularly good, capturing the essence of vine-ripened tomatoes, enhanced by garlic and lemon zest.

If maltagliati is not available, buy good-quality Italian egg pasta lasagne squares. Break them into rough pieces and prepare as described. For a change, top the salad with flakes of hot-smoked salmon, or add a handful of baby basil or rocket leaves, or add all three!

EMILIAN EGG PASTA is a treat. It is made from pasta dough enriched with eggs, and is much more yellow than regular Italian dried pasta. Maltagliati are odd-shaped pieces, scraps if you like (the word means badly cut), the off-cuts from making stuffed pasta. In Italy it is available either fresh or dried.

Summer pasta salad

rich and saucy LASAGNETTE WITH ITALIAN SAUSAGE AND MUSHROOM RAGÙ

SERVES 4 AS A MAIN COURSE OR 6 AS A STARTER

3 tablespoons extra virgin olive oil
1 onion, very finely chopped
250g button mushrooms, sliced
freshly ground black pepper to taste
250g Italian-style sausages (use meaty, well-seasoned sausages)
2 bay leaves
600g (1½ cans) canned Italian tomatoes, mashed
salt
500g lasagnette (small curly-edged pieces of lasagne, or use fusilli or cavatappi)
freshly grated parmesan (parmigiano reggiano) cheese for serving

Heat the extra virgin olive oil in a heavy-based saucepan over a low-to-medium heat and add the onion. Cook until it is a light golden colour, then increase the heat to medium-high and add the mushrooms. Stir to coat them in the onion-flavoured oil, then grind on some black pepper.

Meanwhile, prepare the sausages. Split the skin and discard it, then chop the sausage meat (a bit messy, but necessary).

Add the sausage meat to the pan, increase the heat to high and cook for 2–3 minutes, stirring, and breaking up the meat with a large fork. Add the bay leaves and tomatoes. Bring to the boil and add a few pinches of salt. Turn the heat to low, partially cover with a lid and simmer gently for 30 minutes (break up the sausage meat with a fork as it cooks). The sauce should end up looking like a ragù (meat sauce), moist but not dry.

Meanwhile, cook the pasta in plenty of gently boiling, well-salted water until al dente. Drain briefly and turn into a heated serving dish. Pour the sauce over, toss well and serve immediately with parmesan cheese.

snow white MACCHERONI WITH CAULIFLOWER SAUCE

SERVES 6 AS A STARTER

1 large, very fresh cauliflower
salt
2 bay leaves
150ml extra virgin olive oil
4 large cloves garlic, finely chopped
1 small dried 'bird's eye' chilli, crushed (optional)
freshly ground black pepper to taste
2 tablespoons finely chopped parsley
500g maccheroni (or tubular pasta)
freshly grated parmesan (parmigiano reggiano) cheese for serving

Remove the outer leaves and bulky stem from the cauliflower, then cut the cauliflower in half. Plunge it into a saucepan of boiling salted water, add the bay leaves and cook, uncovered, for 20–30 minutes or until tender in the thickest part (this is not cauliflower à la crunch!). Drain well.

Heat the extra virgin olive oil in a saucepan over a medium heat and add the garlic. Cook until the garlic turns a pale biscuit colour, then add the chilli, if using. Quickly add the cauliflower and use a wooden spoon to break it apart and mash it to a purée. Season with $1/4$ teaspoon of salt and add some black pepper if not using chilli. Add the parsley.

Meanwhile, cook the pasta in plenty of gently boiling, well-salted water until al dente. Drain briefly, then turn the pasta into a heated serving bowl. Quickly toss the sauce through and serve immediately with parmesan cheese.

THIS IS AN UNUSUAL sauce, which also makes an excellent stuffing for baked jacket potatoes. Make it in winter when crisp, snow-white cauliflowers are inexpensive.

The sauce may be prepared ahead but add the parsley when reheating. Allow it to cool completely before covering and don't refrigerate it, as it will turn watery. It can be kept at room temperature for several hours. When ready to use, reheat gently and add the parsley.

When blanching or boiling cauliflower, add a fresh bay leaf to the water; it sweetens the odour.

fast pasta TAGLIATELLE WITH PROSCIUTTO

SERVES 4 AS A STARTER

300g fresh tagliatelle (or fettuccine)
salt
50g butter
350g thinly sliced prosciutto (or use thinly sliced ham off the bone), cut into strips
freshly ground black pepper to taste
50g ($1/2$ cup) freshly grated parmesan (parmigiano reggiano) cheese, plus extra for serving

Cook the pasta in plenty of gently boiling, well-salted water until al dente. This will take only 2–3 minutes.

Meanwhile, heat a large frying pan over a medium heat and, when it is hot, drop in the butter. Add the ham to the pan while the butter is sizzling and cook for 2–3 minutes, stirring.

Drain the pasta and transfer to a heated serving bowl. Tip all the contents of the frying pan over the pasta, grind on some black pepper and sprinkle with the cheese. Toss well and serve immediately with extra cheese.

FRESH PASTA VERSUS DRIED PASTA

I don't know who started the tale, but fresh pasta is not superior to dried pasta. It is different, that's all. Fresh pasta is more tender and delicate, absorbs sauce more readily and is better suited to lighter, delicate sauces, particularly those made with butter and/or cream.

Fresh pasta in Italy is made and consumed within 48 hours at most, or, providing it is not stuffed, is dried in the air and stored until required and used in the same way as dried pasta. Most of the commercially made pastas I have tried outside of Italy have slick, shiny surfaces, sauces don't adhere to them and they feel slimy in the mouth. Italian dried pasta is a far superior product.

Cook fresh pasta more gently than dried, because fast boiling will cause it to break apart, and for only 1–2 minutes, or until just al dente.

crusty top BAKED RIGATONI WITH RICOTTA

SERVES 6 AS A MAIN COURSE

1 large onion, finely chopped
2 cloves garlic, crushed
75ml olive oil
1 teaspoon dried marjoram
freshly ground black pepper to taste
2 x 400g cans Italian tomatoes, mashed
salt
500g rigatoni (or use large pasta shells or other tubular pasta)
50g butter
200g ricotta cheese
50g (½ cup) freshly grated parmesan (parmigiano reggiano) cheese, plus extra for serving

Put the onion and garlic in a heavy-based saucepan with the olive oil and cook gently until lightly golden. Add the marjoram and black pepper, then tip the tomatoes in and add ¼ teaspoon of salt. Bring to the boil, then turn the heat to very low. Cook, uncovered, stirring occasionally, for about 25 minutes or until the sauce is pulpy.

Cook the pasta in plenty of gently boiling, well-salted water until nearly al dente (undercook the pasta because it finishes off cooking in the oven). Drain the pasta well and turn it into a large bowl. Toss half of the butter and 3 tablespoons of the sauce through. Tip half the pasta into a well-buttered ovenproof dish (33cm x 21cm x 5cm deep). Spoon a little sauce over it, then spoon the ricotta cheese on, then coat with a little more sauce. Sprinkle half the parmesan cheese over, then put the rest of the pasta in the dish. Spoon the remaining sauce over the top, sprinkle with the rest of the parmesan cheese and dot with butter.

The pasta can be prepared an hour or two in advance to this point; cover loosely with waxed paper and keep at room temperature.

Bake in an oven preheated to 180°C for 15–20 minutes, or until piping hot and a little crusty on top. Serve immediately with extra parmesan cheese.

IT'S IMPORTANT not to overcook the pasta in the initial cooking stage because it continues to cook in the oven.

holy trinity SPAGHETTI WITH GARLIC AND OIL

SERVES 4 AS A STARTER OR 3 AS A LIGHT MEAL

400g spaghetti
salt
4–6 cloves garlic
250ml (1 cup) extra virgin olive oil
1–3 small dried 'bird's eye' chillies, crushed (optional)
freshly chopped basil or parsley (optional)
freshly grated parmesan (parmigiano reggiano) cheese for serving (optional)

Cook the pasta in plenty of gently boiling, well-salted water until al dente.

While the pasta is cooking, peel the garlic and cut it into fine slivers or chop it very finely. Put the extra virgin olive oil in a small pan, add the garlic and warm gently over a low heat, so the garlic flavours the oil.

Drain the pasta, transfer to a heated serving bowl and pour the infused oil over the pasta. Toss well.

This is a very simple dish to put together. It comes into its own when you are ravenous and want something quick and tasty. There are several ways to finish it off.

- If you want a milder flavour, strain the oil over the pasta and discard the garlic. Alternatively, let the garlic brown in the oil until it turns a pale biscuit colour, then pour it over the pasta. This gives a nutty flavour.
- Add the crushed chilli to the oil with the garlic and, if you like herbs, add these to the oil just before pouring the oil over the pasta.
- Although Italians don't usually serve parmesan cheese with this pasta dish, I think it improves it.
- Ziti with Eggs Fried in Chilli Oil (see page 54) is a different slant on the combination above. It's great when you want something speedy with a real flavour hit.

roman glory FETTUCCINE ALLA CARBONARA

SERVES 4 AS A MAIN COURSE

300g (approximately 8 rashers) smoked bacon, rind removed, cut into small strips
50g soft butter
2 whole eggs
2 egg yolks
120g (1¼ cups) freshly grated parmesan (parmigiano reggiano) cheese
freshly ground black pepper to taste
500g fettuccine
salt
½ cup cream

Heat a large frying pan over a medium heat. When hot, add the bacon. Cook, stirring occasionally, until very crisp. Drain off most of the visible fat and turn off the heat.

Bring a large saucepan of water to the boil. Place an ovenproof serving dish in a warm oven and allow it to get very hot (choose a dish that will hold the heat well, such as thick pottery, chunky china or cast iron).

Cream the butter in a small bowl with a spatula until it is very soft. Break the eggs into another small bowl, add the egg yolks and half the parmesan cheese. Beat well with a fork, adding black pepper to taste.

Cook the pasta in plenty of gently boiling, well-salted water until al dente.

Meanwhile, reheat the bacon in the pan, add the cream and bubble it up. Drain the pasta and transfer it to the very hot dish. Immediately work the butter through with 2 large spoons. Add the hot bacon mixture, then the eggs and cheese. Toss vigorously and serve immediately with the remaining cheese. (The heat of the ingredients and the dish will be sufficient to cook the eggs, but the mixture should remain light, not tacky or scrambled.)

THIS ROMAN DISH of pasta with bacon, eggs and cream makes a substantial main course dish. It's easy enough to make, but ensure you get everything ready before you start to cook the sauce. It is traditionally made with spaghetti, but in our household we enjoy it made with fettuccine. We also like it with extra cheese.

simple saucery FETTUCCINE WITH ROMAN-STYLE MEAT SAUCE

SERVES 4 AS A MAIN COURSE OR 6 AS A STARTER

1 small onion, very finely chopped
1 small carrot, very finely chopped
1 stalk celery, very finely chopped
75g bacon, rind removed, finely chopped
50g butter, plus extra for tossing through pasta
300g prime minced beef
salt
freshly ground black pepper to taste
freshly grated nutmeg
100g chicken livers, rinsed, trimmed and finely chopped
75ml dry red wine
600g (1½ cans) canned Italian tomatoes, mashed
1½ tablespoons Italian tomato paste
½ teaspoon sugar
¼ teaspoon dried oregano
500g fettuccine
freshly grated parmesan (parmigiano reggiano) cheese for serving

Put the onion, carrot, celery and bacon in a saucepan with the butter. Fry gently until the onion is a pale golden colour. Increase the heat to high and add the minced beef. Break the beef up with a fork and cook until it loses its pinkness. Season with ¼ teaspoon of salt, some black pepper and some nutmeg. Add the chicken livers and cook for 2 minutes more.

Turn the heat down to medium, stir in the wine and cook until it has evaporated. Add the tomatoes, tomato paste, sugar and oregano. Bring to the boil, then lower the heat and cook gently, uncovered, for 30 minutes. Partially cover with a lid and cook for 15–30 minutes more, stirring occasionally, until rich and thick.

Cook the pasta in plenty of gently boiling, well-salted water until al dente. Drain briefly and turn into a heated serving dish. Quickly toss a large knob of butter through, then pour the sauce over (don't toss). Serve immediately with parmesan cheese.

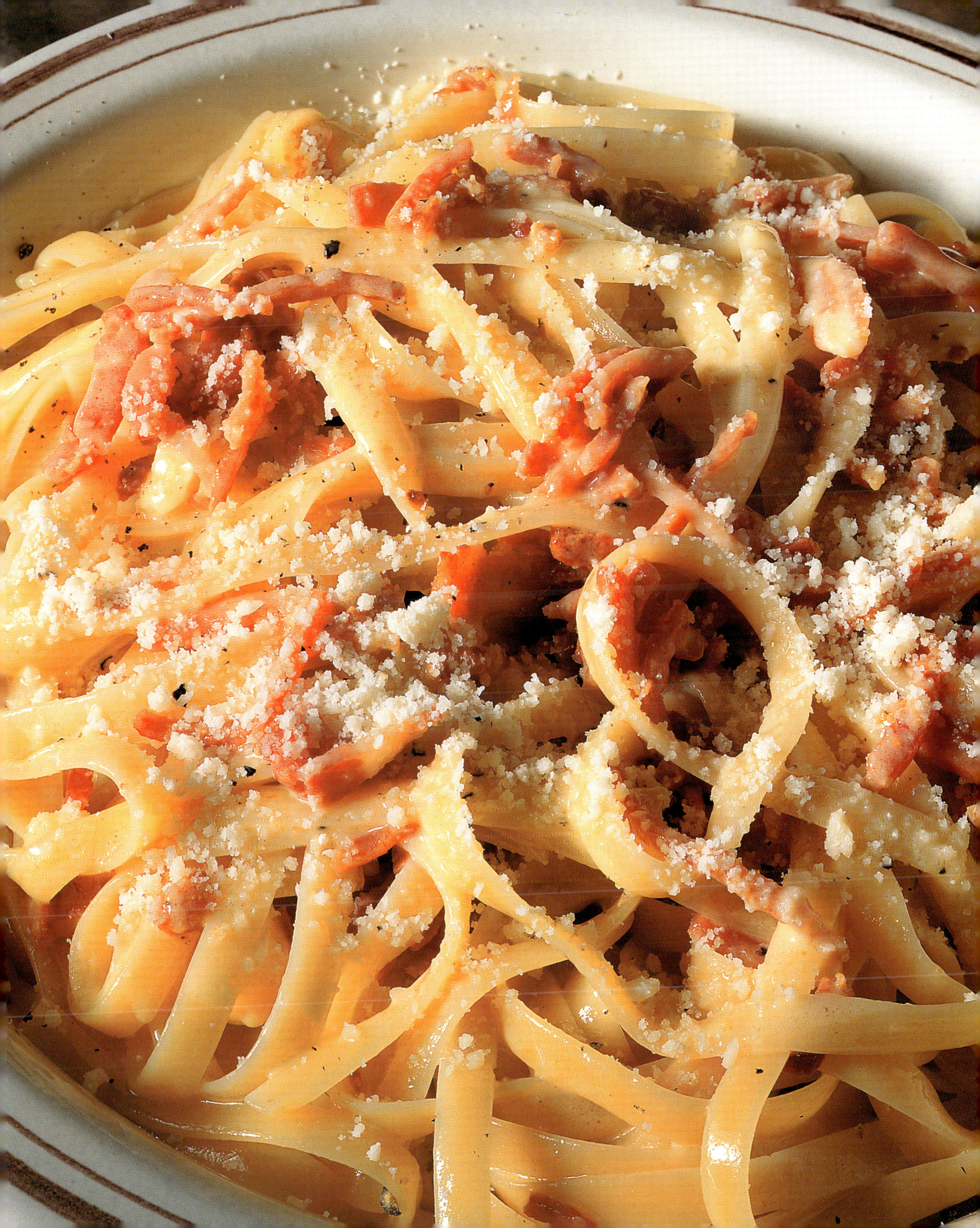

wickedly good ways

VENETIAN FISH	74
FISH ROLLS WITH PINE NUTS	77
STUFFED CHICKEN DRUMSTICKS	77
SPRING CHICKEN	78
CHICKEN WITH LEMON AND CREAM	80
CHICKEN BREASTS WITH BROWNED BUTTER	82
TURKEY TENDERLOINS WITH LEMON AND ROSEMARY	82
QUAIL ROASTED WITH VINCOTTO	83
VEAL FILLET WITH GREEN OLIVES AND FRESH BAY LEAVES	85
SCALOPPINE WITH LEMON	86
SCALOPPINE COLOSSEO	86
SCALOPPINE WITH MELTING MOZZARELLA	87
CRISPY VEAL WITH PARMESAN AND BLACK OLIVES	88
ISANNA'S SCALOPPINE	90
TUSCAN PORK AND BEANS	90
ROAST PORK WITH FENNEL SEEDS	91
ROASTED EYE FILLET WRAPPED IN BACON	92
SELVAPIANA BEEF IN CHIANTI	92
OSSOBUCO	94
LAMB ABRUZZI	95
SAUSAGE COIL WITH HOT POLENTA AND SAUTÉED MUSHROOMS	96
LEG OF LAMB WITH PARMESAN CRUST AND CRUNCHY POTATOES	98

a slick of oil, a slosh of wine

pungent olives, hints of spice

flakes of succulent sea-fresh fish

morsels of fork-tender roasted meat

tantalise and tempt the tastebuds

with fish, fowl & meat

soused seafood VENETIAN FISH

SERVES 8

1kg smallish white fish fillets, skinned
3 eggs
salt
¼ cup milk
100ml olive oil
50g butter
1 onion, finely sliced or chopped
3 cloves garlic, crushed
¼ cup pine nuts
¼ cup raisins, soaked for 10 minutes in boiling water
1 bay leaf, torn in half
freshly ground black pepper to taste
¾ cup white wine vinegar
¾ cup cold water
2 tablespoons coarsely chopped parsley
1 cup dry breadcrumbs (see below)
125ml (½ cup) frying oil

Rinse the fish fillets, and pat them dry with absorbent kitchen paper. Cut each fillet into 2–3 pieces. Break the eggs into a shallow dish, add a few pinches of salt and beat well with a fork. Beat in the milk, then drop in the pieces of fish. Stir gently to coat, then leave to soak for 30 minutes, stirring occasionally.

Heat the olive oil and butter in a large frying pan over a medium heat. Add the onion and garlic and cook gently, uncovered, until soft and transparent. Add the pine nuts, drained raisins and bay leaf. Grind on some black pepper and cook the mixture for 2–3 minutes. Pour the white wine vinegar in, let it bubble away for a minute, then add the water and ¼ teaspoon of salt. Cook gently for about 10 minutes, then stir in the parsley.

When the marinade is ready, prepare the fish. Tip the breadcrumbs onto a piece of absorbent kitchen paper. Turn the fish into a large colander set over a bowl and drain for 5 minutes. Drop the fish pieces into the breadcrumbs, one at a time, and pat on the crumbs.

When all the fish is prepared, heat most of the frying oil in a large frying pan over a medium-high heat. Drop several pieces of fish in and cook until golden. Turn carefully and cook the other side. Transfer to a large serving platter (don't drain them). Continue frying the fish, adding a little more oil if necessary (watch the heat; lower it a little to stop the crumbs from burning if necessary).

When all the fish fillets are done, spoon the marinade over, ensuring each piece of fish is anointed with some of the liquid. Leave to cool, then cover loosely with a ventilated cover. Leave for several hours before serving.

BASED ON AN OLD Venetian method of cooking and preserving fish, this dish is ideal for entertaining because it is made several hours before serving.

DRIED WHITE BREADCRUMBS

Dried white breadcrumbs are used primarily for coating foods that are to be fried. Usually, the items for frying are floured and dipped in beaten egg, which makes a sticky base to which the crumbs adhere. The protein in the egg coagulates when the food is immersed in the fat and this makes an impenetrable wall. For this reason 'egging and crumbing' should be done with great care because if it is patchy the fat will enter the food, making it greasy. Dried white breadcrumbs are used to thicken this protective wall and to give the food a crisp, crunchy exterior, which is also appealing to the eye. Fresh white breadcrumbs should not be used as they contain moisture – this will cause the fat to spit and the crumbs may not adhere. Dried browned breadcrumbs (available commercially) are unsuitable for frying as they will be over-browned before the food is cooked through.

To make dried breadcrumbs, spread a batch of fresh white breadcrumbs in a baking dish and bake in a low oven (120°C) until crisp and dry, but not coloured. Turn them from time to time to ensure they dry evenly. They may take as long as 45 minutes, but don't be tempted to increase the heat. When they are very dry, take them out of the oven and push them through a metal sieve, or blend them in a food processor or liquidiser again until a fine crumb is achieved. If they feel at all moist, return them to the baking dish and continue drying in the oven. When completely cool, store in an airtight container. Dried breadcrumbs will last for many months.

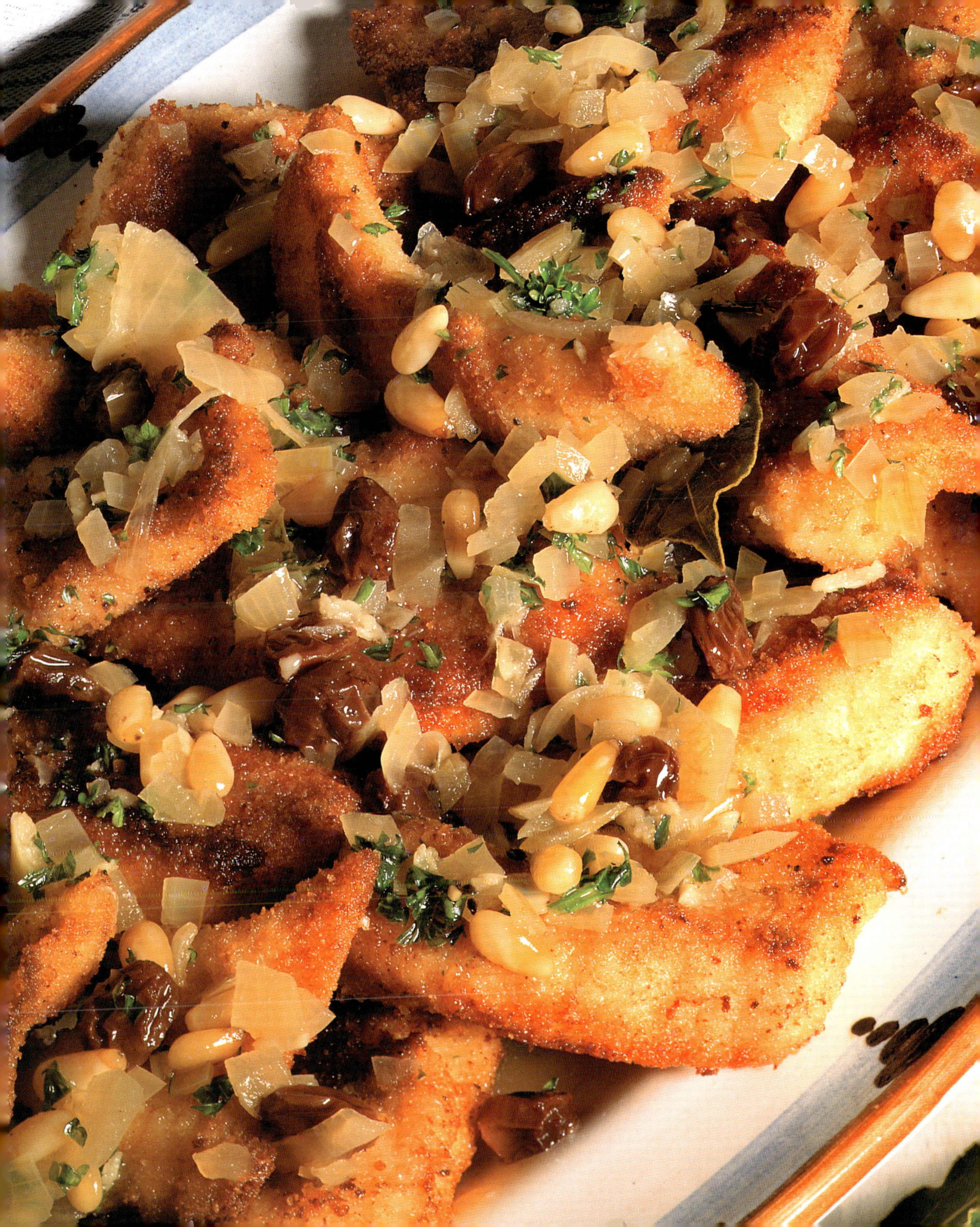

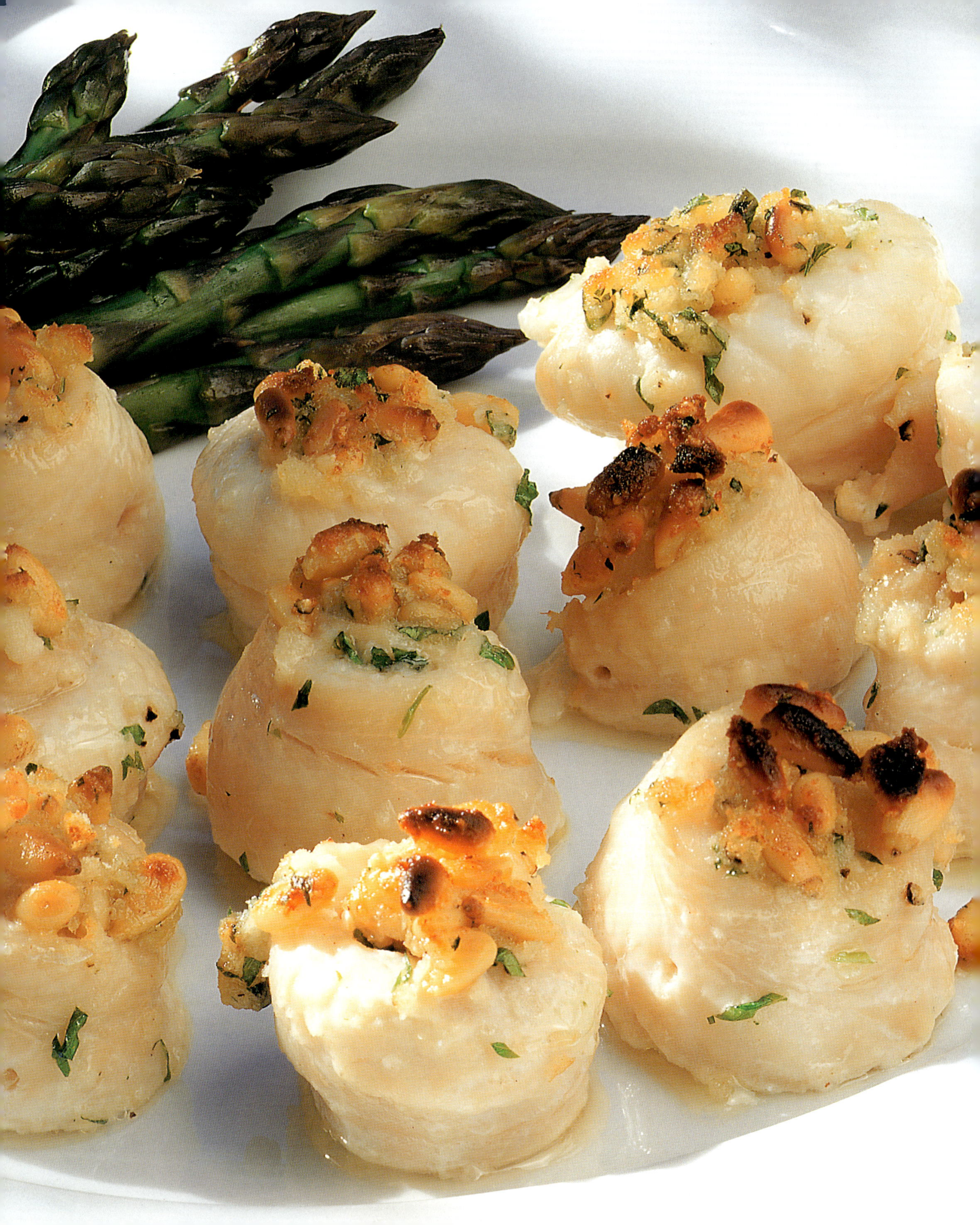

nutty turbans FISH ROLLS WITH PINE NUTS

SERVES 4

1/4 cup pine nuts
4 tablespoons fresh breadcrumbs
4 tablespoons freshly grated parmesan (parmigiano reggiano) cheese
1/4 teaspoon salt
freshly ground black pepper to taste
2 tablespoons chopped parsley
3 tablespoons melted butter
500g even-sized skinned gurnard fillets (or other small, firm, white fish fillets)
white wine

Mix the pine nuts, fresh breadcrumbs, parmesan cheese, salt, black pepper, parsley and half of the melted butter in a small bowl.

Remove any skin from the fish fillets, then rinse the fillets and pat them dry with absorbent kitchen paper. Lay them on a clean board, skin side facing up, and cut each one into 2–3 pieces.

Brush the fish fillets with the rest of the melted butter, then press some of the filling onto each fillet (it tends to fall off, but don't worry – stuff these bits into the tops of the rolls in the next step). Roll up each piece of fish and secure with a toothpick.

Transfer the fish rolls to a shallow, buttered ovenproof dish, then put in any extra bits of stuffing. Splash with a little white wine and cover with a piece of buttered greaseproof paper or aluminium foil.

Bake in an oven preheated to 180°C for 5–7 minutes, or until the fish is just starting to cook (changing in colour from opaque to dull white). Remove the paper. Leaving the dish in the oven, turn on the grill, then grill until the topping is golden and the fish is just cooked. Transfer the fish to a heated serving dish and spoon 2–3 tablespoons of the juices over the top. Serve immediately.

Fish rolls with pine nuts

succulent mouthfuls STUFFED CHICKEN DRUMSTICKS

SERVES 4–6

125g thinly sliced ham, finely chopped
1 large clove garlic, crushed
1 tablespoon chopped marjoram (or 1 teaspoon dried marjoram)
2 tablespoons finely chopped parsley
4 tablespoons freshly grated parmesan (parmigiano reggiano) cheese
1–2 small eggs, lightly beaten (I usually use 1 whole egg and 1 extra yolk)
salt
freshly ground black pepper to taste
12 skinned and boned chicken drumsticks (or use chicken thighs, trimmed of excess fat)
125ml (1/2 cup) olive oil
2 tablespoons butter
1/4 cup plain flour mixed with 1/2 teaspoon salt
125ml (1/2 cup) dry white wine
250ml (1 cup) hot chicken stock

In a bowl mix the ham, garlic, herbs and parmesan cheese and blend in enough beaten egg to turn the mixture into a paste. Season with 1/4 teaspoon of salt and some black pepper. Smear a little of the stuffing on the inside of each drumstick, then seal by pressing the flesh together.

Heat the olive oil in a large heavy-based frying pan over a medium heat. When it is hot, drop in the butter.

Meanwhile, coat the chicken drumsticks with the seasoned flour, dust off the excess, squeeze them gently to seal the coating, then lower them into the hot pan. Sauté for 15 minutes, turning with tongs halfway through the cooking. Pour off the fat, season them with a little salt and black pepper, then pour the wine over. Let the wine evaporate slowly (for about 10 minutes), and turn the pieces of chicken over once. Start adding the hot stock, a little at a time, pouring a teaspoonful of stock over each drumstick. Continue cooking the chicken pieces for about 15 minutes more or until they are just cooked through. Turn them over from time to time and moisten them with more stock.

When done, transfer the chicken drumsticks to a heated serving dish and pour any juices over the top.

favourite flavours SPRING CHICKEN

SERVES 4–6

12 skinned and boned chicken thighs
salt
freshly ground black pepper to taste
1 tablespoon olive oil
2 tablespoons butter
1 tablespoon chopped rosemary
juice of 2 lemons
250g fresh broad beans (or 125g frozen broad beans)
250g maltagliati (see page 67)
½ cup pesto (see page 56)
3 tablespoons cream

THIS COMBINATION of pasta, chicken, pesto and cream, although not traditional (pasta is usually served as a component of a meal), makes stunning eating.

Trim excess fat from chicken thighs. Season the inside of the thighs with a little salt and black pepper and roll up. Tie with string or cotton, or secure with toothpicks. Heat a large heavy-based frying pan over a medium heat and, when hot, add the olive oil. Drop in the butter, then add the chicken thighs while the butter is sizzling. Sprinkle the thighs with a little rosemary, then cook them for about 10 minutes, until they are a good deep-golden colour, turning occasionally. Season with salt and pepper, then pour the lemon juice over. Put on a lid, a little ajar, and cook the chicken gently for about 20 minutes, until cooked through; turn the thighs from time to time.

Prepare the broad beans next. Remove the broad beans from their pods, then drop them into a saucepan of lightly salted boiling water. Bring the water back to the boil, then cook the beans for 5–7 minutes. If using frozen broad beans, cook them for 5 minutes only. Drain, refresh with cold water and drain again. When cool enough to handle, remove the tough outer skins (fiddly but necessary). Set the beans aside.

Meanwhile, cook the pasta in plenty of gently boiling, well-salted water until al dente. Mix the pesto with the cream and add 2 tablespoons of the pasta water to loosen it. Quickly drain the pasta, add it to the bowl and mix the pesto and broad beans through it (if the sauce is a bit clingy, add a little more pasta water). Turn onto a heated platter and top with the chicken thighs. Toss once, then serve immediately. Follow with a watercress salad.

Spring chicken

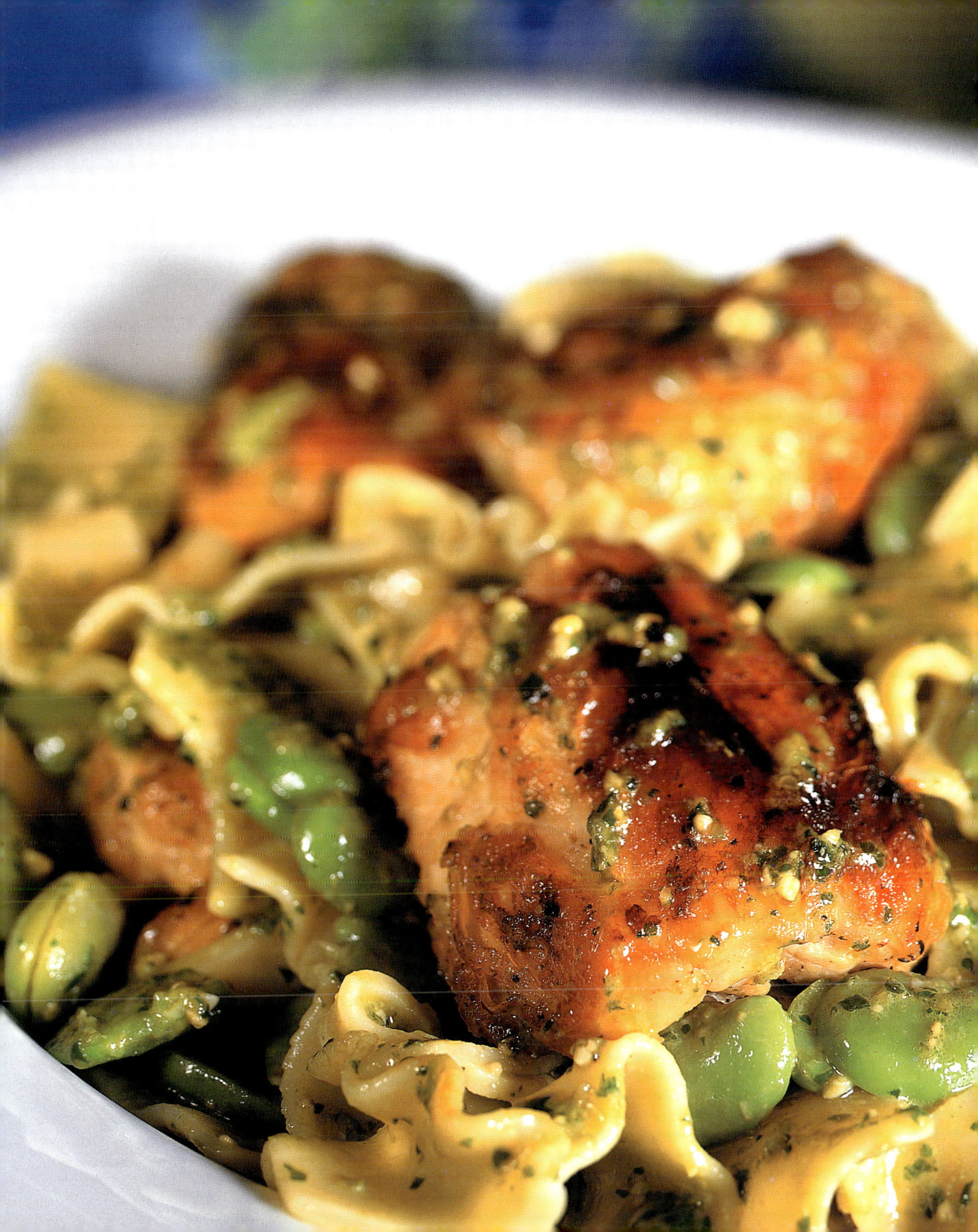

hot chick CHICKEN WITH LEMON AND CREAM

SERVES 6

3 tablespoons olive oil
1 small onion, finely chopped
1.3kg chicken pieces (thighs, drumsticks and wings), skinned where possible
½ teaspoon salt
freshly ground black pepper to taste
2 tablespoons finely chopped rosemary
4 large cloves garlic, finely chopped
3 tablespoons white wine, preferably chardonnay
2 lemons
¾ cup cream

Put the olive oil in a large non-stick frying pan. Set the pan over a medium heat and add the onion. Cook for 2 minutes, then put the chicken joints in the pan. Cook until golden (about 15 minutes), turning often, and spooning the onion on top of the chicken joints; make sure the heat is not too fierce or the onion will burn.

When the chicken is well browned, sprinkle with salt and black pepper and half the rosemary and garlic. Cook for 1 minute, turning the chicken pieces in the seasonings. Pour the wine on and cook for 3–4 minutes until it has evaporated, then pour the strained juice of 1 lemon over the chicken.

Turn the heat to low and cook gently, adding 2–3 tablespoons of water from time to time to keep the chicken moist until it is tender (it'll take about 45 minutes and about ¾ cup of water). Sprinkle with the rest of the rosemary and garlic and the strained juice of the second lemon, then mix the cream in.

Cook for a few minutes more or until the creamy juices have thickened slightly (don't over-reduce the juices). Dish onto a hot plate, spoon the juices over and serve immediately. Although not a traditional accompaniment, I like to serve this chicken with hot buttered noodles and a crisp, green-leaf salad.

HOT BUTTERED NOODLES

Italians don't usually serve pasta as an adjunct to a meal; it is nearly always served as a separate first course. However, pasta noodles work especially well with Chicken with Lemon and Cream because the sauce is rich and creamy, just the sort of thing noodles like to stick to. Pasta has a bit more 'bite' than other starch accompaniments such as potato purée or fluffy grains of rice.

Cook noodles until al dente, drain and tip into a hot dish. Toss a knob of soft butter through and serve immediately.

Chicken with lemon and cream

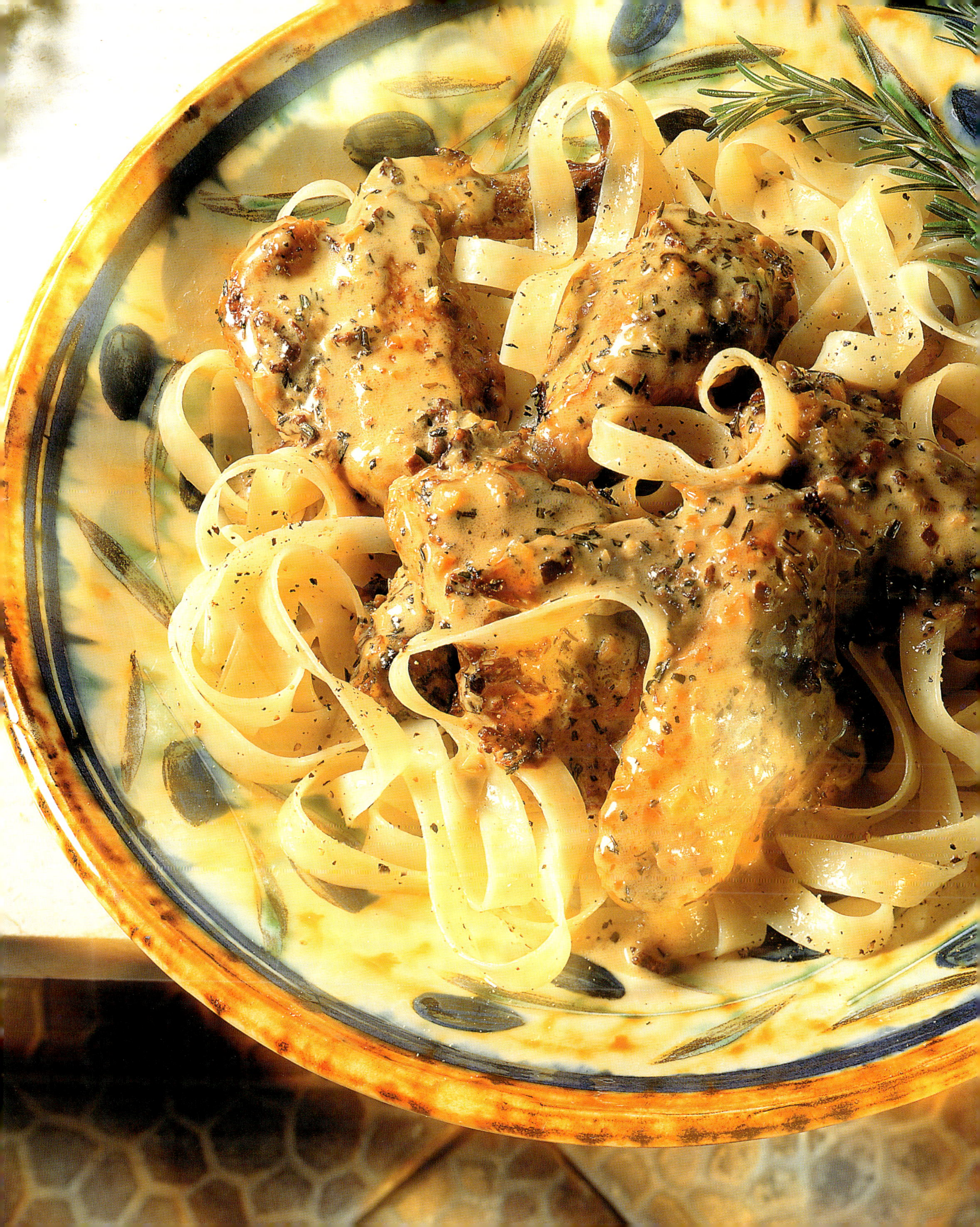

swirling juices CHICKEN BREASTS WITH BROWNED BUTTER

SERVES 4–6

6 chicken breasts, skinned
1 tablespoon olive oil
75g butter
salt
freshly ground black pepper to taste
juice of 2 lemons
2 tablespoons finely chopped parsley
1 lemon, thinly sliced

Cut each chicken breast into 3–4 pieces. Protect the meat with a plastic bag and beat with a mallet until the pieces of chicken are of an even thickness.

Heat the olive oil in a heavy-based frying pan over a medium heat, then drop in the butter. Add the chicken breasts and sauté for about 5 minutes until golden. Turn and cook the other side. Sprinkle the chicken with a little salt and grind on some black pepper. Transfer to a heated dish.

Increase the heat under the frying pan and let the butter colour to a light nut brown; it should smell very nutty. Immediately pour the lemon juice in, swirl the pan, then add the herbs. Use a metal spoon to scrape up any browned bits.

Return the chicken to the pan, turn each piece over in the herb butter and allow the chicken to reheat briefly. Tip the contents of the pan onto a heated serving dish, garnish with lemon and serve immediately.

ALTHOUGH NOT TRADITIONAL, I like to add a tablespoon of chopped mint along with the parsley.

fragrant and fresh TURKEY TENDERLOINS WITH LEMON AND ROSEMARY

SERVES 6

600g turkey tenderloins
2 tablespoons plain flour mixed with ¼ teaspoon salt
olive oil
butter
salt
freshly ground black pepper to taste
1 small onion, finely chopped
grated zest and juice of 2 lemons
1 tablespoon chopped rosemary, plus extra to garnish
¾ cup cream

Pat the turkey tenderloins dry with absorbent kitchen paper. Coat them with the seasoned flour. Heat a heavy-based frying pan over a medium heat and, when it is hottish, drop in a tablespoon of olive oil and a knob of butter and swirl the pan. Add the tenderloins while the butter is melting. Cook over a medium heat until browned, turn and cook the second side until the meat is nearly cooked through; it should be pink and juicy. Season with salt and black pepper and transfer to a side dish.

Add another knob of butter to the pan and drop in the onion. Cook gently until tender and browned, about 8 minutes. Add the lemon zest and return the turkey tenderloins to the pan. Season them well and add the lemon juice, rosemary and cream. Let the mixture bubble up for a minute or two, until the turkey is hot again. Transfer the turkey tenderloins to a hot serving plate and continue bubbling the sauce until it is thickish. Pour the sauce over the turkey and serve straight away.

spicy bite QUAIL ROASTED WITH VINCOTTO

SERVES 4

4 quail
2 tablespoons olive oil, plus a little extra for cooking the quail
2 tablespoons vincotto
grated zest and juice of 2 limes
1 teaspoon pink peppercorns, crushed or ground
small piece of cinnamon bark, broken up
1 teaspoon ground coriander seeds
1 teaspoon fennel seeds
good grinding of sea salt

Rinse the quail inside and out and pat dry with absorbent kitchen paper. Tie the legs together with string, or use a short bamboo skewer or sturdy toothpick to keep them together.

Put the 2 tablespoons of olive oil, vincotto, lime zest and juice, pink peppercorns, cinnamon bark, coriander and fennel seeds and salt in a shallow dish. Mix well and add the quail. Spoon the marinade over the quail, cover the dish with plastic food wrap and refrigerate the quail for several hours; turn them over in the marinade from time to time. Bring to room temperature before carrying on with the dish.

Heat a small ovenproof dish (cast iron is good) over a medium heat. When it is hot, add a little extra olive oil and smear it around the inside of the dish. Put in the quail and brown them all over, turning with tongs. The aim is to get the birds a deep golden brown, but not to burn them, so watch the heat. Pour the marinade in and add ¼ cup of water. Transfer the dish to an oven preheated to 180°C and cook for 30–40 minutes. During this time baste and turn the quail three or four times, and as soon as the juices look as if they are bubbling, or are about to catch (the vincotto can burn very easily), add a little more water.

I LIKE TO SERVE quail with rice or orzo and, very unItalian, I know, a salsa of thinly sliced green mango dressed with chopped mint, fresh red chilli, lemon juice and salt. Delicious!

VINCOTTO

Vincotto is a concentrated syrupy essence made by cooking the must of late-harvested negroamaro and malvasia grapes over a low flame for hours. The mixture is then transferred to oak casks where it is blended with a 'mother' must and left to mature. The secret recipe belongs to the Calogiuri family, in Leece, Italy.

I have added spices to the marinade and included lime to give the quail a fresh finish – New World Italian!

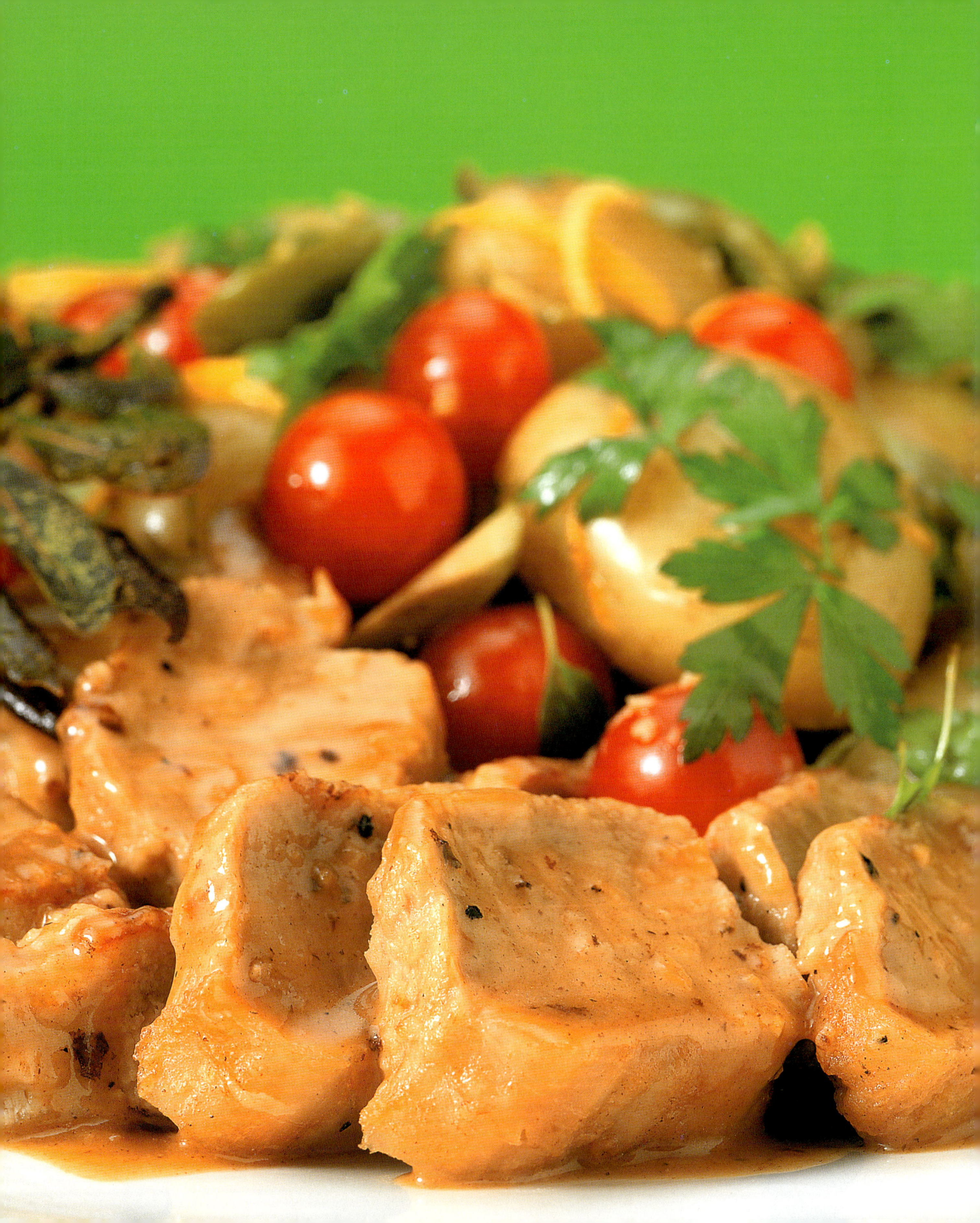

christmas colours VEAL FILLET WITH GREEN OLIVES AND FRESH BAY LEAVES

SERVES 6

1kg new baby potatoes, scrubbed
6 x 150g veal loin fillets
1 tablespoon olive oil
knob of butter
3 tablespoons plain flour
fresh bay leaves
salt
freshly ground black pepper to taste
¼ cup dry white wine
2 cloves garlic, crushed
1 cup large green olives, chopped
pared strips of lemon zest from 1 lemon
2 tablespoons extra virgin olive oil
1 tablespoon chopped marjoram
1 cup cherry tomatoes
1 tablespoon torn parsley leaves

Steam the potatoes until they are just tender. (If the potatoes are not new, just small, peel them first.)

Remove any silvery skin from the veal fillets and pat them dry with absorbent kitchen paper. Choose a large frying pan that has a lid, or a large casserole dish. Heat the olive oil in the pan or casserole over a medium heat. When it is hot, drop in the butter. Pass the pieces of fillet through the flour and put half of them in the pan (or all of them if they will fit) while the butter is sizzling. Cook on both sides until a good brown colour and transfer them to a plate when done. Repeat with the other pieces of fillet. While the meat is browning, add the bay leaves and let these brown too, covering the pan or casserole with a splatter screen if you have one (the bay leaves tend to spit!). Return all the fillets to the pan, sprinkle with salt, grind on some black pepper and pour the wine in. Immediately cover with the lid, turn the heat to low and cook for about 7 minutes, or until the meat is just cooked but still juicy and slightly pink. Turn off the heat and let the meat rest with the lid on for 5 minutes.

While the meat is cooking, heat the garlic, olives and lemon zest in a pan with the extra virgin olive oil. Cook for 2–3 minutes until hot, then add the potatoes and marjoram. Cook gently, tossing, until piping hot (be careful not to break up the potatoes). Stir the tomatoes and parsley through the potatoes and olives and tip into a bowl.

Transfer the meat to a board and reduce the pan juices over a medium heat until they are syrupy. Slice the meat, arrange on a heated plate and pour the juices over. Serve immediately with the potato and olive salad.

Veal fillet with green olives and fresh bay leaves

splash of vermouth
SCALOPPINE WITH LEMON

SERVES 4

500g veal scaloppine
2 lemons
4 tablespoons plain flour mixed with ½ teaspoon salt
1 tablespoon olive oil
2–3 tablespoons butter
salt
freshly ground black pepper to taste
250ml (1 cup) dry white vermouth (or dry white wine)
thin slices of lemon to garnish

Prepare the veal as described in Scaloppine Preparation (see page 88), cutting each slice of meat into 2–3 pieces. Remove the zest from the lemons and set aside. Put the veal in a shallow dish and pour the juice from 1 lemon over it. Cover and refrigerate for up to 1 hour.

Coat the veal with the seasoned flour, dusting off the excess. Set a large frying pan over a medium heat and add the olive oil. When it is hot, drop in 2 tablespoons of the butter. While it is sizzling, add half the veal pieces to the pan (or as many as will fit without overlapping) and cook until they are golden brown on both sides. Sprinkle with salt and grind on some black pepper. Transfer the veal to a plate, and repeat the procedure with the rest of the veal, adding a little more butter if necessary.

When all the veal is cooked and transferred to the plate, pour the previously mixed dry vermouth, lemon zest and juice from the second lemon into the pan. Bubble up, scraping up any sediment.

Once the mixture is syrupy, return the veal to the pan and turn the pieces over to coat them in the lemony juices. Transfer to a heated serving plate, garnish with lemon slices and serve immediately.

fiery inferno SCALOPPINE COLOSSEO

SERVES 4

500g veal scaloppine
4 tablespoons plain flour mixed with ½ teaspoon salt
2 eggs, beaten with ¼ teaspoon salt
½ cup fine dry breadcrumbs (see page 74)
3 tablespoons freshly grated parmesan (parmigiano reggiano) cheese
extra salt
1 tablespoon olive oil
3–4 tablespoons butter
extra salt
3 large cloves garlic, sliced
4–6 small dried 'bird's eye' chillies, crushed

Prepare and coat the veal, adding the parmesan cheese to the breadcrumbs, as in the recipe for Crispy Veal with Parmesan and Black Olives (see page 88).

Set a large frying pan over a medium heat. When hot, add the oil and 2 tablespoons of the butter. While the mixture is sizzling, add half the veal pieces to the pan (or as many as will fit without overlapping) and cook until golden brown on both sides (take care not to let them burn and add extra butter if required).

When the pieces of veal are cooked, transfer them to a serving platter. Sprinkle lightly with salt. Add 1 tablespoon of butter to the pan and, when it has melted, add the sliced garlic. Cook for a few minutes, then add the crushed chillies. Continue cooking until the garlic is pale golden and fragrant. Immediately spoon the buttery chilli mixture over the veal and serve.

LITTLE SQUARES of browned veal, topped with slivers of garlic that have been cooked until nutty and crisp and spiked with chilli, is an old Biuso family favourite. To ring the changes, I've coated the veal in breadcrumbs and parmesan cheese, but you can omit this step if you prefer.

napolitana beauty SCALOPPINE WITH MELTING MOZZARELLA

SERVES 4

1 medium eggplant (aubergine)
olive oil
500g veal scaloppine
4 tablespoons plain flour mixed with ½ teaspoon salt
2 tablespoons butter
extra salt
150g mozzarella 'bocconcini' in whey, drained and sliced
handful of small basil leaves
freshly ground black pepper to taste
1½ cups homemade tomato sauce, spiked with chilli (use your favourite recipe or the Puttanesca Sauce on page 54)

Slice the eggplant into rounds and pat dry with absorbent kitchen paper. Heat a 5mm depth of olive oil in a heavy-based frying pan over a high heat until it is smoking. Drop in as many slices of eggplant as will fit and cook quickly on both sides until a deep golden colour. Transfer to a plate lined with kitchen paper and repeat with the other slices of eggplant. (The eggplant can be fried a few hours before required. Alternatively, oven-bake the eggplant slices as described on page 36.)

Prepare the veal as described in Scaloppine Preparation (see page 88), cutting each slice of meat into 2–3 pieces. Coat the veal with the seasoned flour, dusting off the excess. Set a large frying pan over a medium heat, add 1 tablespoon of olive oil and, when it is hot, drop in the butter. While the mixture is sizzling, add half the veal pieces to the pan (or as many as will fit without overlapping) and cook until they are golden brown on both sides (take care not to let them burn). Transfer to a plate when they are done and continue cooking the rest of the veal, adding a little more butter if necessary.

When all the veal is cooked, return it to the pan, but remove the pan from the element. Increase the heat of the element to high. Sprinkle the veal with salt. Cut the eggplant slices in halves or quarters and top each piece of veal with eggplant followed by a slice of mozzarella. Scatter the basil leaves over, grind on some black pepper and put a lid on the pan (improvise with aluminium foil if you don't have a lid).

Set the pan back over a high heat and cook for 2–3 minutes until the cheese has only just melted. Transfer the veal to a heated serving plate and serve immediately with the heated tomato sauce.

golden crumbs CRISPY VEAL WITH PARMESAN AND BLACK OLIVES

SERVES 4

500g veal scaloppine
75g (¾ cup) freshly grated parmesan (parmigiano reggiano) cheese
¼ cup dry breadcrumbs (see page 74)
salt
2 eggs, beaten with a pinch of salt
olive oil
1 tablespoon butter
1 large onion, sliced
1 clove garlic, crushed
20 basil leaves
100g (approximately 20) black olives, halved and pitted
freshly ground black pepper to taste

Prepare the veal as described in Scaloppine Preparation (see opposite), cutting each slice of meat into 2–3 pieces. Mix the parmesan cheese and breadcrumbs with ¼ teaspoon of salt. Pass the slices of meat through the beaten egg, letting the excess drip off, then coat with the crumb mixture. Put the pieces of veal on a tray in a single layer as they are coated; they can be prepared up to 1 hour before cooking.

Set a large frying pan over a medium heat. When hot, add 2 tablespoons of olive oil and the butter. While the mixture is sizzling, add half the veal pieces to the pan (or as many as will fit without overlapping) and cook until golden brown on both sides (take care not to let them burn). Transfer the cooked veal to a heated plate and keep it warm while cooking the rest of the meat; add more oil and butter if necessary.

Meanwhile, put the onion and garlic and 2 tablespoons of olive oil in a small frying pan, set it over a gentle heat, and cook until soft and lightly golden. Add the basil leaves and olives, grind on some black pepper and heat through for 1 minute.

Arrange the veal on a heated serving plate and spoon the olive garnish down the centre. Serve immediately.

ADDING PARMESAN CHEESE to the breadcrumb crust gives these pieces of veal an appetising, golden crisp crust and a flavour boost.

SCALOPPINE PREPARATION

Scaloppine is the Italian name for the thin slices of veal cut from a single muscle off the top of the animal's leg. In France, the same cut is known as an escalope. In English the names scallop and schnitzel are used, but not scallopini, which is the name for small star-shaped squash. Piccata, coming from the verb picchiare, meaning beaten, is another Italian name used for this cut.

It is essential that the scaloppine be cut from a single muscle from the top of the leg (called the top round) and that the meat be cut across the grain. If the meat is cut with the grain, it will shrivel up on cooking and be tough to eat. The slices of veal then need to be lightly flattened with a meat mallet to make them uniformly thin. Do not bash the meat, as it easily tears and turns to shreds. Cover the meat with a clean plastic bag or waxed paper, and apply a gentle pressure with the mallet, sliding it along the surface of the meat as you do so. This stretches the meat without damaging the tissues.

Crispy veal with parmesan and black olives

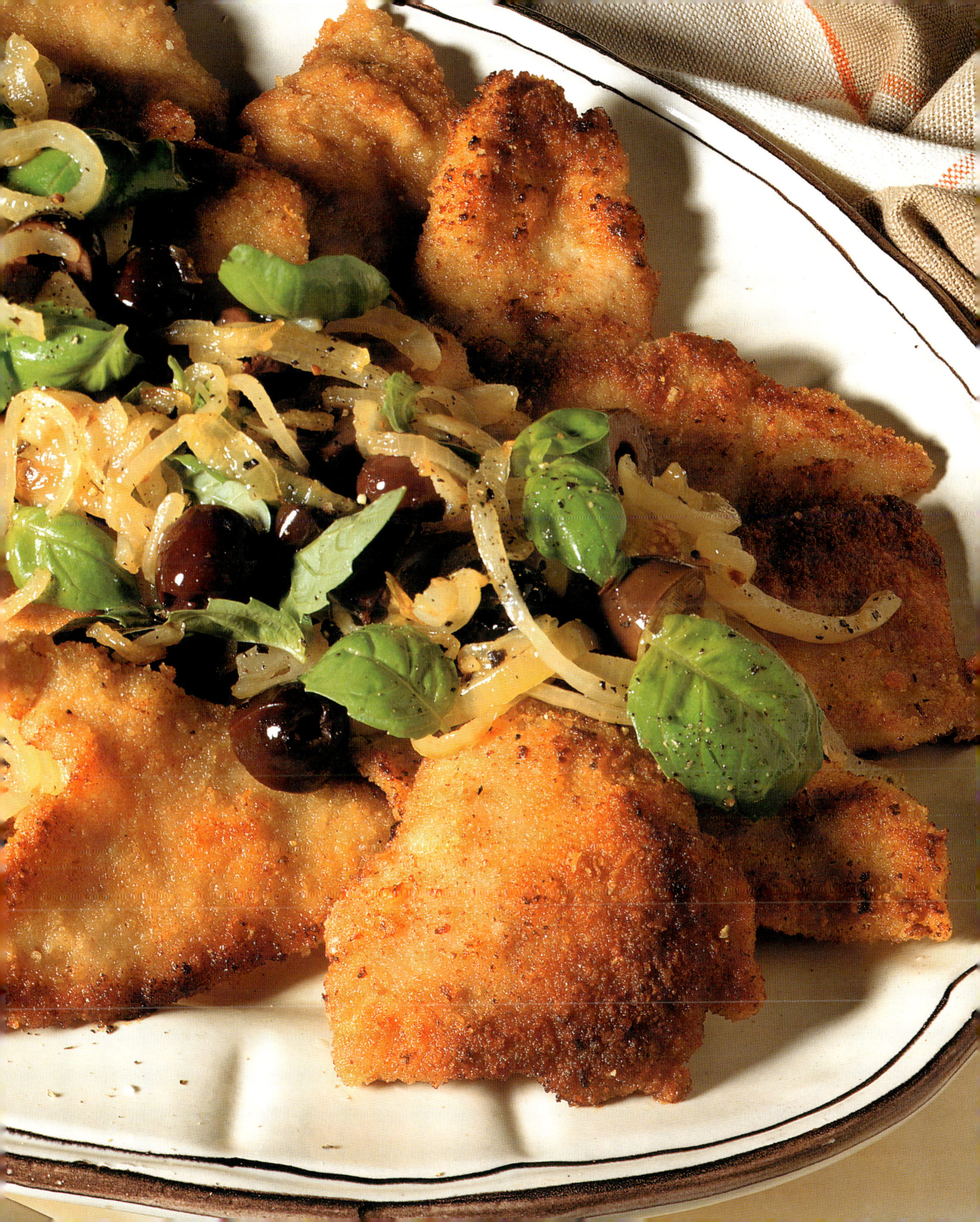

bubbling parmesan ISANNA'S SCALOPPINE

SERVES 4

500g veal scaloppine
4 tablespoons plain flour mixed with ½ teaspoon salt
2 large eggs beaten with ¼ teaspoon salt
¾ cup dried breadcrumbs (see page 74)
1½ tablespoons olive oil
2–3 tablespoons butter
extra salt
100g thinly sliced prosciutto (or use thinly sliced ham)
50g piece of parmesan (parmigiano reggiano) cheese
¼ cup cream
freshly ground black pepper to taste
freshly grated nutmeg

Prepare the veal as described in Scaloppine Preparation (see page 88), cutting each piece of meat into 2–3 pieces. Coat the veal with the seasoned flour, dusting off the excess, then coat with the beaten eggs. Let the excess egg drip off, then coat the veal pieces with breadcrumbs. Put the pieces of veal on a tray in a single layer as they are done; they can be prepared up to 1 hour before cooking.

Set a large frying pan over a medium heat. When hot, add the olive oil and 2 tablespoons of the butter. While the mixture is sizzling, add half the veal pieces to the pan (or as many as will fit in without overlapping) and cook until golden brown on both sides (take care not to let them burn). Transfer them to an ovenproof serving platter or plate. Sprinkle the meat lightly with salt. Cook the rest of the veal, adding a little more butter to the pan if necessary.

Cut the prosciutto or ham into squares and the parmesan cheese into thin slices (don't worry about it crumbling). Top each piece of meat with a piece of prosciutto and a little parmesan cheese.

Mix the cream, black pepper and nutmeg together, then spoon it over the veal pieces. Put the platter under a hot grill, cook for 2–3 minutes or until golden and crisp. Serve immediately.

ANOTHER TEMPTING recipe from my sister-in-law's Emilian kitchen (Emilia Romagna is a region in Italy). I enjoy this dish served with rice.

stave off winter TUSCAN PORK AND BEANS

SERVES 6

1 cup (225g) cannellini beans (if not available, use white beans of your choice but be aware that they may take longer to cook)
3 tablespoons extra virgin olive oil
1 small onion, finely chopped
½ carrot, finely chopped
1 small stalk celery (choose an inner stalk), finely chopped
300g pork spare ribs (buy them 'in the piece', not cut into individual ribs, cut from the short end)
2 fresh bay leaves
1 teaspoon finely chopped rosemary
1 tablespoon coarsely chopped flat leaf parsley
freshly ground black pepper to taste
200g (½ a regular can) Italian tomatoes, well mashed
salt

Rinse the beans then soak overnight in water to cover. Drain, put them in a saucepan and cover generously with water. Bring to the boil, removing any scum as it rises. Lower the heat and cover with a lid (set the temperature so that the liquid is boiling gently without boiling over – the beans will cook more quickly like this). Cook for 30–40 minutes, or until nicely tender. Drain, reserving the liquid (don't forget to put a bowl under the strainer!). Cover the beans with a piece of absorbent kitchen paper until required.

Put the extra virgin olive oil in a medium-sized saucepan with the onion and set the pan over a medium heat. Cook gently until lightly coloured. Add the carrot, celery, pork ribs, bay leaves, rosemary and parsley. Grind on plenty of black pepper. Cook for 10 minutes, stirring often.

Stir in the tomatoes and beans and 1 litre of the bean cooking water (make up to 1 litre with water if necessary). Bring to the boil. Lower the heat and cook, uncovered, for 30 minutes. Stir in 1½ teaspoons of salt, then mash some of the beans with a potato masher to thicken the soup. Dish into soup bowls and serve hot.

salt 'n' crackle ROAST PORK WITH FENNEL SEEDS

SERVES 10

2 tablespoons finely chopped rosemary
1 tablespoon chopped sage
1 teaspoon fennel seeds
2 large cloves garlic, finely chopped
1.6kg loin of pork, with crackling scored and bones chined
olive oil
salt
white wine
extra herbs to garnish

Mix the rosemary, sage, fennel seeds and garlic together. Rub the mixture over the meat and bones, tucking it into the cuts in the meat (but not over the crackling). Rub the crackling generously with olive oil, then sprinkle well with salt. Sit the meat in a snug-fitting but low-sided roasting dish.

Roast the meat for 30 minutes in an oven preheated to 220°C or until the fat has started to crackle. Lower the heat to 180°C and continue cooking for 40–60 minutes or until the meat is cooked through (test with a skewer; the juices should be clear). Scrape up any browning bits during cooking, but do not baste the crackling.

Transfer the meat to a board and rest it for 10 minutes. Tilt the roasting tin, then scoop off nearly all the fat. Set the pan over a medium heat and splash in 2–3 tablespoons of wine. Bubble up.

Meanwhile, carve the meat into slices about 5mm thick, cutting through the chined bones. If the crackling is difficult to cut through, take it off in large pieces, remove the fat from the back and cut the crackling into chunks with scissors. Arrange the meat on a hot plate, spoon the hot juices over and garnish with herbs. Put the crackling on a separate plate and serve immediately. If serving the pork cold, slice the meat more thinly.

THIS IS AN EASY-TO-DO yet impressive meat dish that provides tender, tasty meat with irresistible crackling. The pork needs to be chined (chining means to cut in between the bones to make it easier to slice), and your butcher can do this for you in a matter of minutes.

THE CRACKLINGIEST CRACKLING

The secret of superb, evenly crackled crackling is to keep everything off it (stuffing, basting liquids, etc) apart from a generous coating of oil and salt. Use a shallow-sided roasting tin. High sides on the tin block out the direct heat and prevent the fat on the sides of the joint from getting hot enough to crackle (or they can trap some steam and soften the crackling). Cook on a very high heat until the fat has started to crackle. Do not cover the meat once it is cooked. If serving the meat cold, remove the crackling and refrigerate it separately on a plate (don't cover it) until it is cold. Serve within 24 hours.

crackling pancetta ROASTED EYE FILLET WRAPPED IN BACON

SERVES 6

1kg fillet of beef, cut from the thick end
1 tablespoon chopped rosemary
2 tablespoons olive oil
1 clove garlic, crushed
1 teaspoon salt
½ teaspoon freshly ground black pepper
200g thinly sliced pancetta (Italian bacon), or substitute prosciutto

Remove any fat and the silverskin from the beef. Mix the rosemary, 1 tablespoon of the olive oil, the garlic, salt and black pepper together in a shallow dish. Roll the beef in the mixture then wrap it in pancetta and tie it on with string as best you can.

Heat the remaining tablespoon of olive oil in a roasting tin over a high heat and carefully lower the beef in. Turn the beef quickly in the hot oil then place in an oven preheated to 210°C and cook for 15 minutes for rare to medium-rare, or until it is done to your liking. Remove the beef from the oven and let it rest for 10–15 minutes.

Remove the string from the beef. Put absorbent kitchen paper around the edges of the chopping board to absorb the juices. Slice the meat into thick, even slices. Rest the sliced meat for 1 minute, mop up the juices, then transfer to the plate and serve immediately.

tuscan touch SELVAPIANA BEEF IN CHIANTI

SERVES 6

1kg piece of beef scotch fillet (or use veal)
salt
freshly ground black pepper to taste
2 cloves garlic, finely chopped
1 tablespoon finely chopped rosemary
3–4 fresh sage leaves, chopped
3 tablespoons olive oil
3 tablespoons chianti (or full-bodied red wine) – serve the rest of the wine with the meal

Make a small cut in the centre of the meat, then use the rounded handle of a wooden spoon to push through the meat to form a tunnel.

In a small bowl mix together ½ teaspoon of salt, black pepper to taste, the garlic, rosemary and sage. Stuff this mixture into the tunnel in the meat, using the handle of the wooden spoon to help push it in. Tie the meat into a good shape with string and grind on plenty of black pepper.

Heat a heavy-based casserole (choose one in which the meat fits snugly) over a medium-high heat and add the olive oil. When it is hot, lower the beef in and brown well on all sides, turning with tongs.

Turn the heat to low and cook, covered with a lid, for 20 minutes, turning the meat once. Remove the lid, turn the meat, and pour the wine over. Cover with the lid again and cook for 10 minutes more. Turn off the heat and rest the beef for 10 minutes before slicing. This produces medium-rare beef, but if you prefer the meat cooked to medium, allow an extra 10 minutes' cooking time before adding the wine.

Transfer the beef to a board and sprinkle generously with salt. Scoop any fat off the juices in the roasting tin, then reduce the juices over a high heat. Remove the string from the meat and slice thickly. Arrange on a heated serving platter, pour the juices from the casserole over the meat and serve.

TUSCANY IS FAMOUS for its beef and, in this dish, which I first sampled at the Selvapiana vineyard in Tuscany, the savoury glaze comes from using chianti wine.

Roasted eye fillet wrapped in bacon

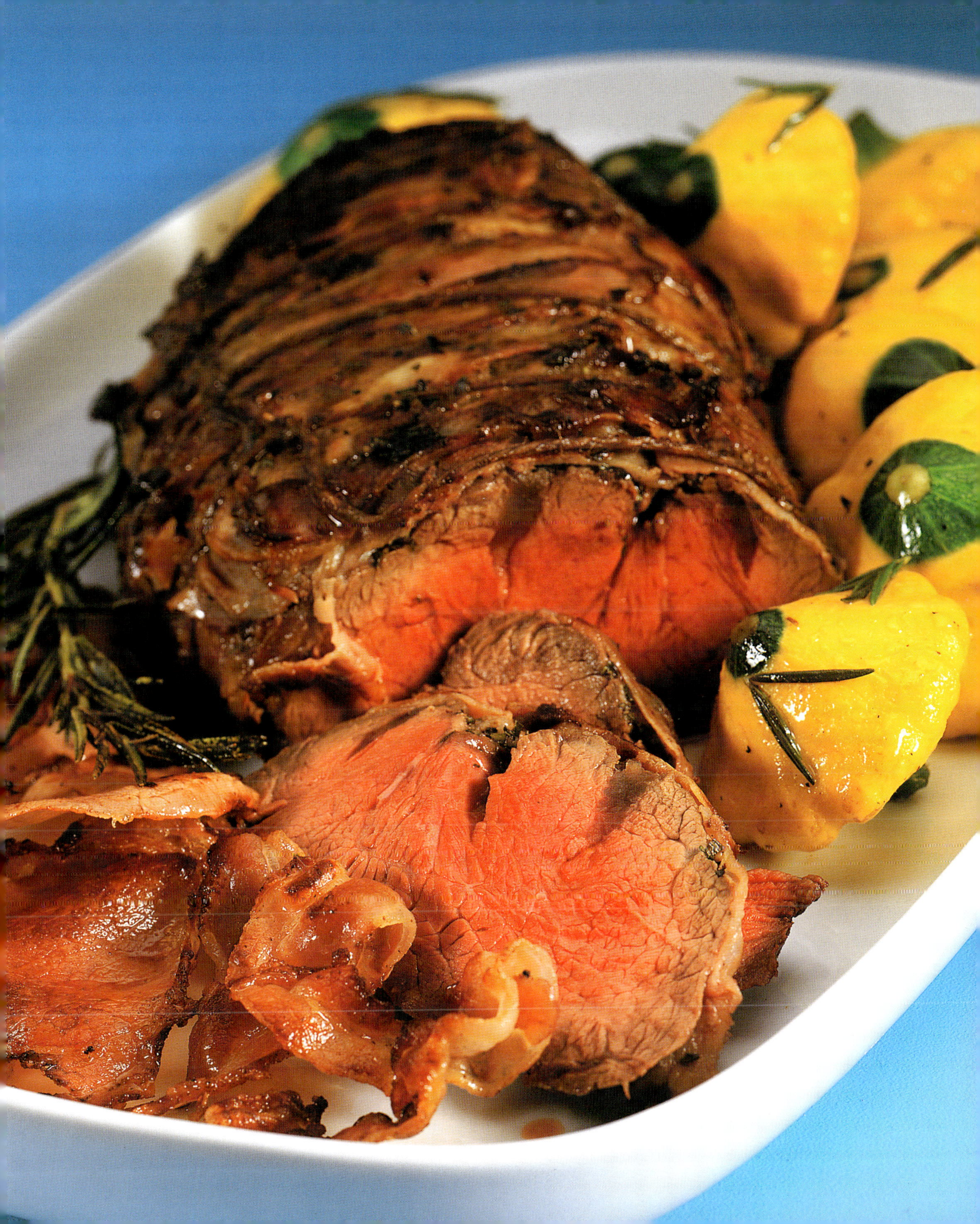

lemon-fresh OSSOBUCO

SERVES 6

75ml olive oil
1 large onion, finely chopped
1 large clove garlic, crushed
1 tablespoon butter
12 pieces ossobuco (shins of young veal) (approximately 1.5kg)
¼ cup plain flour mixed with ¼ teaspoon salt
¾ teaspoon salt
freshly ground black pepper to taste
300ml dry white wine
300ml chicken stock (if you don't want to use wine, use 600ml chicken stock)
several sprigs fresh thyme
2 bay leaves, halved
400g can Italian tomatoes, mashed

GREMOLADA
2 tablespoons finely grated lemon zest
2 tablespoons finely chopped parsley
2 large cloves garlic, finely chopped

Heat the olive oil in a large heavy-based frying pan over a low-to-medium heat. Add the onion and garlic and cook gently until soft but not coloured. Tilt the pan to allow the oil to drain, then using a slotted spoon transfer the onion mixture to a heavy-based casserole. Reheat the oil in the pan and, when it is quite hot, drop in the butter.

Meanwhile, coat half the veal pieces with the seasoned flour. Brown the veal on both sides, then transfer to the casserole, standing the pieces side by side (this helps keep the marrow, which many consider a delicacy, inside the bone). Repeat with the second batch of veal. Season the meat well with salt and black pepper.

Add the remaining flour to the frying pan and mix it in with a metal spoon (if the pan is dry, add a knob of butter and allow it to melt before adding the flour). Cook for 2–3 minutes, stirring, then pour the wine in. The mixture will thicken immediately. Have ready the chicken stock and pour it in. Add the thyme and bay leaves and bring to the boil. If there is room in the pan, add the tomatoes, return the stock mixture to the boil and pour it over the veal. If the pan is full (which it probably will be), pour most of the boiling stock mixture over the meat, then add the tomatoes to the pan, heat through, pour over the meat and mix all together gently. Cover with a tight-fitting lid.

Transfer the casserole to an oven preheated to 170°C and cook for $1\frac{1}{2}$–2 hours or until the meat is fork-tender. Turn the meat carefully two or three times during cooking.

Mix the gremolada ingredients together in a small bowl. Remove the casserole from the oven, lift off the lid and sprinkle with the gremolada. Serve immediately with Risotto Milanese (see page 41).

OSSOBUCO is a rich stew made from an inexpensive cut of veal (it can be made with beef, but it will be stronger in flavour and require longer cooking). It is traditionally served with Risotto Milanese, a risotto flavoured and coloured with saffron (see page 41). In Italy, risotto is nearly always served as a first course, like pasta, but in this instance the two dishes are served together and complement each other perfectly.

Gremolada is sometimes spelled gremolata.

shepherd's treat LAMB ABRUZZI

SERVES 6

3 tablespoons finely chopped streaky bacon
3 cloves garlic, crushed
1 tablespoon finely chopped rosemary
2 tablespoons finely chopped parsley
freshly ground black pepper to taste
1.5–2kg leg of lamb, trimmed of excess fat
2 tablespoons olive oil
125ml (½ cup) balsamic vinegar (or red wine vinegar)
1 teaspoon salt
2 tablespoons freshly grated parmesan (parmigiano reggiano) cheese
3 tablespoons fresh white breadcrumbs
2 tablespoons soft butter

Mix the bacon, garlic, rosemary, parsley and a little black pepper in a small bowl. Make a dozen or so deep incisions in the meaty parts of the lamb and force the stuffing into these slits, using the end of a teaspoon.

Put the olive oil in a roasting tin and place in an oven preheated to 190°C. When the oil is hot, add the lamb, coating it in the hot oil to seal. Grind over some black pepper and roast the meat for 45 minutes, basting occasionally. Pour the balsamic vinegar over, sprinkle with the salt and return to the oven for a further 15 minutes.

Meanwhile, mix together the parmesan cheese, breadcrumbs and butter. Spread this over the top of the lamb and return it to the oven for another 15 minutes. Remove the lamb from the oven and it let rest at room temperature, covered loosely with aluminium foil, for 15 minutes before slicing. (This produces a moist pink roast but, if you prefer the lamb a little more cooked, allow an extra 10–15 minutes in the initial cooking stage.)

Transfer the lamb to a chopping board. Tilt the roasting tin, scoop off and discard the fat, then bubble up the juices over a medium heat for a minute or two. Slice the lamb thinly, arrange it on a serving plate, pour the pan juices over and serve immediately.

I'VE COOKED HUNDREDS of lamb dishes over the years, but this one is tops. It's succulent and tender, and its crisp coating of parmesan cheese makes it absolutely delicious.

spicy spiral SAUSAGE COIL WITH HOT POLENTA AND SAUTÉED MUSHROOMS

SERVES 6

½ quantity Basic Polenta (see page 42)
3-metre length of sausage (see opposite)
3–4 wooden skewers
75g butter
500g button mushrooms, thickly sliced
2 large cloves garlic, crushed
freshly ground black pepper to taste
½ teaspoon salt
2 tablespoons coarsely chopped parsley
1 teaspoon finely chopped rosemary

Make the polenta first and, while it is cooking, cook the sausages and mushroom sauce. (This will keep you busy but, providing everything is prepared, it can be done. Alternatively, the mushrooms can be cooked ahead, cooled, then reheated in the microwave – and you can opt for quick-cooking polenta.)

Curl the sausage into a large, preferably non-stick, frying pan. Secure the sausage coil with the skewers, pushing each skewer right through the flat coil of sausage from one side to the other.

Set the cold pan over a medium-high heat (you shouldn't need any oil) and cook until the sausage is lightly browned underneath. Turn it over and cook the second side until it is lightly browned, then lower the heat and cook gently, turning once more, until it is cooked through (if any liquid accumulates, pour it off). Remove the sausage from the pan, pull out the skewers and drain briefly on absorbent kitchen paper.

While the sausage is cooking, and while you intermittently stir the polenta, sauté the mushrooms. Heat a large frying pan over a medium heat, then drop two-thirds of the butter in. When it is sizzling, increase the heat to medium-high and drop the mushrooms in. Toss them in the butter, then cook, stirring often, until any liquid evaporates and the mushrooms are starting to brown.

Stir the garlic through, grind on some black pepper and continue cooking until the garlic is lightly browned. Sprinkle with the salt and add the herbs. Turn off the heat.

Now co-ordinate the meal. To finish off, turn the hot polenta into a heated serving bowl and top with the sausage coil. Quickly reheat the mushrooms over a high heat and add the last of the butter. As soon as it melts, pour the contents of the pan over the sausage and polenta. Serve immediately.

MAMMA ROSA'S TRICK

Keeping sausage meat in an uninterrupted loop, twirling it into a coil and securing it with skewers is a trick I learned from my mother-in-law. Apart from a novel presentation, it's a lot easier to turn the sausage coil over during cooking than it is to deal with a pan full of hot, splattering sausages.

You will need to order the sausage from a sausage maker (many butchers make their own sausages). Just tell them to give you an unbroken length of sausage, preferably a thinner sausage, about 2–3 meters long. Make sure you use a good-quality flavoursome sausage, not the sawdust kind!

Sausage coil with hot polenta and sautéed mushrooms

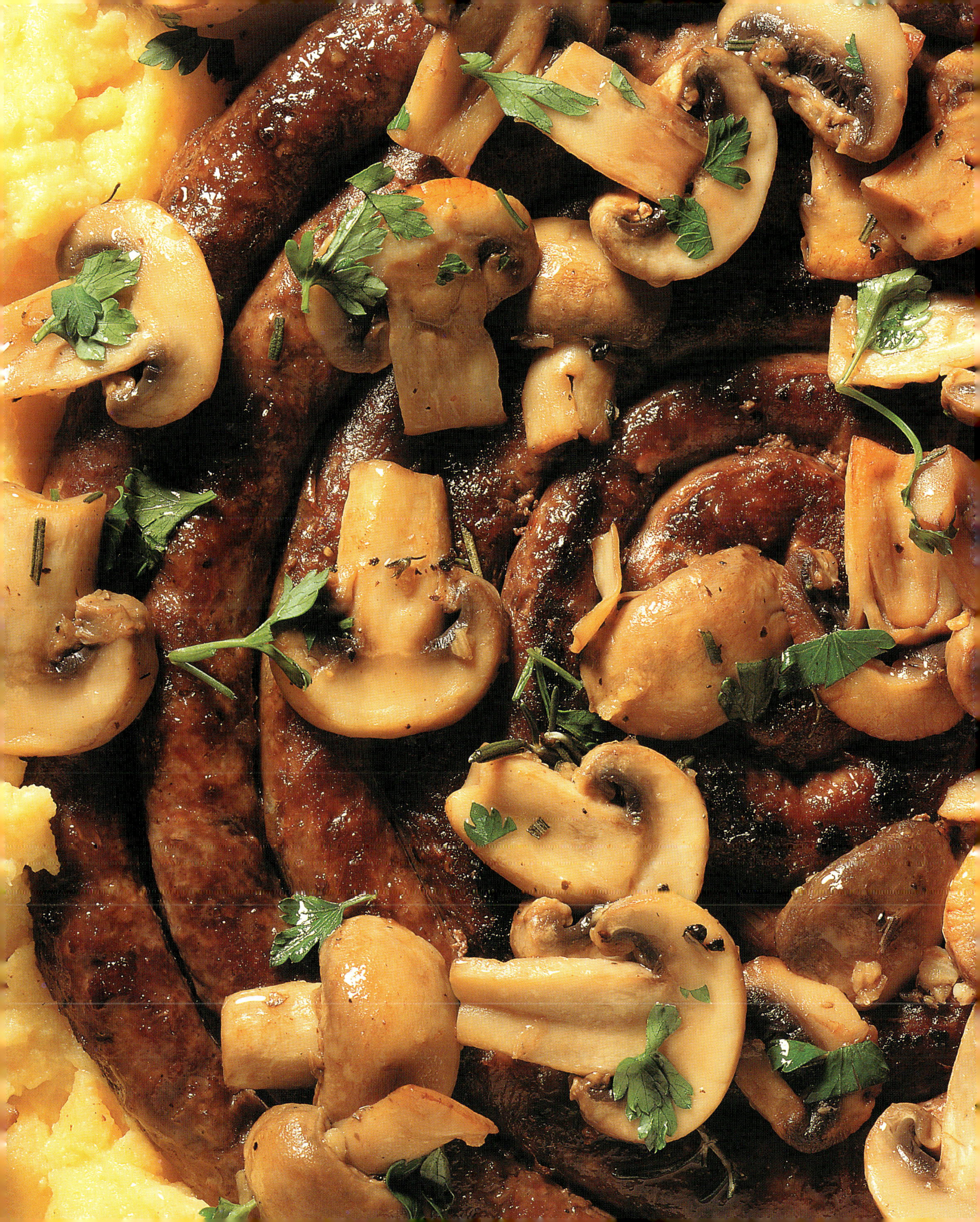

splashed with wine LEG OF LAMB WITH PARMESAN CRUST AND CRUNCHY POTATOES

1 leg of lamb, partially boned, weighing approximately 1.8kg (ask the butcher to remove the aitchbone, leaving the shank bone in)
3 cloves garlic, sliced
rosemary sprigs
½ cup white wine
1.5kg roasting potatoes (starchy ones), peeled and cut into large chunks
olive oil
salt
3 tablespoons fresh breadcrumbs
½ cup freshly grated parmesan (parmigiano reggiano) cheese
freshly ground black pepper to taste
3 tablespoons soft butter

Trim as much fat as possible from the lamb. Stud the lamb with slivers of garlic and sprigs of rosemary. Put it in a roasting tin and set this over a medium element. Heat for 3–4 minutes until it starts to sizzle, then pour the wine over.

Meanwhile, rub the potatoes with olive oil and salt and set these around the lamb; the tin should be crowded.

Roast the meat and potatoes in an oven preheated to 180°C for 60 minutes, basting and turning the potatoes from time to time. In a small bowl mix the breadcrumbs, parmesan cheese, black pepper to taste, ½ teaspoon of salt and the butter. Remove the lamb from the oven and spread this over the top. Return the lamb to the oven and cook for a further 10–15 minutes, or until it is done to your liking (this should produce pink, juicy lamb with a good crust on top).

Transfer the lamb to a board and let it rest for 15 minutes. Continue cooking the potatoes while the lamb rests. Slice the lamb into thin pieces and arrange on a heated serving platter. Serve the potatoes separately. Accompany with a green salad.

THIS DISH IS MODELLED on Lamb Abruzzi (see page 95), with the addition of potatoes, which cook until crusty around the lamb. Omitting the bacon from the lamb makes it less gamey. A good family roast main course.

Leg of lamb with parmesan crust and crunchy potatoes

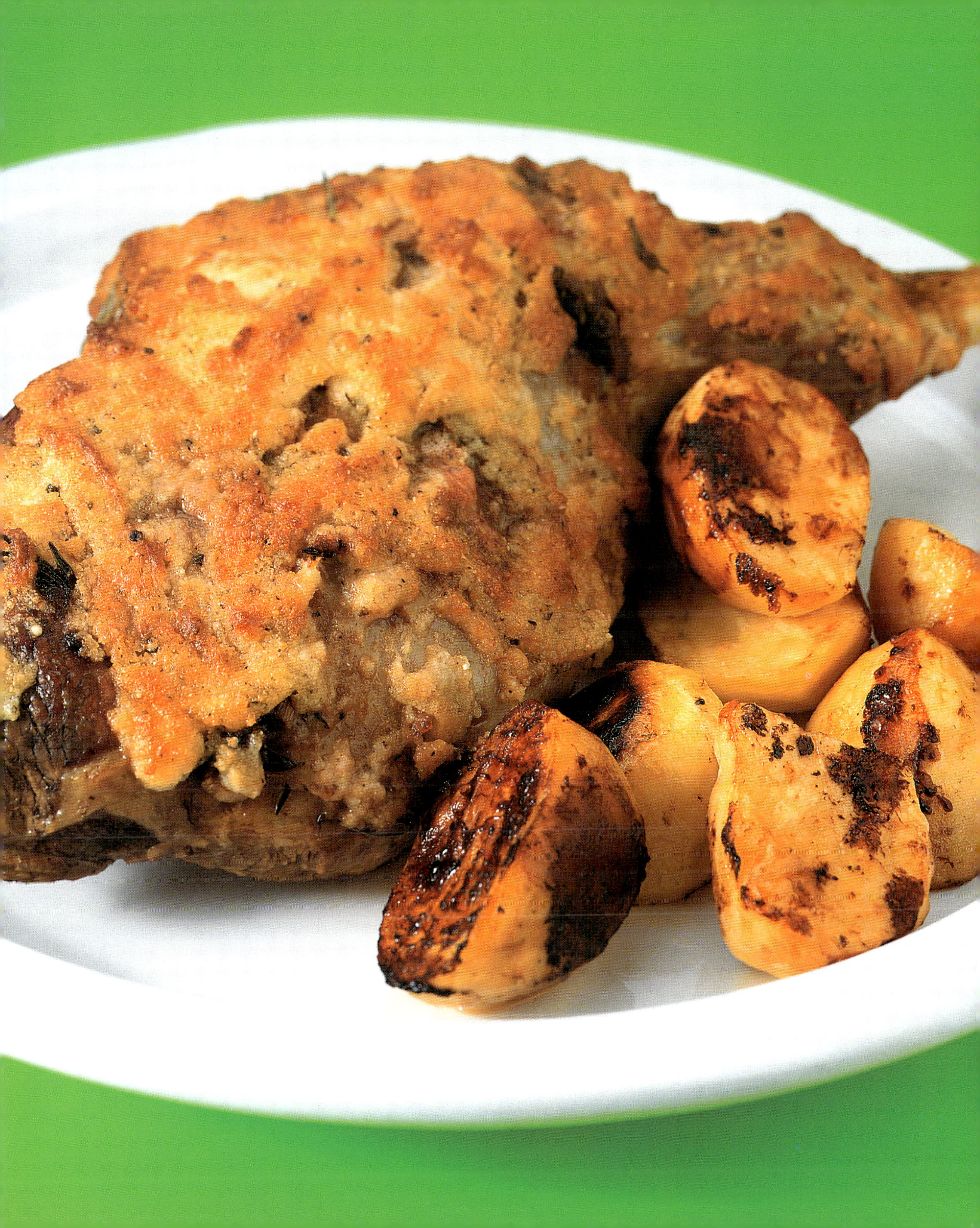

vegetables

CRUNCHY POTATO STICKS	103
PEPERONATA	103
ROASTED POTATO STICKS WITH WHITE WINE	104
BUTTER BEANS AND POTATOES	104
LEAFY GREENS IN THE PAN	104
GLAZED CARROTS	105
WHITE BEANS STEWED WITH ROSEMARY AND GARLIC	105
POTATOES WITH ROSEMARY	106
CARROTS WITH GREMOLADA	106
RED LEAVES ON THE GRILL	109
'SUFFOCATED' CAULIFLOWER	109
FENNEL, SWEET TOMATO AND OLIVE SALAD	110
CHICK PEAS AND TOMATO	110
BABY POTATOES ON ROSEMARY STALKS	112
STUFFED BABY ZUCCHINI	112
ROASTED FENNEL	114
BABY PEAS WITH SAUTÉED PROSCIUTTO	114
BARBECUED EGGPLANT WITH BALSAMIC DRESSING	114
SALAD OF RED LEAVES WITH CAPER DRESSING	116
ZUCCHINI, BASIL AND BLACK OLIVE SALAD	116

taut asparagus, beans with snap

peppers as bright as traffic lights

crinkly green leaves, feathery herbs

glossy eggplants and sun-warmed tomatoes

fresh and flavoursome from the earth

to inspire

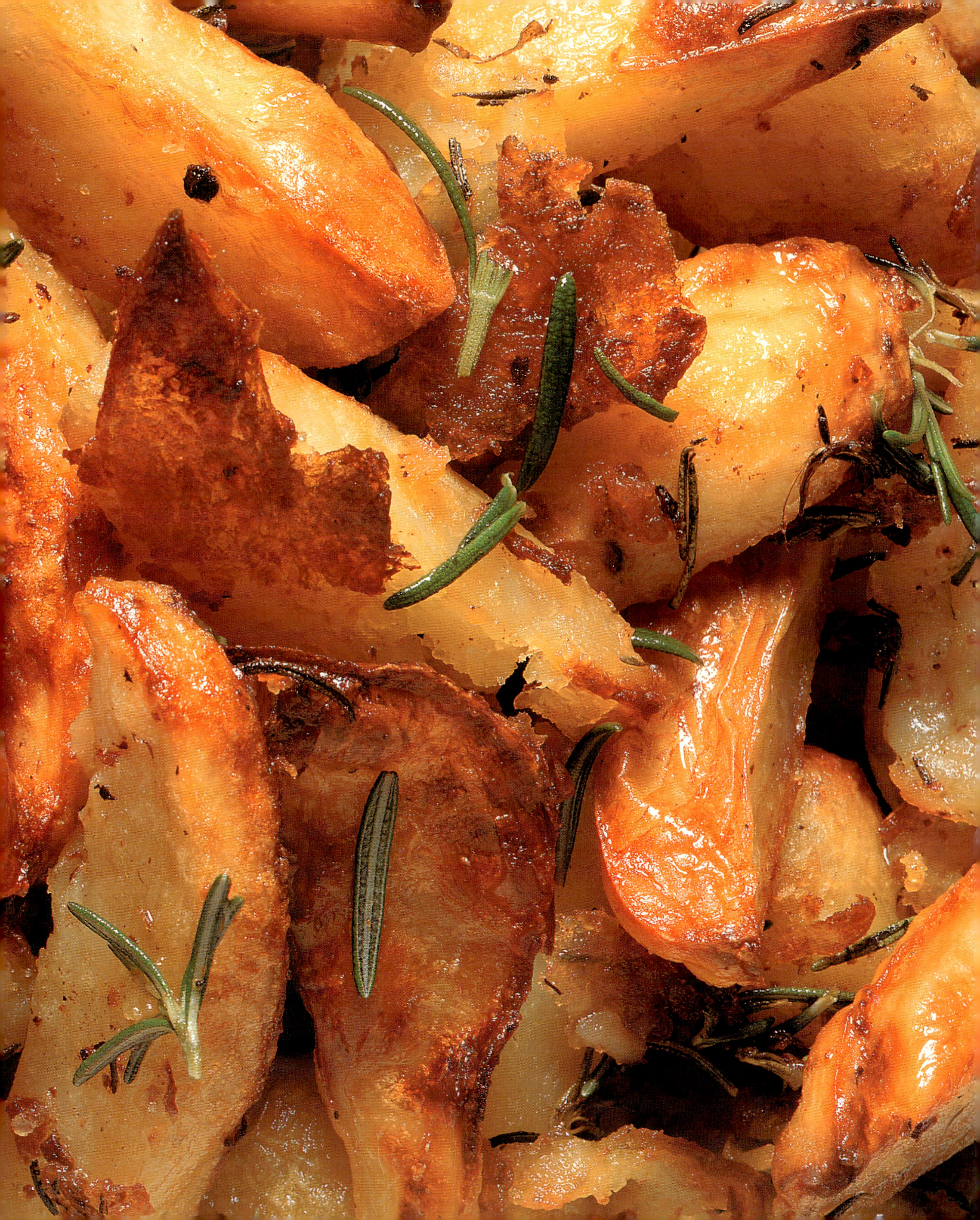

irresistible CRUNCHY POTATO STICKS

SERVES 6

2kg roasting potatoes, peeled
3 tablespoons olive oil
2 tablespoons butter
1 teaspoon salt or to taste
2 tablespoons finely chopped rosemary

Cut the potatoes into rough chunks and dry on absorbent kitchen paper. Put them in a roasting tin, drizzle with the olive oil and dot with butter. Sprinkle the salt and the rosemary over the top.

Cook the potatoes in an oven preheated to 180°C for 1¼ hours, turning occasionally with a fish slice, or until they are crisp and golden.

sweet peppers PEPERONATA

SERVES 6

3 tablespoons extra virgin olive oil
1 tablespoon butter
1 onion, finely sliced
4 large red peppers (capsicums), cores and seeds removed, cut into chunks
2 cloves garlic, crushed
½ teaspoon salt
freshly ground black pepper to taste
6 ripe vine-ripened tomatoes (or flavoursome outdoor tomatoes) (approximately 750g), peeled, cored and roughly chopped (flick out as many seeds as possible)
½ cup small basil leaves

Heat the extra virgin olive oil in a large frying pan over a medium heat and, when it is hot, drop in the butter. Add the onion and fry gently until it is lightly coloured, then add the peppers, garlic, salt and black pepper. Stir well to combine and cook for 10 minutes.

Lower the heat, put in the tomatoes and cook, uncovered, for about 30 minutes, or until the tomato liquid is reduced (stir often to prevent catching on the bottom of the pan).

Transfer half of the peperonata to a serving bowl and scatter half the basil leaves over, then pile the rest of the peperonata on top (the warmth of the peppers draws out the musky flavour of the basil and helps it permeate through).

Just before serving, scatter the remaining basil leaves over (not earlier, as they will soften and darken if put on top while the peperonata is still warm).

Crunchy potato sticks

crunchy fingers ROASTED POTATO STICKS WITH WHITE WINE

SERVES 6

2kg large roasting potatoes
2 tablespoons olive oil
125ml (½ cup) dry white wine
½ teaspoon salt
freshly ground black pepper to taste
2 tablespoons butter, cut into small cubes

Cut the potatoes into thickish fingers. Turn onto a clean teatowel or absorbent kitchen paper, pat dry, then transfer to a roasting tin.

Pour the olive oil and wine over the potatoes and sprinkle them with salt and black pepper. Toss the potatoes in the mixture, then dot them with the butter.

Bake in an oven preheated to 200°C for 1¼–1½ hours, turning often. Don't worry if the potatoes catch on the bottom of the tin – the caught bits turn deliciously crunchy by the end of the cooking time. Serve hot.

summery salad BUTTER BEANS AND POTATOES

SERVES 6

1kg new waxy potatoes, scrubbed
salt
2 tablespoons extra virgin olive oil
1 red onion, chopped
1 clove garlic, crushed
1 tablespoon chopped basil
6 vine-ripened tomatoes, quartered
½ teaspoon salt
freshly ground black pepper to taste
700g butter beans, topped and tailed
1 cup water
1 tablespoon chopped marjoram

Steam the potatoes with a little salt, or boil them in salted water until just tender.

Put the extra virgin olive oil in a roomy saucepan over a medium heat and add the onion. Cook for several minutes until it is softening and starting to colour. Add the garlic and basil, then the tomatoes, salt, black pepper and butter beans. Add 1 cup of water and bring to the boil. Lower the heat, cover with a lid and cook for 15 minutes, stirring often. Add the marjoram and potatoes and cook for 5 minutes more, turning carefully, then tip into a serving bowl. Serve at room temperature.

sweet 'n' hot LEAFY GREENS IN THE PAN

SERVES 6

1 tablespoon pine nuts
large bunch of silverbeet (or Swiss chard or spinach), trimmed and roughly chopped
salt
small knob of butter
1 clove garlic, crushed
freshly ground black pepper to taste
freshly grated nutmeg to taste
1 tablespoon freshly grated parmesan (parmigiano reggiano) cheese

Put the pine nuts in a shallow ovenproof dish and toast in a moderate oven (180°C) for about 10 minutes or until they are lightly browned. Cool, then store in an airtight container until required.

Plunge the silverbeet into boiling salted water and cook, uncovered, for about 7 minutes, or until it is barely tender. Drain, refresh with cold water, and drain again. (This can be done ahead.)

Put the butter in a large pan with the garlic and set over a medium heat. Press excess water out of the silverbeet, then add the silverbeet to the pan. Grind on some black pepper and grate a little nutmeg over. Cook until it is very hot, stirring often (but don't let it fry). Pour off any liquid that accumulates. Remove from the heat, stir the parmesan cheese through and tip into a hot dish. Scatter the toasted pine nuts over the top and serve immediately.

ONLY THE GREEN leaves of the silverbeet are usually used in this dish. The white stalks are often cooked separately, turned into a gratin, or crumbed and fried. To avoid wastage, I have used the leaves and stalks in this recipe.

what a caper GLAZED CARROTS

SERVES 6

650g young carrots, peeled
2 tablespoons extra virgin olive oil
2 cloves garlic, crushed
¼ teaspoon salt
freshly ground black pepper to taste
125ml (½ cup) water
2 tablespoons capers, roughly chopped
1 tablespoon finely chopped parsley

Cut the carrots into short lengths. Shape the ends with a vegetable peeler if you prefer a uniform look.

Heat the extra virgin olive oil in a saucepan over a low heat, and add the garlic. Cook gently until the garlic turns a pale biscuit colour, then add the carrots. Stir to coat them in the garlic oil, then sprinkle with salt and black pepper and add ¼ cup of water.

Cover and cook for 10 minutes. Swirl the pan and add another ¼ cup of water, cover with a lid, and cook for 5–10 minutes more or until the carrots are just tender.

Remove the lid and continue cooking for another 5 minutes or until the water has evaporated. You should be left with beautifully glazed carrots (be careful not to let them fry).

The carrots may be prepared ahead up to this point. Cool quickly and set aside.

Five minutes before serving time, add the capers and parsley to the carrots and heat through carefully.

imbued with rosemary WHITE BEANS STEWED WITH ROSEMARY AND GARLIC

SERVES 6

400g (2 cups) dried white beans
75ml extra virgin olive oil
2 tablespoons finely chopped rosemary
3 large cloves garlic, peeled
100g bacon, rind removed, finely chopped
¾ teaspoon salt
freshly ground black pepper to taste

Soak the beans for several hours in cold water to cover. Drain, then put them in a heavy-based casserole. Pour the extra virgin olive oil over and mix in the rosemary, garlic and bacon. Add 3½ cups of water and bring to the boil over a high heat. Remove any scum, then cover with a lid. Transfer to an oven preheated to 170°C.

Cook for 1½ hours, stirring occasionally, until the beans are tender. The beans will still be swimming in liquid, but most of this will be absorbed as they sit. Sprinkle with the salt and grind on some black pepper. Carefully stir through, then cover with a lid and leave to cool before serving.

The beans should retain their shape and be covered in a creamy coating. Delicious! Refrigerate when cool and consume within three days (they are good warmed or at room temperature).

ROSEMARY, garlic and olive oil give these beans a distinctive aroma and taste. Don't be alarmed by the 'soupy' look – it's how it should be. Try them with good sausages, or a rustic chicken or pork dish.

addictive POTATOES WITH ROSEMARY

SERVES 4–6

1kg roasting potatoes, peeled and cubed
125ml (½ cup) olive oil
6 large cloves garlic, very finely chopped
1 tablespoon finely chopped rosemary
½ teaspoon salt
freshly ground black pepper to taste
50ml white wine vinegar

Turn the potato cubes onto a clean teatowel or absorbent kitchen paper and pat dry.

Put the olive oil in a large heavy-based frying pan and heat over a medium-high heat. Add the potato cubes, toss in the oil and cook for 2–3 minutes. Cover with a lid (leaving it slightly ajar for steam to escape), turn to low and cook very gently for 1 hour, turning potato cubes often until they are crisp. Watch the heat; if it is too high, the potatoes will form a hard, glazed surface on the outside, yet remain uncooked on the inside.

Remove the lid, increase the heat to medium and add the garlic and rosemary. Sprinkle with the salt and grind on some black pepper. Cook for 3–4 minutes or until the garlic takes on a little colour. Pour the white wine vinegar over the potatoes and toss well. Cook for 2–3 minutes more, then tip all the contents of the pan into a hot serving dish and serve immediately.

pungent sprinkle CARROTS WITH GREMOLADA

SERVES 4

GREMOLADA
1 large clove garlic, peeled
2 tablespoons finely chopped parsley
grated zest of 1 lemon

700g carrots, peeled and cut into chunks on the diagonal (or any shape you like)
salt
butter

Chop the garlic clove coarsely with a knife, then chop finely along with the parsley and lemon zest. Transfer to a small dish, cover and set aside.

Put the carrots in the top of a steamer set over a saucepan of boiling water. Sprinkle lightly with salt, cover with a lid and steam until they are crisp-tender (or cook them in a microwave or by conventional boiling). Transfer them to a heated serving dish, dot with a little butter and sprinkle with the gremolada. Serve immediately.

Potatoes with rosemary

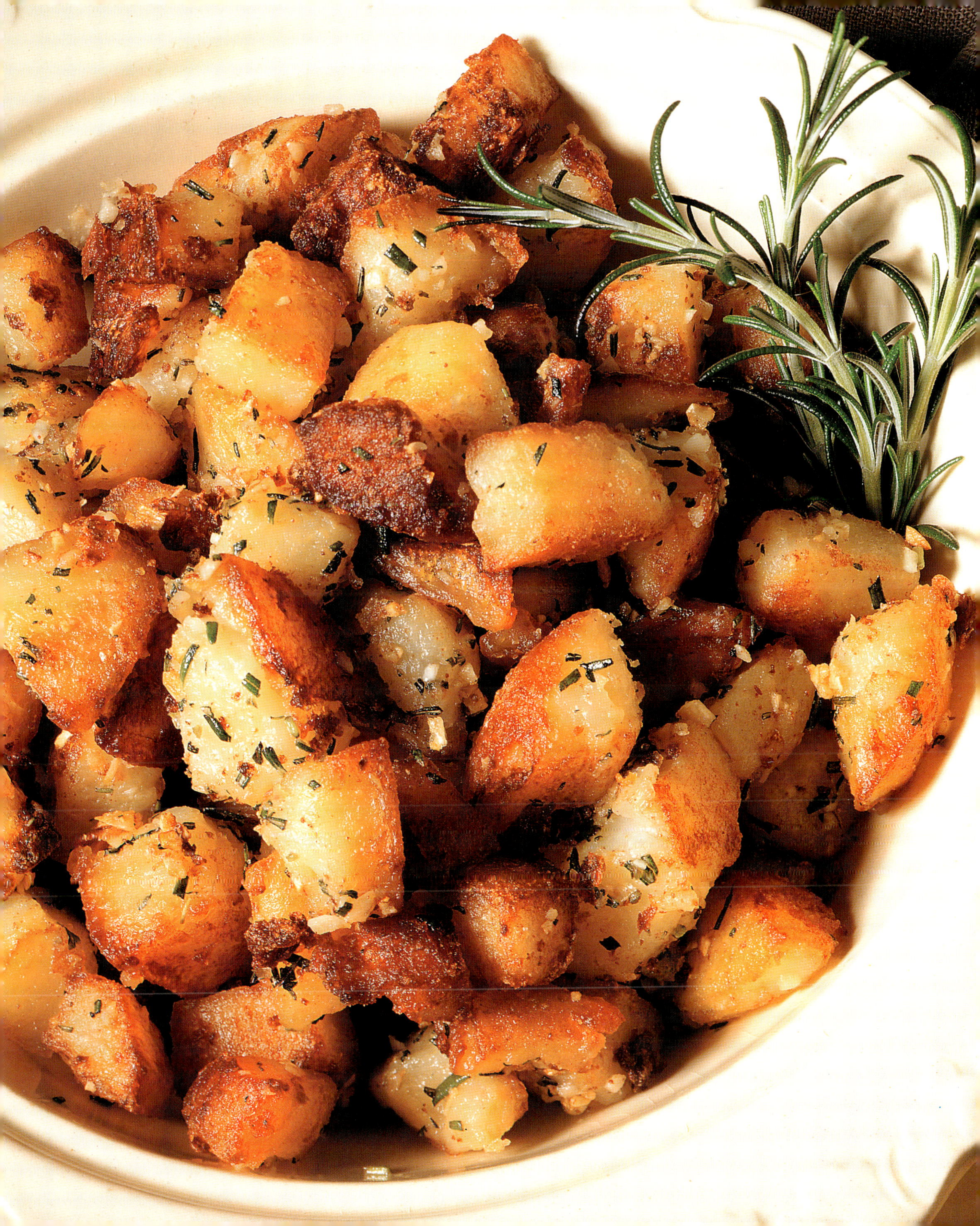

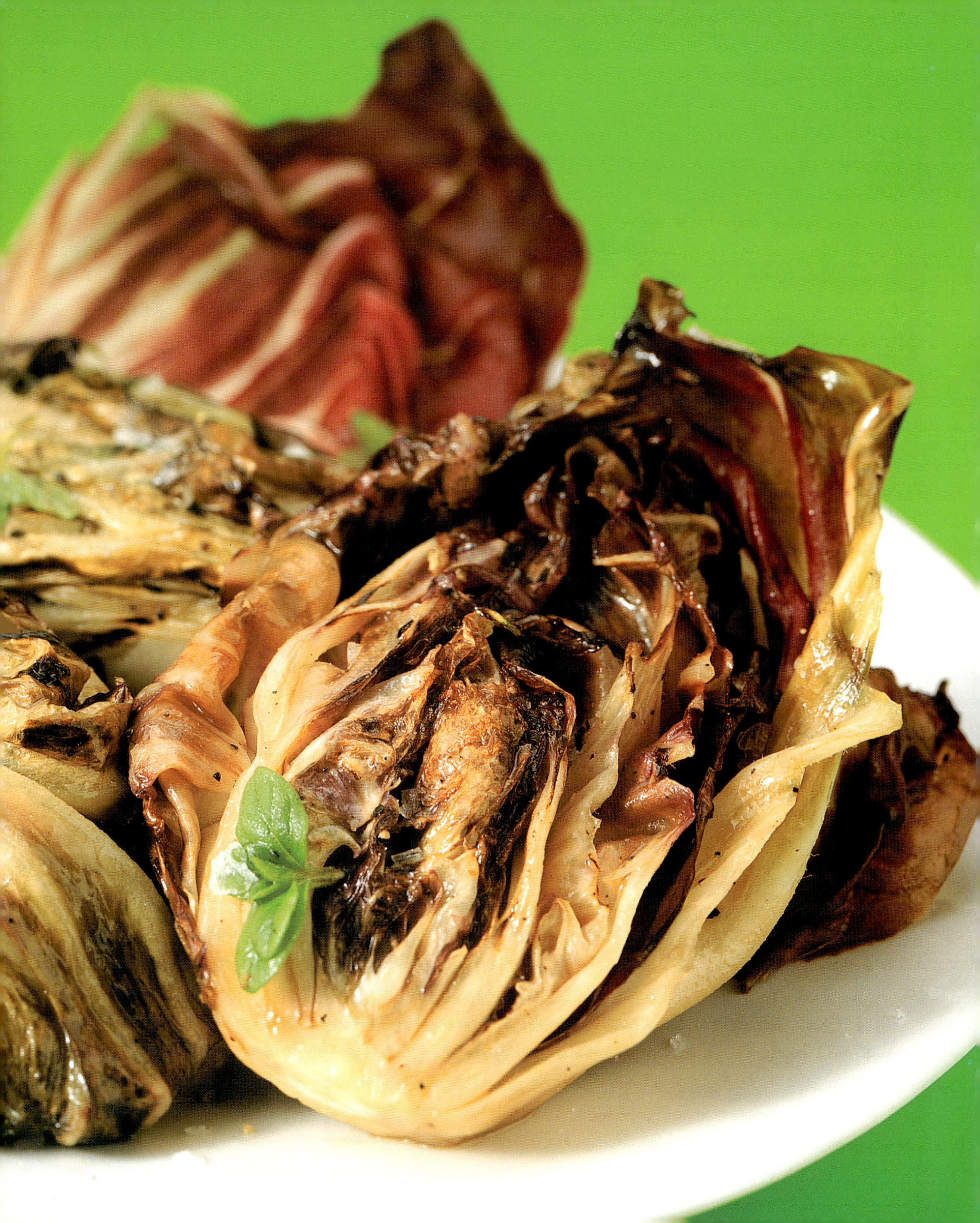

sweet and sour RED LEAVES ON THE GRILL

SERVES 4–6

¼ cup pine nuts
4 balls radicchio (or chicory), trimmed and outer bitter leaves removed
2 tablespoons extra virgin olive oil
1 tablespoon fresh marjoram leaves
¼ teaspoon salt
freshly ground black pepper to taste
1 tablespoon balsamic vinegar

Toast the pine nuts in a small dry pan, or fry them in a little hot oil.

Cut the balls of radicchio in half or into quarters if large. Mix the extra virgin olive oil in a large bowl with the marjoram, salt and black pepper and put in the radicchio. Toss well. Cook gently, on a barbecue plate that has just been heated, until the radicchio is lightly browned – watch the heat doesn't get too fierce or the radicchio will burn and the bitter flavour, which is pleasant in a small dose, will become too much. Turn onto a plate and drizzle with balsamic vinegar and a little extra oil. Season with extra salt and black pepper, toss well, scatter the pine nuts over and serve hot or hottish.

BARBECUING RADICCHIO is not as silly as it sounds, providing you strip back the bitter, strong-tasting outer leaves and barbecue it over a gentle heat. The radicchio will retain some of its bitterness, but this is part of its character. The other ingredients add tiers of complexity to the char-grilled radicchio. Use the best extra virgin olive oil and balsamic vinegar you can afford.

I think radicchio cooked like this tastes like artichokes.

steaming spices 'SUFFOCATED' CAULIFLOWER

SERVES 6

¼ cup extra virgin olive oil
2 large cloves garlic, peeled and lightly crushed
1 medium cauliflower, cut into florets, washed and shaken dry
¼ teaspoon salt
freshly ground black pepper to taste
125ml (½ cup) dry white wine
2 tablespoons pine nuts
1½ tablespoons raisins
3 small dried 'bird's eye' chillies, crushed (optional)
1 tablespoon finely chopped parsley

Heat the extra virgin olive oil in a large frying pan over a low heat. Add the garlic cloves and fry gently until they are golden brown; remove and discard.

Add the cauliflower florets, toss them quickly in the oil, cover the pan with a lid and cook for 5 minutes, shaking the pan occasionally. Lift off the lid, sprinkle with the salt and grind on some black pepper. Pour the wine in and stir the pine nuts and raisins through. Put the lid back on, bring to the boil, then lower the heat and simmer gently for 10–15 minutes, or until it is done to your liking.

Remove the lid and allow the liquid to evaporate until it is syrupy. Stir the crushed chillies and parsley through. Transfer to a serving bowl and allow it to cool. Toss well before serving.

Red leaves on the grill

fresh crunch FENNEL, SWEET TOMATO AND OLIVE SALAD

SERVES 6–8

2 fennel bulbs (if the fennel is slim, increase the quantity to 4)
1½ cups sweet cherry tomatoes, halved
50g (approximately 10) black olives
1 teaspoon lemon juice
½ teaspoon salt
freshly ground black pepper to taste
2 tablespoons coarsely chopped parsley
3 tablespoons extra virgin olive oil

Prepare the fennel by trimming away the root end, and removing stems and bruised parts. Slice into thinnish strips and put in a bowl with the cherry tomatoes and olives.

Whisk the lemon juice, salt, black pepper and parsley together in a small bowl, then blend in the extra virgin olive oil. Pour over the salad, toss well and serve.

summer fragrance CHICK PEAS AND TOMATO

SERVES 6

150g (¾ cup) dried chick peas (or 2 cups canned, drained chick peas)
90ml extra virgin olive oil
4 cloves garlic, peeled and flattened with a mallet
1 tablespoon finely chopped rosemary leaves
200ml (½ can) canned Italian tomatoes, mashed
salt
freshly ground black pepper to taste

If using dried chick peas, soak them for several hours in cold water to cover. Drain and tip into a saucepan. Cover generously with cold water and bring to the boil. Boil for 10 minutes, then drain, rinse and return to the clean saucepan. Cover with cold water again, bring back to the boil, then lower the heat and cook gently until the chick peas are tender (about 1 hour); top up with water from time to time if necessary. When the chick peas are cooked, drain them and flick off as many of the loose skins as possible.

Heat the extra virgin olive oil in a saucepan over a medium heat and drop in the flattened garlic cloves. Cook gently until they are a pale brown colour, then lift them out with a slotted spoon and discard. Add the rosemary, then the tomatoes, a few pinches of salt and plenty of black pepper. Cook, uncovered, over a medium heat, for 20–25 minutes or until the tomato separates from the oil. Add the chick peas and cook for 5 minutes more, turning over in the sauce. Transfer to a serving bowl and serve at room temperature.

Fennel, sweet tomato and olive salad

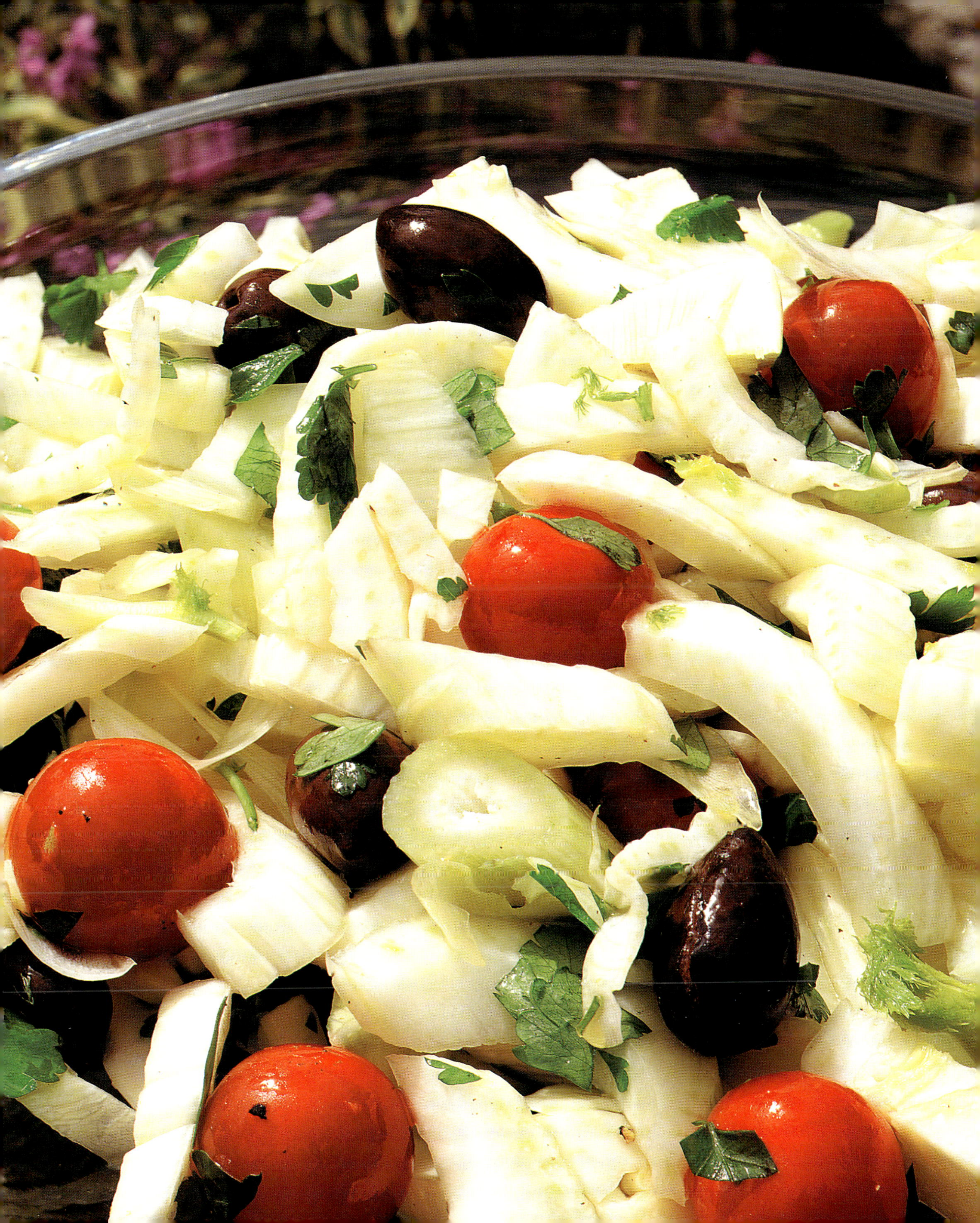

scented skewers BABY POTATOES ON ROSEMARY STALKS

SERVES 4–6

1kg freshly dug small potatoes, scrubbed
3 small dried 'bird's eye' chillies, crushed
4 tablespoons extra virgin olive oil
½ teaspoon salt
12 long, firm stalks of rosemary

Cook the potatoes until they are nearly tender (preferably steam them; alternatively, cook them gently in water). When the potatoes are cool, cut them in half. Put the chillies, extra virgin olive oil and salt in a shallow rectangular dish. Thread the potato chunks onto the rosemary stalks. If this is difficult to do, carefully make holes with a fine skewer first. Gently brush the potatoes with the flavoured oil. Cook them on a hot barbecue plate until they are golden, anointing them with the oil marinade during the cooking. Serve hot.

SKEWERING baby potatoes on rosemary stalks gives them a wonderfully resinous rosemary fragrance. Finishing them over the barbecue grill imparts a whiff of smokiness. The potatoes must be waxy ones (sometimes sold as salad potatoes) to ensure they will hold together on the skewers (starchy potatoes will fall off). Choose firm, woody stalks of rosemary. If you're buying the herb, it's a good idea to dry the stalks for a day or two before using them.

baked and bubbling STUFFED BABY ZUCCHINI

SERVES 3 AS A MAIN COURSE OR 6 AS A STARTER

1 small onion, finely chopped
50g butter
1 clove garlic, crushed
6 firm zucchini (courgettes)
¼ teaspoon salt
freshly ground black pepper to taste
1 tablespoon finely chopped parsley
1 egg
½ cup fresh breadcrumbs
100g (1 cup) freshly grated parmesan (parmigiano reggiano) cheese
¾ cup Quick Tomato Sauce (see page 30)

Put the onion in a small saucepan with the butter, cover and cook gently until it is soft. Remove the lid, add the garlic and cook, uncovered, until the onion and garlic are a light golden brown. Transfer to a mixing bowl.

Slice the zucchini lengthways. Using a teaspoon, carefully gouge out the flesh without piercing the skin. Chop the flesh finely and add to the cooked onion with the salt, black pepper, parsley, egg, breadcrumbs and three-quarters of the parmesan cheese. Mix well and spoon into the zucchini shells.

Spread the tomato sauce over the base of a baking dish and place the filled zucchini halves in it. Sprinkle with the remaining parmesan cheese and bake in an oven preheated to 180°C for about 20 minutes or until the cheese is golden brown and the zucchini are done to your liking.

Baby potatoes on rosemary stalks

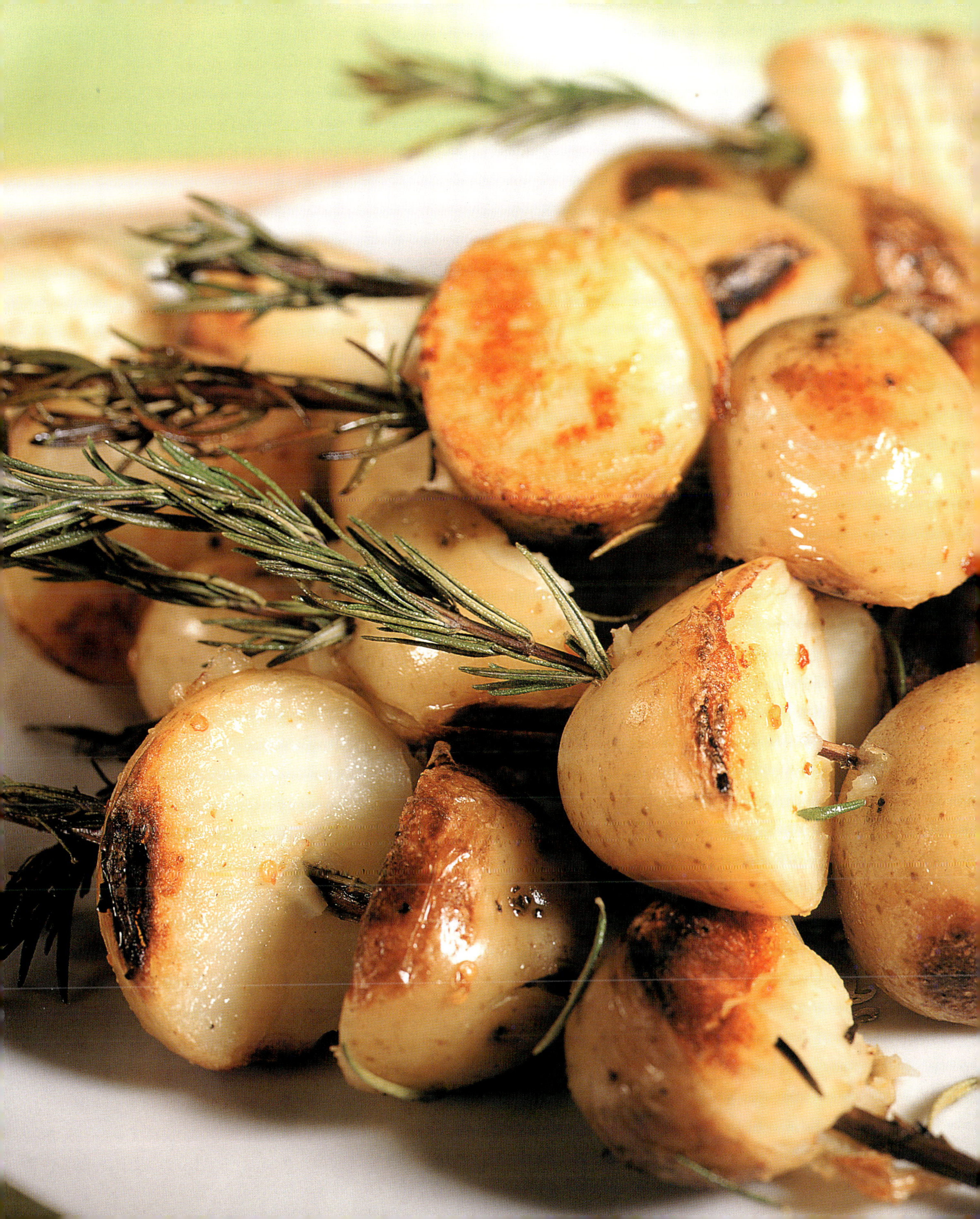

squeeze of lemon ROASTED FENNEL

SERVES 4

3–4 medium fennel bulbs
extra virgin olive oil
freshly ground black pepper to taste
lemon segments

Trim the fennel bulbs then cut them into quarters through the root. Rub them generously with extra virgin olive oil, put them in a shallow-sided ovenproof dish and grind on some black pepper. Cook the fennel in an oven preheated to 200°C for 20–30 minutes, or until it is tender and lightly browned, turning once. Serve with grilled or barbecued fish, rabbit or chicken, or use in a risotto. Accompany with segments of lemon to squeeze over.

piselli perfection BABY PEAS WITH SAUTÉED PROSCIUTTO

SERVES 4

2 tablespoons olive oil
1 clove garlic, finely chopped
70g prosciutto or ham, diced
freshly ground black pepper to taste
¼ teaspoon salt
1kg fresh peas, podded, or use 300g frozen baby peas
2 tablespoons finely chopped parsley

Put the olive oil and garlic in a small saucepan and set over a medium heat. Cook until the garlic is a light nut-brown colour. Add the ham or prosciutto and cook briefly, stirring. Grind on some black pepper, add the salt and peas and pour in ¼ cup of water. Cover with a lid and cook for about 15 minutes. (If using frozen peas, cook them with 3 tablespoons of water for about 5 minutes.)

Check the seasoning, stir in the parsley, and serve.

smoke-imbued BARBECUED EGGPLANT WITH BALSAMIC DRESSING

SERVES 4

1 large eggplant (aubergine)
salt (optional, see note below)
extra virgin olive oil

BALSAMIC DRESSING
1 tablespoon balsamic vinegar
¼ teaspoon salt
freshly ground black pepper to taste
1 large clove garlic, crushed
12 fresh large basil leaves, roughly chopped
2 tablespoons extra virgin olive oil

Cut the eggplant into thickish slices and pat dry with absorbent kitchen paper. Brush the slices on both sides with the extra virgin olive oil. Cook on a hot barbecue plate, turning often, until they turn a deep golden brown. Finish cooking over the barbecue grill to impart a smoky flavour.

Blend the balsamic vinegar, salt, black pepper, garlic and basil leaves in a bowl. Whisk in the olive oil and spoon the dressing over the eggplant slices while they are still warm. Serve hottish or at room temperature.

TO SALT OR NOT TO SALT

Most eggplant recipes recommend that you sprinkle the sliced or cut eggplant with salt before cooking. The salt draws out any bitter juices. The step is well worthwhile if the eggplants are bitter, but unnecessary if they're not. How do you tell whether an eggplant is bitter or not? It is not easy. In my experience, immature eggplants, which are heavy for their size, and those tinged with a fair amount of green underneath the skin (visible when you slice or cut them), will be bitter, and are best salted as a precaution. If you've ever eaten a bitter eggplant, you will know it is not worth taking the risk.

Roasted fennel

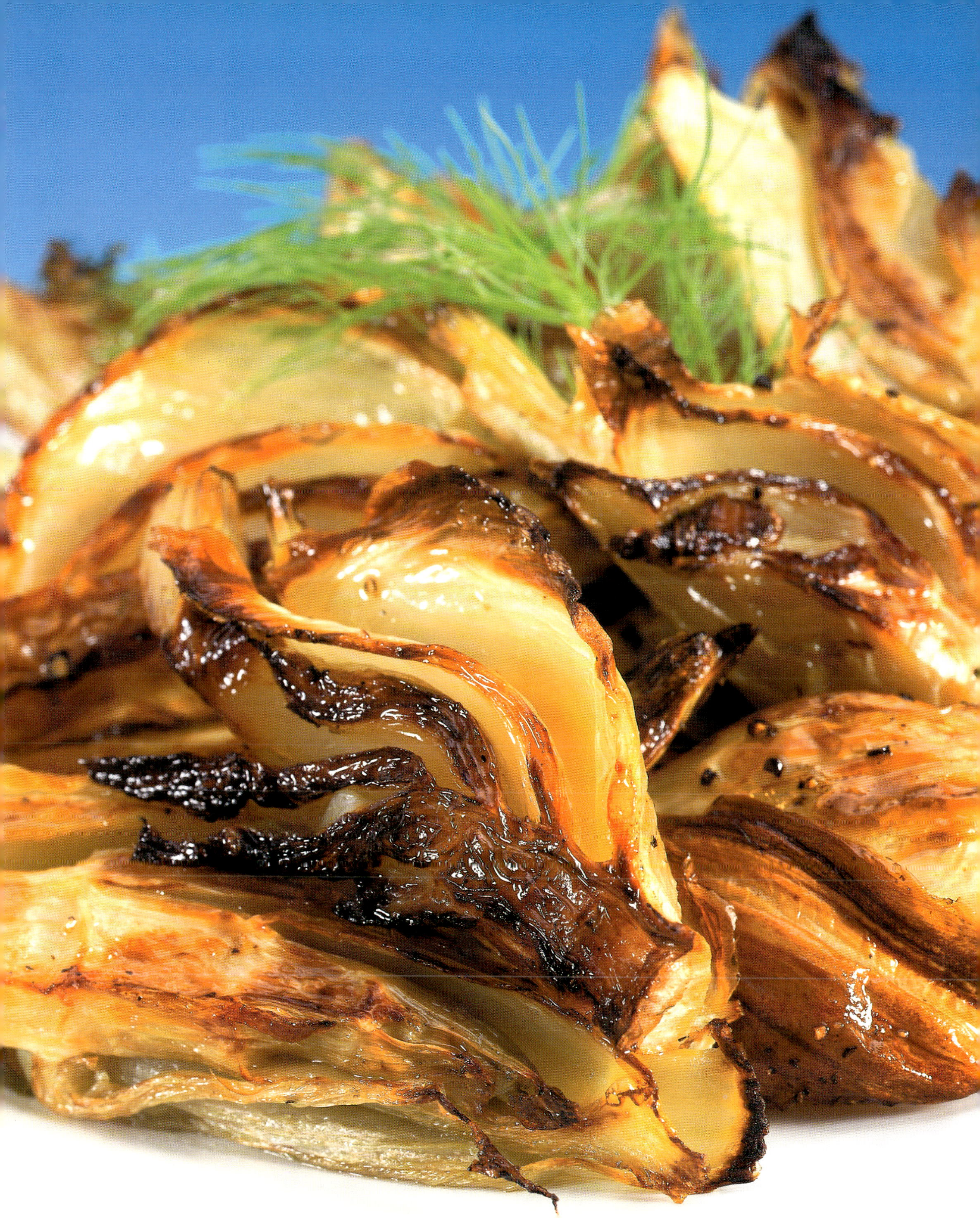

tangy bite SALAD OF RED LEAVES WITH CAPER DRESSING

SERVES 4–6

1 tablespoon white wine vinegar
1 tablespoon capers, drained
1 clove garlic, crushed
1 tablespoon coarsely chopped parsley
125ml (½ cup) extra virgin olive oil
50g (½ cup) freshly grated parmesan (parmigiano reggiano) cheese
3–6 radicchio or chicory heads (use 3 large or 6 small ones)

Blend the white wine vinegar, capers, garlic and parsley together in a food processor fitted with the chopping blade. While the machine is running, dribble in the extra virgin olive oil, then stop the machine, scatter the parmesan cheese over and process briefly until it is blended. (The dressing can be prepared several hours ahead to this point; store it covered at room temperature.) Alternatively, make it by hand – blend all the ingredients, except the olive oil, in a bowl with a fork. Slowly mix in the oil.

Wash and dry the radicchio, then tear it into bite-sized pieces and place in a salad bowl. Pour the dressing over, toss very well, then serve. Although the salad is at its best when first dressed, leftovers are delicious, too.

CAPERS, GARLIC AND PARMESAN cheese make a gutsy dressing that stands up well against the bitterness of radicchio or chicory. Be warned; it's very moreish!

mustard punch ZUCCHINI, BASIL AND BLACK OLIVE SALAD

SERVES 6

12 small firm zucchini (courgettes)
200g (1 cup) small black olives
2 tablespoons white wine vinegar
1 tablespoon finely chopped basil
½ teaspoon salt
freshly ground black pepper to taste
1 clove garlic, crushed
1 teaspoon Dijon mustard
4 tablespoons extra virgin olive oil

Trim the zucchini and slice into chunks on the diagonal. Put them in a bowl with the olives.

Make the dressing by blending together the white wine vinegar, basil, salt, black pepper, garlic and mustard, then whisk in the extra virgin olive oil. Pour over the salad and stir well. Marinate for 1–24 hours, depending on how crunchy you like the zucchini. Toss again before serving.

Salad of red leaves with caper dressing

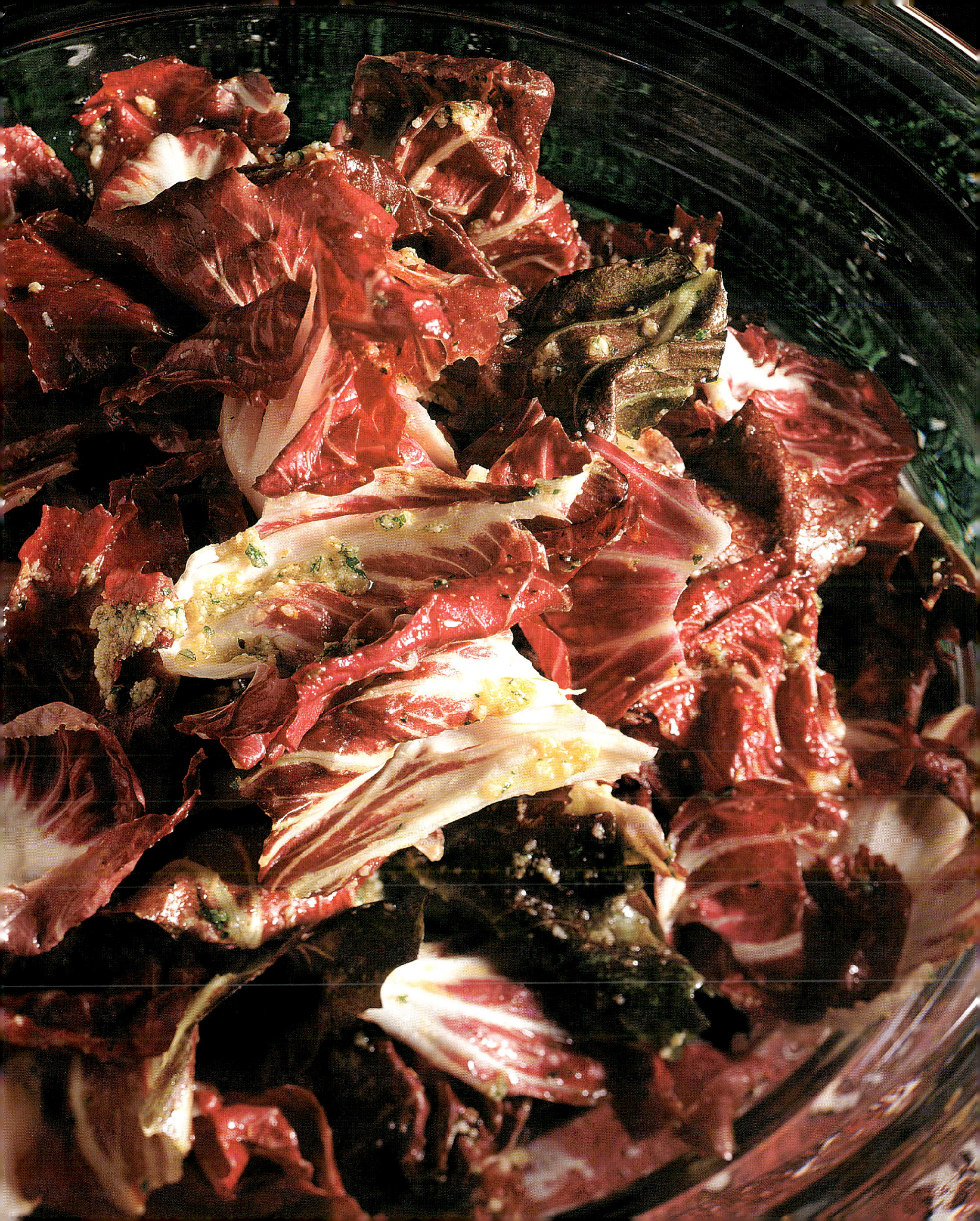

seriously good

LEMON RICOTTA FLAN	120
STRAWBERRIES WITH RICOTTA CREAM	120
PEACHES STUFFED WITH AMARETTI	122
MASCARPONE FRUIT NESTS	122
FRUITY CRÊPES WITH CHOCOLATE SAUCE	125
GRILLED PANETTONE WITH PEACHES OR NECTARINES	126
GLAZED BERRIES	127
LATE SUMMER FRUIT SALAD	127
LATTICE-TOPPED RICE PUDDINGS	128
MACEDONIA	128
HONEYMOON CAKE	130
CRUMBLY ALMOND CAKE	132
BAKED PEACHES WITH RUM	132
PINOLATA	135
CURD CAKE WITH GLAZED BERRIES	137
HAZELNUT AND AMARETTI CUPOLA	138

perfect apricots with a rosy blush

crumbling flakes of buttery pastry

pillows of vanilla-scented whipped cream

seductive fragrances to tease your senses

go on, lick your fingers!

sweets

tangy sweet LEMON RICOTTA FLAN

SERVES 8

1 quantity rich shortcrust pastry (see page 135)
300g ricotta cheese
150g (scant ¾ cup) castor sugar
grated zest of 2 lemons
3 eggs, at room temperature
¼ cup strained lemon juice
icing sugar for dusting

Make the pastry and line a 23cm flan ring with it. (There will be some left over – see the note on Rich Shortcrust Pastry on page 135.) Chill for 30 minutes, then bake 'blind' for 10 minutes (see page 136).

The filling is quickly made in a food processor. Alternatively, use a hand-held electric beater. Process the ricotta cheese to break it up, then, with the machine running, pour in the castor sugar. Process until it is well blended, then add the lemon zest. With the machine running, drop in the eggs one at a time, and process until they are amalgamated, scraping the sides of the bowl if necessary. Blend in the lemon juice.

Pour the mixture into the pastry case, then transfer the flan to an oven preheated to 200°C. Bake for 15 minutes, then lower the heat to 170°C and bake for 15–20 minutes more or until the custard is just set and lightly golden.

Slide the flan onto a cake rack to cool. Before serving, sift icing sugar over the top. This tart is best eaten the day it is made.

THIS TANGY-SWEET flan is a favourite with those who don't have an excessively sweet tooth. It seems to have just the right balance of creaminess, sweetness and lemony tang.

sweet fruit STRAWBERRIES WITH RICOTTA CREAM

SERVES 4

SUGARED STRAWBERRIES
2 punnets strawberries (approximately 4 cups), hulled and sliced
juice of 1 lemon
castor sugar

RICOTTA CREAM
250g ricotta cheese
2 eggs, separated
50g (scant ¼ cup) castor sugar
finely grated zest of 1 lemon
50g top quality tangy glacé fruits (e.g. apricots or tangerines), finely chopped
1 tablespoon kirsch (optional)
150ml cream
2–3 amaretti biscuits (optional)

Mix the strawberries in a bowl with the lemon juice and castor sugar to taste. Cover and refrigerate for 2–3 hours.

Sieve or process the ricotta cheese, then blend in the egg yolks, castor sugar and lemon zest, and beat or process until the mixture is smooth. Blend in the chopped glacé fruits (and the kirsch if using).

Whip the cream until it is thick but still softish, and fold it into the ricotta mixture. Next, whip the egg whites to a firm snow and fold into the mixture. The ricotta cream can be used immediately or prepared 2–3 hours before required; cover and keep refrigerated.

When ready to assemble the dessert, spoon the strawberries into 4 chilled glasses and top with the ricotta cream. Crumble the amaretti biscuits over the top and serve immediately.

For a change, omit the kirsch and macerate the strawberries in Amaretto liqueur instead of lemon juice.

Lemon ricotta flan

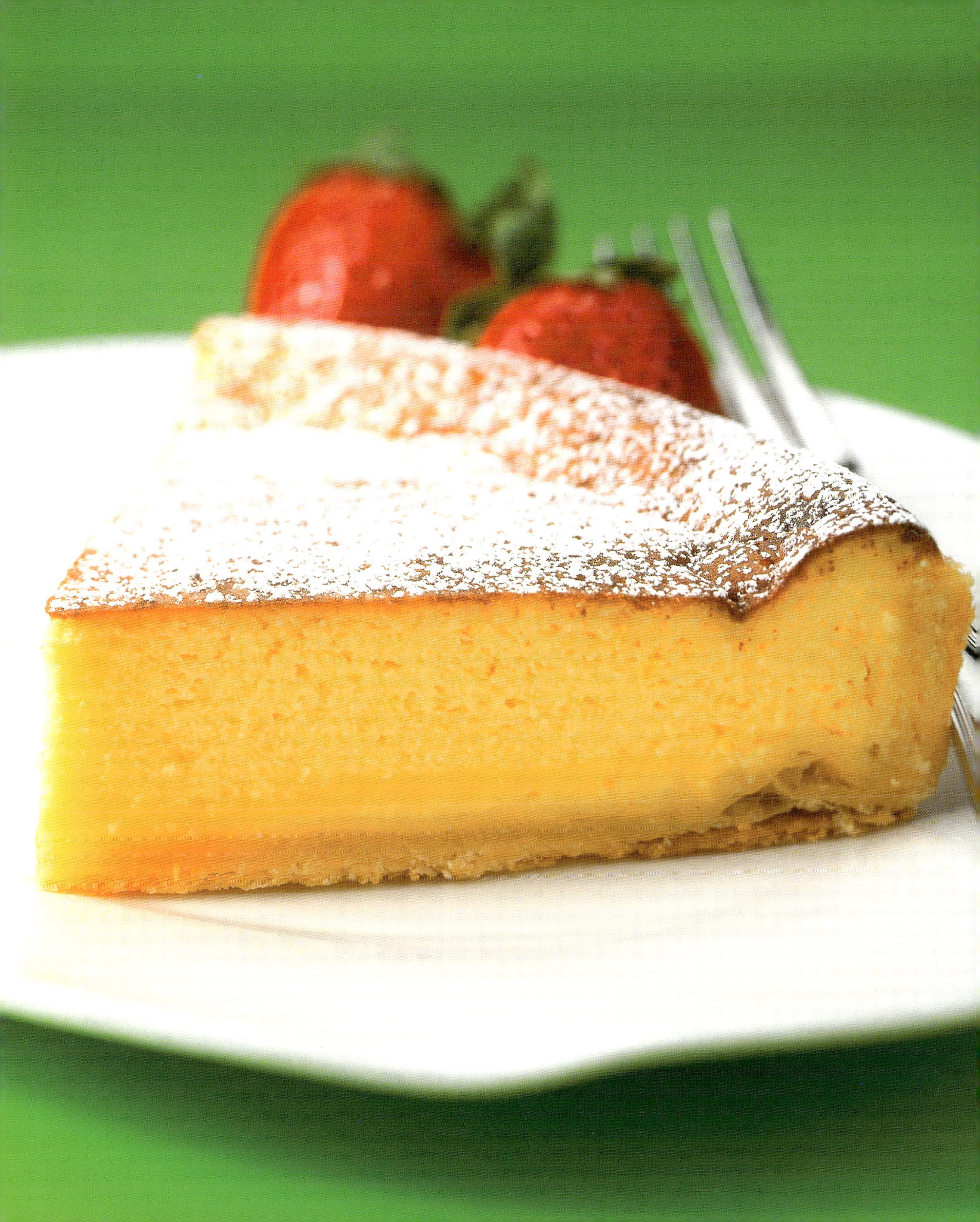

crumbling cookies PEACHES STUFFED WITH AMARETTI

SERVES 6

¾ cup coarsely crushed amaretti biscuits
¼ cup castor sugar
4 tablespoons cocoa powder
100ml fruity, dry white wine
6 medium or 12 smallish peaches or nectarines, ripe but firm
butter

MASCARPONE CREAM
300g mascarpone cream
125ml (½ cup) cream
castor sugar to taste

Put the crushed amaretti biscuits in a bowl with the castor sugar. Sieve the cocoa powder over, then add 2 tablespoons of the wine and mix.

Cut the peaches in half through their natural indentations, twist, then pull apart and extract the stones. Put the peaches in a shallow baking dish, cut side up. Put a teaspoonful of the amaretti mixture in the cavity of each peach, then top with a small pat of butter. Pour the remaining wine over the top. Bake in an oven preheated to 180°C for 30 minutes or until the fruit is tender.

Meanwhile, gently mix together the mascarpone cream ingredients in a bowl, then mound in soft peaks on individual plates. Arrange the baked peaches on the plates and pour any juices over the cream. Serve immediately. These are best eaten the day they are made.

IF PEACH STONES are difficult to extract, cut them out with a serrated grapefruit knife. Cut off any flesh adhering to the stones, chop finely and add to the amaretti mixture in the bowl.

splash of cointreau MASCARPONE FRUIT NESTS

SERVES 4

1½ tablespoons honey
1½ tablespoons Cointreau
4 passionfruit
250g mascarpone cream
1 tablespoon castor sugar
selection of fresh fruit, peeled, pipped and sliced or segmented as appropriate

Mix the honey, Cointreau and passionfruit pulp together in a small bowl.

Beat the mascarpone cream and castor sugar together until the mixture is smooth. Place a small mound of mascarpone onto each plate, then make a hollow in the centre. Pour the passion fruit syrup into the hollows, then surround the mascarpone with segments and slices of fresh fruit. Serve immediately. Accompany with sweet crisp biscuits.

FANS OF RICH cream and fruit desserts will be in raptures over this combination. Choose from juicy pears, kiwifruit, bananas, mandarins and persimmons.

Peaches stuffed with amaretti

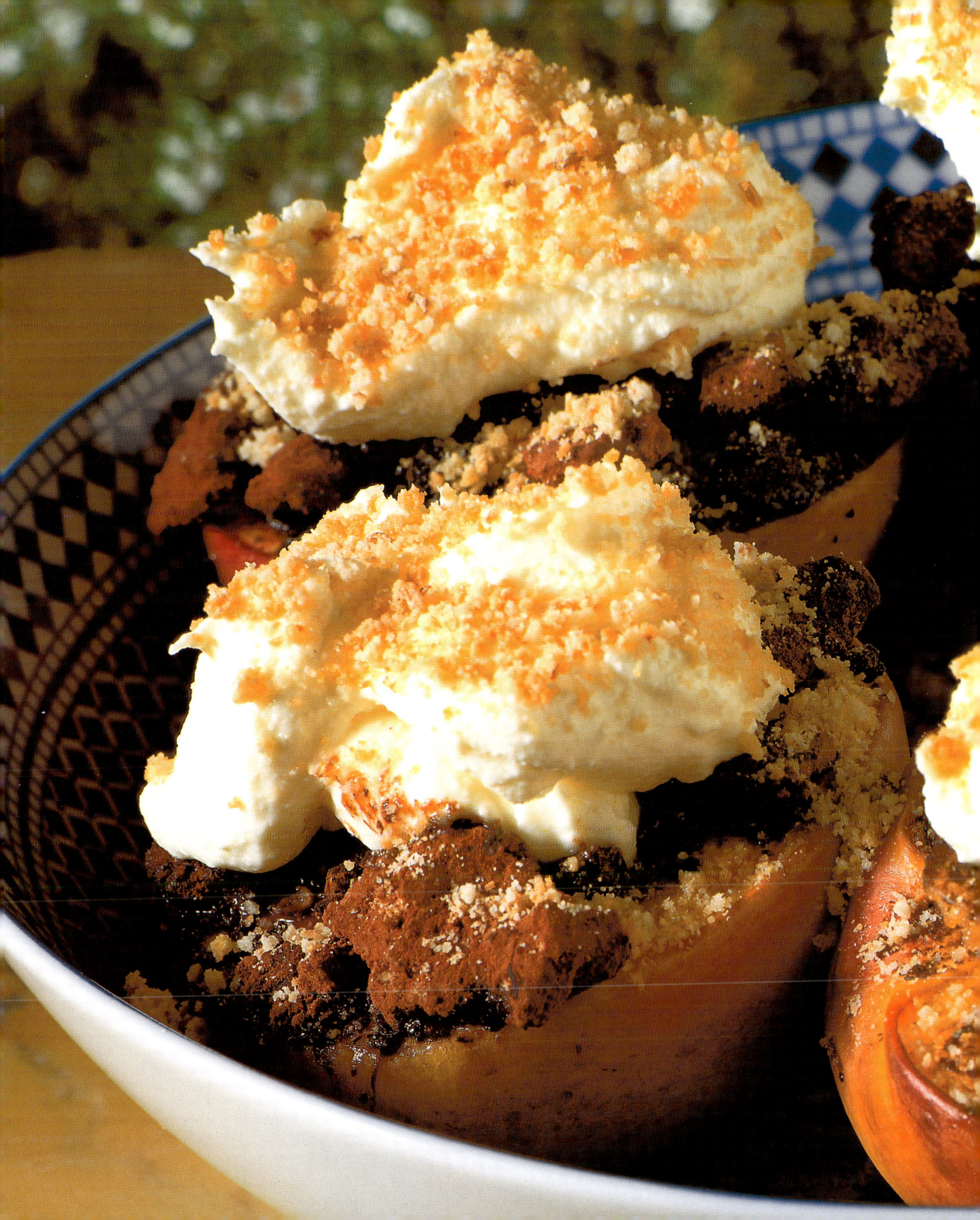

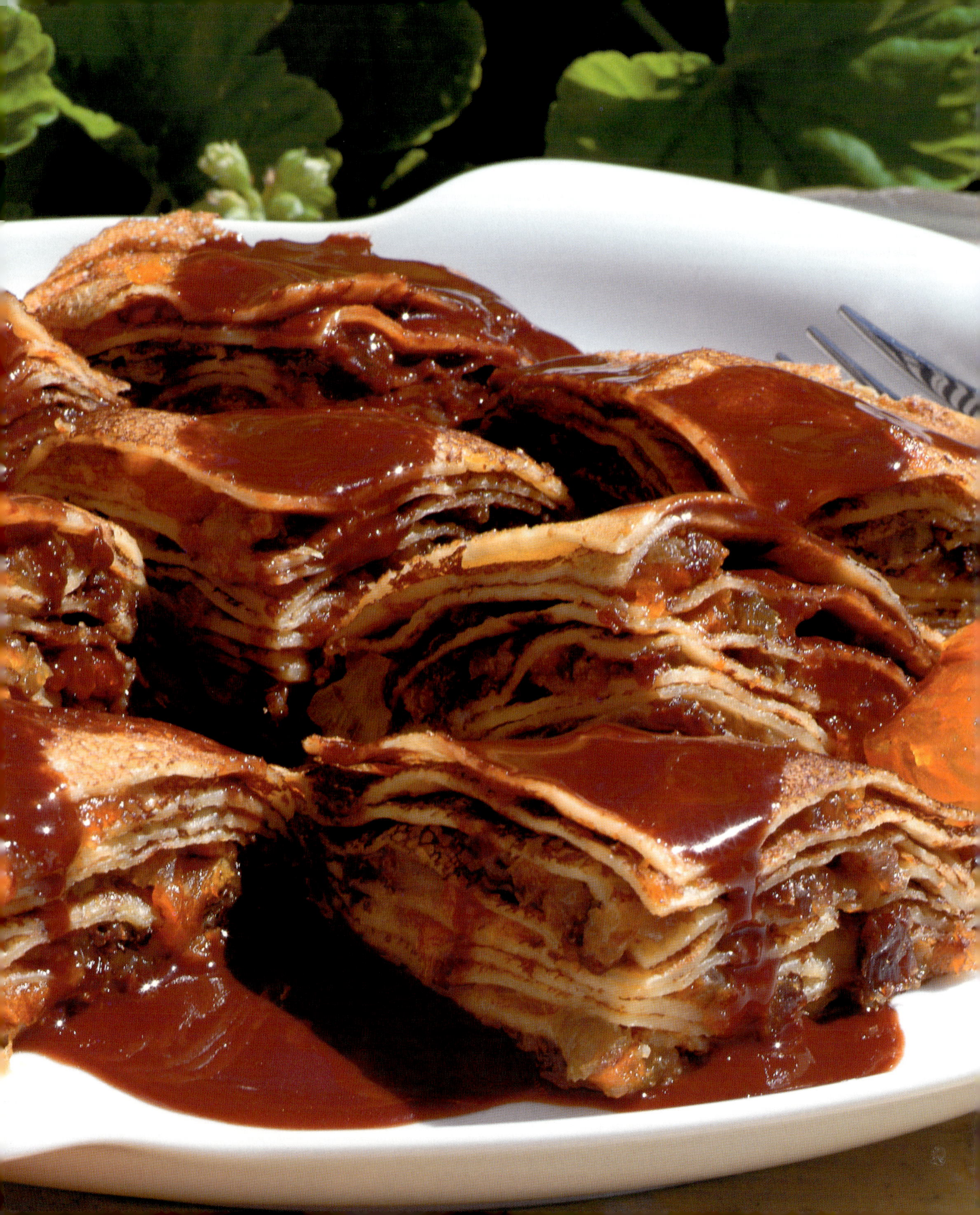

chocolate tutti frutti FRUITY CRÊPES WITH CHOCOLATE SAUCE

SERVES 4

50g (approximately 6) dried apricots, finely sliced
½ cup sultanas
½ cup mixed peel or glacé fruits, chopped
⅓ cup raisins
2 tablespoons dark rum
1 tablespoon lemon juice
1 tablespoon melted butter, plus a little extra
16 crêpes (see opposite)
Chocolate Sauce (see opposite)
300ml cream, lightly whipped, for serving

Put the apricots, sultanas, mixed peel and raisins in a bowl with the rum and lemon juice and leave to macerate for 2 hours. Transfer to the bowl of a food processor (or liquidiser), add the tablespoon of butter and process the mixture briefly until it is finely chopped (don't turn it into a paste).

Lightly butter a shallow, rectangular ovenproof dish and place 2 crêpes side-by-side on the bottom of the dish. Form 2 crêpe stacks, spooning a little of the fruit mixture on top of each crêpe. Finish both crêpe stacks with a plain crêpe. Cover and refrigerate until they are required.

When ready to finish off the crêpes, cover the dish with aluminium foil and put in an oven preheated to 180°C for 15 minutes to heat through.

Transfer the crêpes to a board and cut each stack into quarters. Arrange the crêpe triangles on a heated serving plate and pour the warmed chocolate sauce over the top. Serve the whipped cream separately.

CHOCOLATE SAUCE

60g chocolate chips or chopped chocolate
2 tablespoons castor sugar
1 teaspoon cocoa powder
1 teaspoon vanilla essence
300ml water
1 teaspoon arrowroot mixed with 1 tablespoon water

Put the chocolate chips, castor sugar, cocoa powder, vanilla essence and water in a small saucepan and heat gently, stirring often, until the chocolate melts. Simmer gently for 20 minutes, then add the dissolved arrowroot. Bring to a gentle boil, stirring, and simmer for 1 minute more. Remove from the heat and cool. Refrigerate when cool and rewarm when required.

CRÊPE BATTER

115g plain flour
pinch of salt
1 whole egg
1 egg yolk
approximately 325ml milk
1 tablespoon melted butter

Sift the flour and salt into a deep mixing bowl and make a well in the centre. Drop in the egg and the egg yolk. Use a wooden spoon to blend the eggs together, gradually drawing in the flour as you go, then start adding the milk, keeping the mixture to the consistency of thick cream. Continue stirring until all the flour is drawn in (you will have used about half the milk by this time). Beat well together, then add the melted butter and remaining milk.

Cover the batter and leave to one side for 30 minutes (this softens the starch grains in the flour and makes the crêpes lighter). Before making the batter into crêpes, check the consistency – it should be like a thin cream. If necessary, thin with a little milk.

Fruity crêpes with chocolate sauce

Choose a small heavy-based pan, 12–18cm in diameter, preferably with sloping sides to make it easier to turn the crêpes over. Lightly grease the pan with oil or butter and heat it over a medium-high heat until it just starts to give off a haze. Pour in a spoonful of batter and quickly swirl it around the pan, coating the entire base, then pour any excess batter back into the bowl. It should take about 1 minute to cook the first side. Loosen with a palette knife, then either flip or turn over and cook the second side. Put the crêpes on a cooling rack as they are made. If necessary, oil or butter the pan occasionally (if bad sticking occurs, wipe the pan with a piece of absorbent kitchen paper dipped in oil and salt, wipe clean and start again).

When all the crêpes are made, wrap them in plastic food wrap and refrigerate them until they are required. Otherwise, layer them, separating the crêpes with a sheet of waxed paper between them (this makes it easy to peel off the crêpes when required), wrap and freeze. To thaw, separate the number of crêpes you want, and leave them at room temperature for 5–10 minutes. Use as directed.

EASY TO MAKE, this batter produces light, crisp crêpes.

MAKING CRÊPE BATTER IN A FOOD PROCESSOR
Use the same quantities as for making by hand. Put the egg, egg yolk, melted butter and milk into the processor bowl fitted with the chopping blade. Whizz for a few seconds, stop the machine, sprinkle the flour and salt over and whizz again for 30 seconds. Pour into a bowl and leave to rest for 30 minutes.

caramelised crusts GRILLED PANETTONE WITH PEACHES OR NECTARINES

SERVES 6

1 panettone (approximately 500–600g)
small bottle botrytised riesling or muscat-flavoured dessert wine (serve remaining wine with the dessert)
6 white peaches or nectarines
castor sugar
cream
1 tablespoon soft floral-scented honey

Cut the panettone into 12 wedges. Lay them on an oven tray and drizzle with $\frac{1}{2}$ cup of wine.

Skin the fruit if necessary and slice into wedges, working your way around the stone. Put the fruit in a bowl and splash on 2–3 tablespoons of wine.

Dust the panettone slices generously with castor sugar on both sides. Toast under a preheated grill until the sugar is starting to caramelise.

Meanwhile, whip the cream with the honey until it is just holding shape.

Serve the panettone slices on individual plates with dollops of the cream and some of the fruit alongside.

sugared fruits GLAZED BERRIES

SERVES 4

1 punnet berries (approximately 2 cups), hulled (choose from strawberries, blackberries, raspberries, blueberries, or a combination)
1–2 tablespoons castor sugar
1 tablespoon lemon juice

Hull the strawberries. If they are large, cut them into slices or quarters. Put them and any other berries in a bowl with the castor sugar and lemon juice, stir well and leave to macerate for 2–3 hours, covered and refrigerated.

blushing apricots LATE SUMMER FRUIT SALAD

SERVES 6

grated zest and juice of 1 lemon
juice of 1 orange
1 punnet strawberries (approximately 2 cups), hulled and sliced
500g plump, just-ripe apricots
fresh mint leaves

Put the lemon zest and citrus juices in a bowl. Add the sliced strawberries. Slice the apricots into smallish wedges and add to the strawberries. Toss well, ensuring all the fruit is covered with juice. Cover and chill for 2–3 hours. The fruit can be prepared several hours ahead if required.

Tear the mint leaves into small pieces and scatter over the fruit. Serve the fruit salad on its own, or with a slice of sponge or brioche, or with a scoop of vanilla ice cream.

wafts of caramel LATTICE-TOPPED RICE PUDDINGS

SERVES 6

30g (approximately 4) dried apricots
¾ cup Italian rice – arborio, vialone nano, carnaroli
500ml (2 cups) milk
½ cup castor sugar
¼ teaspoon ground cinnamon
grated zest of 1 lemon
75g unsalted butter, plus extra for greasing the moulds
3 egg yolks
icing sugar for dusting

Soak the apricots for several hours (or until tender) in enough hot water to cover them. Drain, then chop roughly.

Bring 1 litre of water to the boil, tip in the rice and cook at a gentle boil for 5 minutes. Drain. Rinse the pan and put in the milk and castor sugar. Stir until the sugar dissolves, then return the rice to the pan and add the cinnamon and lemon zest. Cook over a low heat for 15 minutes, stirring often, especially towards the end of cooking (the rice mixture should be creamy, not dry or liquid). Stir in the butter, then mix in the apricots and egg yolks.

Spoon into 6 buttered moulds or ramekins. Sit them inside a shallow baking dish (for easy movement) and bake in an oven preheated to 170°C for 30 minutes or until they are lightly golden on top. Allow the puddings to cool, then unmould them. Sieve a little icing sugar over the top.

Heat a metal skewer over a gas flame or an electric element until it is very hot (be sure to wear an oven glove) then, using the hot end, mark out a lattice pattern on the top of the puddings; reheat the skewer as necessary.

The puddings are best eaten at room temperature, but they can be cooled, refrigerated and served the day after they are made.

refreshing taste MACEDONIA

SERVES 6

grated zest of 1 lemon
3 tablespoons lemon juice
300ml freshly squeezed orange juice
2 tablespoons castor sugar
¼ cup Amaretto liqueur (optional)
2 bananas
1.5kg assorted fruit (e.g. strawberries, cherries, plums, grapes, pineapple, peaches, nectarines)
½ honeydew melon

Put the lemon zest and citrus juices in a bowl. Add the castor sugar and stir until it is dissolved, then add the Amaretto liqueur, if using.

Prepare the fruit by washing, peeling, hulling and deseeding as necessary. Slice it into attractive rounds, cubes or slivers. You can use a melon-baller to shape the melon into balls.

Add each fruit to the bowl as it is prepared, dunking it in the syrup to prevent it browning. Cover the bowl with a plate and refrigerate for at least 3 hours. Mix well before serving.

IF HONEYDEW MELON is not available, don't substitute rock melon because it will overpower the other fruits.

If Amaretto liqueur (an almond-flavoured liqueur from Italy) is not on hand, substitute Cointreau, or a fruity liqueur of your choice.

Lattice-topped rice puddings

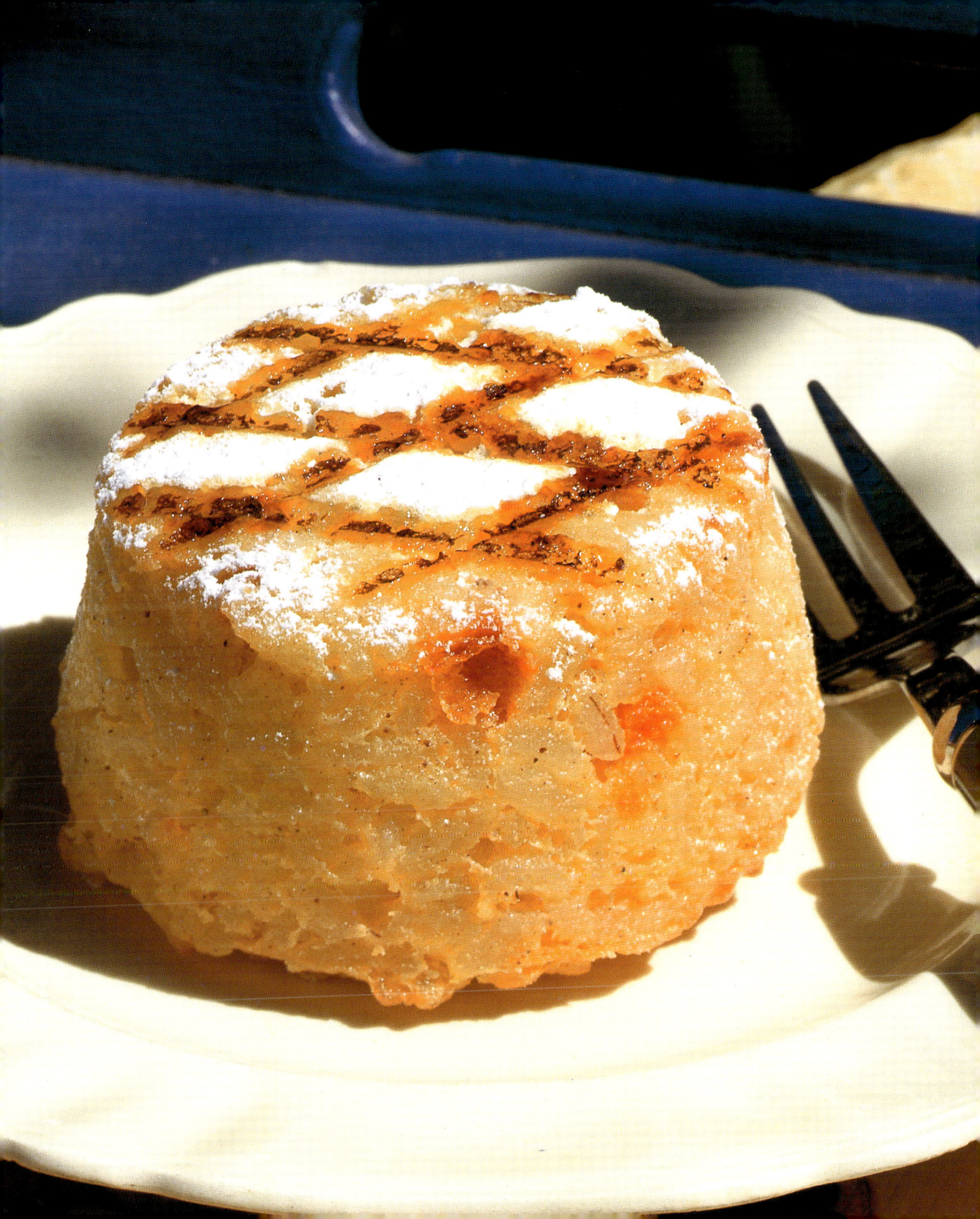

la luna miele HONEYMOON CAKE

SERVES AT LEAST 8

melted butter, castor sugar and plain flour to prepare the tin
100g butter
1 lemon
3 medium, tart cooking apples
4 eggs
½ cup castor sugar
1 cup flour
pinch of salt
1 level teaspoon baking powder
icing sugar for dusting

Prepare the tin first according to the instructions opposite.

Melt the butter gently, then set aside to cool. Grate the zest from the lemon and set aside. Peel and core the apples, then slice them thinly. Put the apples in a large bowl and squeeze the juice of the lemon over. Toss well.

Break the eggs into the bowl of a large food mixer (or food processor). Beat with the whisk until they are blended, then pour the castor sugar in slowly. Continue beating until the mixture leaves a thick trail off the up-held beaters (this may take up to 5 minutes). Sprinkle the lemon zest over and transfer to a large bowl.

Sift the flour, salt and baking powder together onto a piece of paper, then sift half of it over the egg mixture. Fold in lightly with a large spoon. Pour the cooled melted butter around the sides of the bowl, then fold in until it is only just amalgamated. Sieve the rest of the dry ingredients over and fold in. Drain off any juice from the sliced apples, then very carefully fold the apples into the sponge mixture.

Transfer the mixture to the prepared tin. Smooth the surface lightly with a knife and place in an oven preheated to 180°C. Bake for about 40 minutes or until the cake is firm but springy to the touch, a rich golden colour and is pulling away slightly from the sides of the tin. Remove from the oven and rest it for 10 minutes. Invert onto a cooling rack and leave the cake to cool completely. Sift icing sugar over before slicing the cake into wedges.

HONEYMOON CAKE TIN PREPARATION

Choose a 23cm diameter cake tin. Cut a disk of non-stick baking paper for the base and a strip to go around the sides. Fold the long edge of the strip over by 5cm, then nick the edges of the paper with scissors. Brush one side of the paper with melted butter, then sprinkle it generously with castor sugar. Tap off the excess. Dust with flour, then tap off the excess. Put the strip of paper, sugared side facing inwards, around the sides of the tin, making sure the folded edge sits flat, then fit the circle of paper in the centre (this should sit on top of the folded over 'nicked' edge of the strip of paper, holding everything in place).

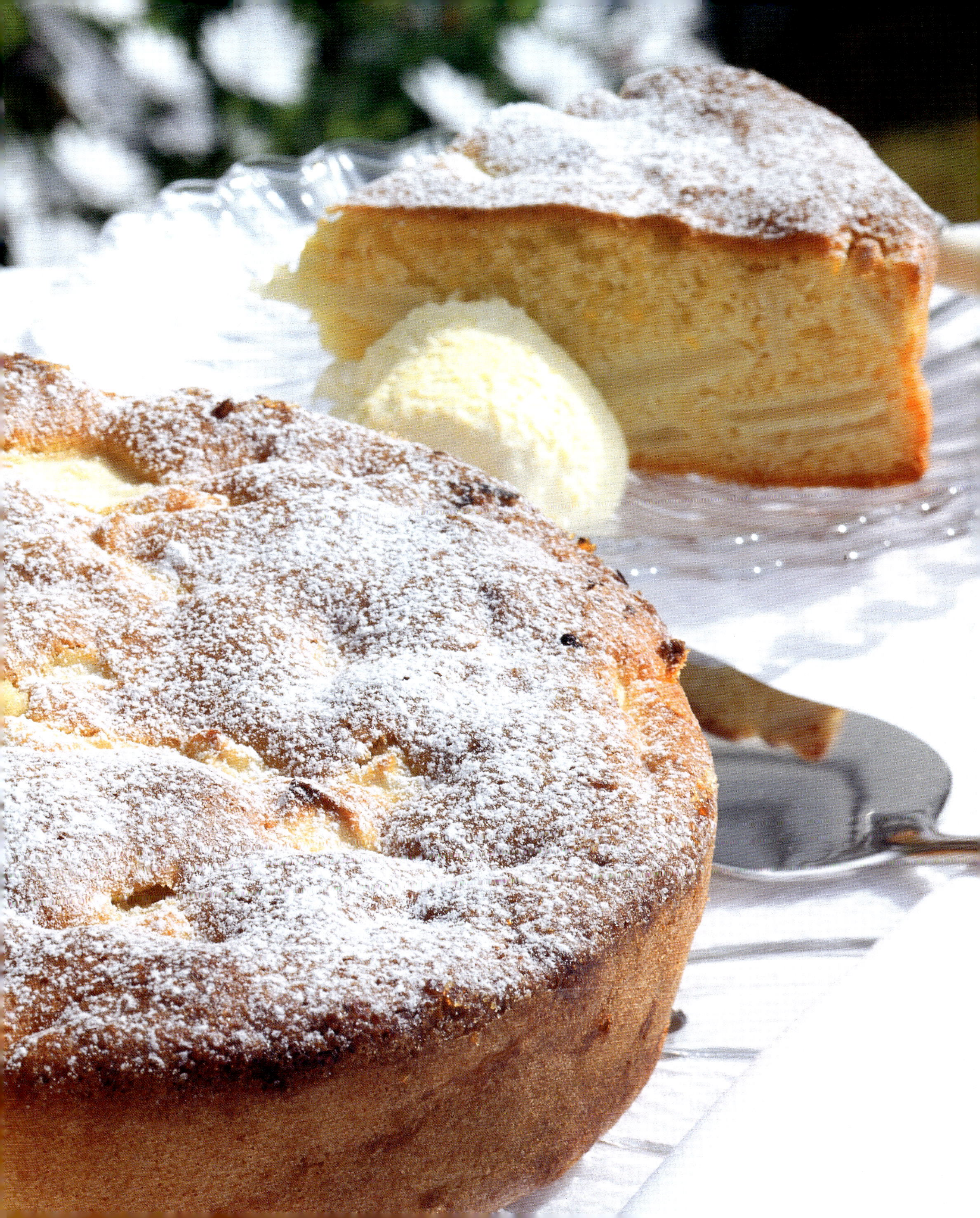

sweet and raisiny CRUMBLY ALMOND CAKE

SERVES AT LEAST 8

125g (¾ cup) unblanched almonds
1 cup plain flour
½ cup granulated sugar
½ cup finely ground corn meal
grated zest of 1 lemon
120g butter, softened
2 egg yolks, at room temperature
icing sugar for dusting
Vin Santo for serving

Put the almonds in a small saucepan, cover with water, bring to the boil, then cool and flick off the skins. Transfer the almonds to a shallow ovenproof dish and toast them in an oven preheated to 180°C until they are a pale brown colour. Cool, then chop in a food processor. Stop the machine and tip in the flour, granulated sugar and corn meal. Blend, then sprinkle the lemon zest on and drop in the butter and egg yolks. Process until it is well mixed and crumbly.

Butter a shallow 23cm round ovenproof dish (or sandwich tin) and line with a disk of baking paper, then press the mixture into the tin. Dust with icing sugar and bake in an oven preheated to 180°C for 35–40 minutes. If the cake starts to brown too quickly, lower the heat.

Mark into small portions while still warm. When cool, store in an airtight container. At serving time, splash with a little Vin Santo or serve the Vin Santo separately, in small glasses.

WHEN I SERVED this cake to the Marchese de Frescobaldi (head of the Frescobaldi Wine Estate in Tuscany) he said it was as good as any he had eaten in Tuscany. Try it with a drop of Frescobaldi's Vin Santo.

If you don't have a food processor, chop or grind the almonds finely, then mix everything together in a large bowl using a strong fork, adding the ingredients in the same order as above.

VIN SANTO

This sweet, or semi-dry wine, is made from grapes left to dry until they turn raisiny. The wine is then transferred to small barrels and left to age for at least 2 years. It is often served with hard biscuits, called cantucci, which are dipped into the Vin Santo to soften them.

exotic fragrance BAKED PEACHES WITH RUM

SERVES 6

6 ripe but firm peaches
butter
175ml dark rum
½ cup brown sugar

Cut the peaches in half through their natural indentations, twist, then pull apart and extract the stones. Smear a little butter over the bottom and sides of a shallow ovenproof dish and put in the peaches, cut side up. Spoon a little rum over the cut surfaces, then spoon the rest into the cavities. Sprinkle the brown sugar over and dot each peach half with a little butter.

Bake the peaches in an oven preheated to 180°C for 30 minutes or until they are very tender when pierced with a skewer, basting twice during cooking.

Cool the peaches, basting them twice more. Serve warm or at room temperature, with ice cream or cream. Do not refrigerate the peaches because they will become soggy.

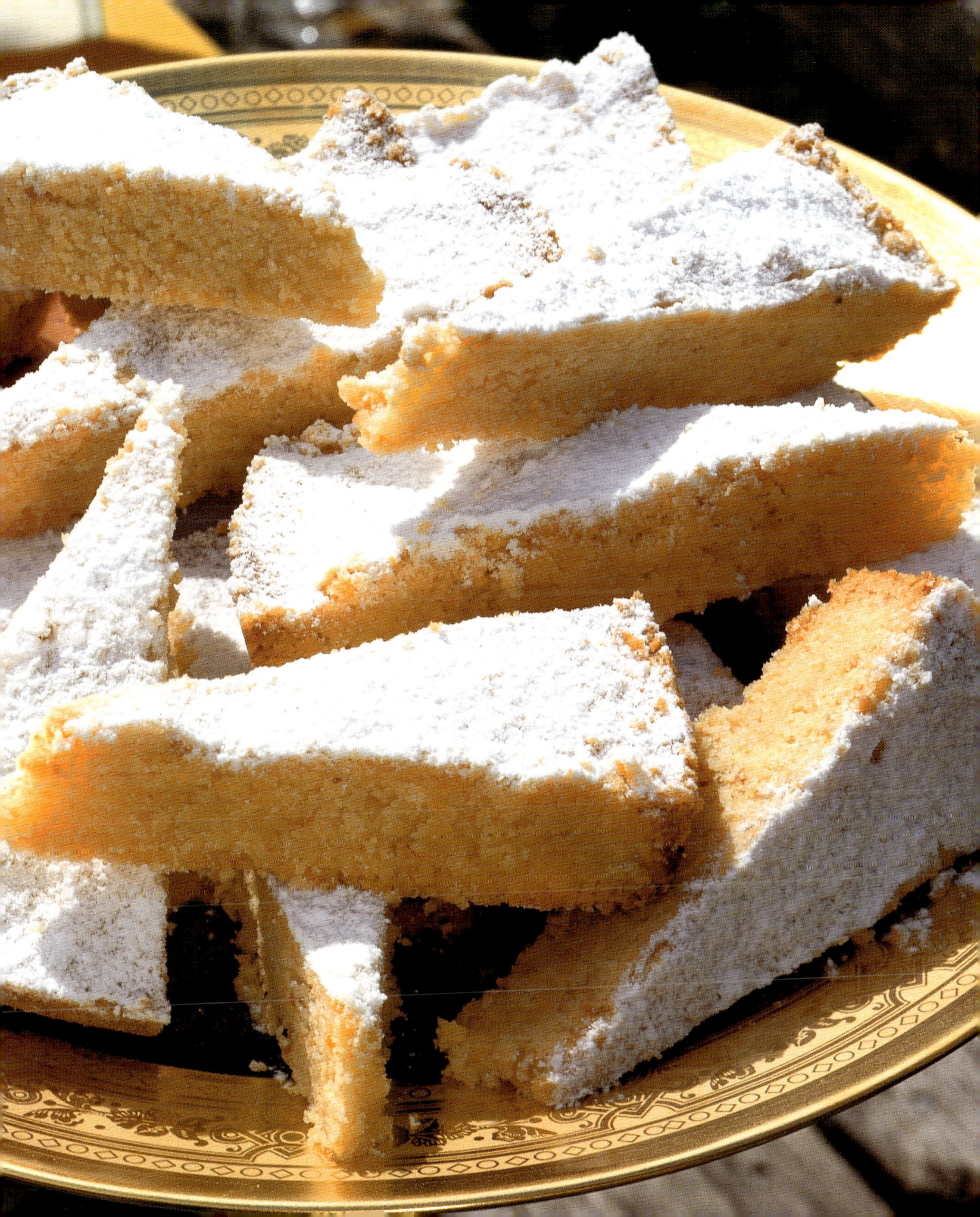

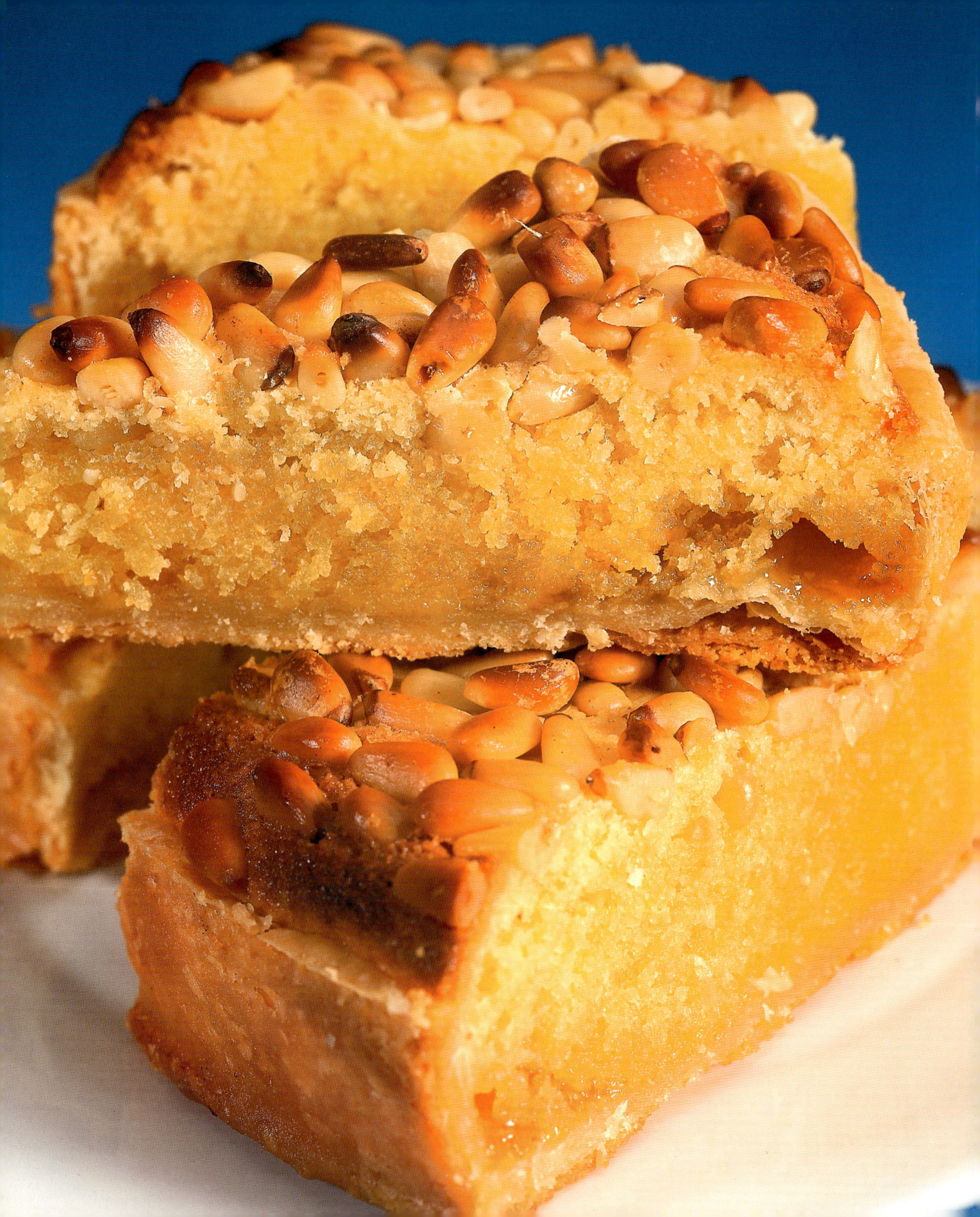

nut-studded PINOLATA

SERVES 8–10

1 quantity rich shortcrust pastry (see opposite)
125g butter, softened
3/4 cup castor sugar
3 tablespoons plain flour
2 eggs plus 2 egg yolks, lightly beaten together
1 3/4 cups ground almonds
1 cup pine nuts
6 tablespoons apricot jam or apricot conserve
cream for serving

Make the pastry and line a 25cm flan ring with it. (There will be some left over – see the note on Rich Shortcrust Pastry opposite.) Chill for 30 minutes, then bake 'blind' for 10 minutes (see page 136).

Put the butter in a warmed bowl and beat with an electric mixer until it is light and creamy. Beat in the castor sugar by degrees and continue beating until the mixture is well creamed. Sprinkle the flour over, then, with the machine running, beat in the eggs and egg yolks by degrees. (This can be done in a food processor.) Fold in the almonds and 1/3 cup of the pine nuts.

Spread the apricot jam or conserve over the pastry case, then put in the almond filling. Smooth the surface with a knife and sprinkle the rest of the pine nuts over the top.

Bake for about 40 minutes in an oven preheated to 180°C or until the pastry is browned and crisp on the base (drape a piece of aluminium foil over the top of the pie to deflect top heat once the pastry has coloured). Cool for 5 minutes, then remove the flan ring and transfer the tart to a cooling rack. Serve at room temperature with cream.

RICH SHORTCRUST PASTRY

225g plain flour
pinch of salt
170g butter, softened until pliable
1 egg yolk
4–5 tablespoons ice-cold water (chill the water in the freezer)

Sift the flour and salt into a large mixing bowl. Cut the butter into large lumps and drop it into the flour. Using 2 knives, cut the butter through the flour until the pieces of butter are like small marbles. Use your fingertips to rub the butter into the flour until the mixture resembles coarse breadcrumbs.

Mix the egg yolk and 3 tablespoons of water together and add it all at once to the flour mixture; if the pastry seems a little dry and flaky during mixing, sprinkle the extra tablespoon of water, or part of it, on the dry flakes. Stir with a knife to combine. Lightly knead with your hands and turn out onto a cool, dry, lightly floured surface. Knead briefly until it is smooth. Wrap in plastic food wrap and refrigerate for 30 minutes.

Roll out thinly with a lightly floured rolling pin and line into a flan ring. Cut off excess pastry, fold it up and re-roll. Cut out small tartlet bases or line into a small dish and freeze for later use.

PASTRY MADE IN THE FOOD PROCESSOR

Put the flour, salt and cubed butter in the bowl of a food processor fitted with the metal chopping blade. Process until the mixture resemble breadcrumbs. Mix the egg yolk and water and pour it over the flour and butter mixture. Pulse until the mixture forms clumps. Turn it out onto a dry work surface and knead lightly, with a little flour if necessary, until it is smooth. Wrap in plastic food wrap and chill for 45 minutes.

CRISP PASTRY

A flan ring placed on a baking tray produces a crisper base to the pastry, as any moisture can freely run out from underneath the flan ring and evaporate. In a flan dish the moisture is trapped and can cause the pastry to become soggy.

RICH SHORTCRUST PASTRY

This is a useful pastry, which has an initially crisp, then melt-in-the-mouth texture and buttery taste. If you take the time to make it, you'll find it's superior in every way to commercially made pastry.

A 20cm flan ring or dish requires rich shortcrust pastry made with 170g plain flour, but I always make a standard 225g batch of pastry (the old 8oz quantity), because the ingredients are easier to work with (ever tried splitting an egg?). Any leftover pastry can be used to line a smaller flan, tartlet tins or a small pie dish. It is no more difficult to make a double batch of pastry (450g plain flour). This makes enough pastry to line 3 x 20cm flan rings.

If you want to freeze the pastry, it is more convenient to do this after lining the flan ring or tins. Once frozen, the pastry shape/s can be slipped out of the rings or tins (freeing them for other uses) and stored in a sealed plastic freezer bag for 6 months. This allows you to collect tartlet bases until you have enough for a recipe and, if you have made a double batch of pastry, you will have extra flan bases on hand when you want to put a quick meal together. Thaw the pastry cases for 5 minutes at room temperature, then slip them back into their rings or tins. Cook once thawed, but while the pastry is still well chilled.

BAKING BLIND

To bake blind, the pastry is first lined with paper, then filled with baking beans and baked. Paper is used to make the removal of the beans easier and to prevent the beans becoming embedded in the pastry. I use tissue paper rather than greaseproof paper – greaseproof paper becomes dry and brittle and the sharp creases in the paper can cut the pastry when you remove it from the flan. Tissue paper, if well crinkled, moulds easily into any shape, is soft after baking and can be lifted out without disturbing the pastry. Baking beans are used to support the pastry until it is cooked or set in position. (Don't waste money on expensive metal pellets, as you can use inexpensive ingredients such as small pasta shapes, rice or dried beans, but replace them periodically).

PARTIALLY BAKING BLIND

This produces crisper pastry (particularly useful when the filling is very moist or if your oven does not have good bottom heat – the most common cause of soggy pastry). This method is also used when the filling is quick-cooking (in other words, it would cook before the pastry).

FULLY BAKING BLIND

This method is used when the pastry case is to be filled with a cooked filling or a combination of a cooked filling and raw ingredients (such as custard and fresh fruit).

For recipes in this book, bake pastry blind for 10–15 minutes in an oven preheated to 180°C or until the pastry rim is set in position.

soft to bite CURD CAKE WITH GLAZED BERRIES

SERVES 6

70g butter, softened
150g (scant ¾ cup) castor sugar
300g ricotta cheese
2 eggs, at room temperature
2 tablespoons semolina
60g (generous ⅓ cup) raisins
70g (approximately ¾ cup) ground almonds
finely grated zest of 2 lemons
strained juice of 1 lemon
icing sugar and strawberries to garnish
200ml cream for serving

Whip the butter in the food processor until it is smooth, then, with the machine running, pour in the castor sugar. Process until it is well blended, then add the ricotta cheese. Process until it is smooth. Separate the eggs and put the whites in a grease-free bowl. With the machine running, drop in the egg yolks one at a time. Transfer the curd mixture to a bowl and mix in the semolina, raisins, ground almonds, lemon zest and juice.

Whisk the egg whites until they are stiff but not dry, then fold them carefully into the curd mixture using a large spoon.

Turn the mixture into an 18–20cm diameter sandwich tin lined with a disk of baking paper. Smooth the top and bake in an oven preheated to 170°C for 35–40 minutes, or until it is lightly browned and firmish. Cool for 10 minutes in the tin, then turn out onto a cake rack and leave to cool. (The cake can be baked several hours before required.)

Transfer the cake to a serving plate, dust with icing sugar and garnish with a few strawberries. Whip the cream lightly, transfer to a serving bowl and serve with the curd cake and Glazed Berries (see page 127).

QUICKLY MADE in a food processor (or use a hand-held electric beater), this curd cake has a nutty taste and slightly crumbly texture. Served with glazed berries, it is very moreish.

DECORATING THE CURD CAKE

Put the curd cake on a serving plate and lay several thin strips of paper over the surface, forming a striped pattern. Sift icing sugar over and remove the paper strips carefully, trying not to dislodge the icing sugar on top (try not to sneeze!).

Put whipped cream into a piping bag fitted with a 'rose' nozzle and pipe a ruffle of rosettes around the border on the top of the cake.

STORING EGG WHITES

Store leftover egg whites for meringue-making or other desserts. Store them in a scrupulously clean plastic container, cover with a lid and refrigerate. They will keep for up to 6 weeks (they can also be frozen for several months).

creamy crunch HAZELNUT AND AMARETTI CUPOLA

SERVES 6–8

300ml cream
½ vanilla pod
¼ cup icing sugar
4 eggs
10 amaretti biscuits, partially crushed (approximately 1 cup crushed biscuits)
100g (¾ cup) hazelnuts, toasted (see opposite), skinned and coarsely chopped
6 large ripe peaches
lemon juice
2 tablespoons castor sugar
50ml dessert wine
1 punnet strawberries (approximately 2 cups), hulled, sliced if large

Choose a bowl with a 1.25–1.5 litre capacity (5–6 cups) and line it with aluminium foil. Put the cream in another bowl, split the vanilla pod open lengthwise and scrape the seeds into the cream. Whip with an electric or rotary beater. As the cream starts to thicken, add the icing sugar, and beat until it is stiff.

Separate the eggs, placing the yolks in the bowl with the cream, and the egg whites in a grease-free bowl. Blend the egg yolks through the cream with the amaretti biscuits and ½ cup of toasted hazelnuts. Whisk the egg whites until they are stiff, then carefully fold them through the cream mixture with a large spoon. Spoon into the prepared foil-lined bowl and freeze. Once frozen, cover the top of the bowl with aluminium foil to avoid contamination and unwanted odours (don't cover it before it's frozen as the foil will stick to the ice cream). The dessert can be stored frozen for several days.

Plunge the peaches for 20 seconds into a saucepan of boiling water sharpened with a tablespoon of lemon juice. Lift out and plunge into a bowl of cold water. Peel and cut into halves or slices. Put the castor sugar and wine in a bowl and stir until the sugar dissolves. Add the strawberries and peaches to the bowl (best done no longer than 1 hour before serving).

Turn the frozen 'cupola' onto a large plate and peel off the aluminium foil. Spoon the fruit around the sides and drizzle the top and sides with the juices. Scatter the remaining hazelnuts over the top and serve immediately.

HOMEMADE ice cream always brings praise but, when it is chock-full of hazelnuts and crushed amaretti biscuits and served with peaches and strawberries in a sweet honeyed wine, don't be surprised if you catch your guests licking their plates!

TOASTING HAZELNUTS

Put the hazelnuts in a shallow ovenproof dish and toast in an oven preheated to 180°C for about 10 minutes or until a golden colour is visible through the burst skins. Rub vigorously in a clean cloth to remove skins.

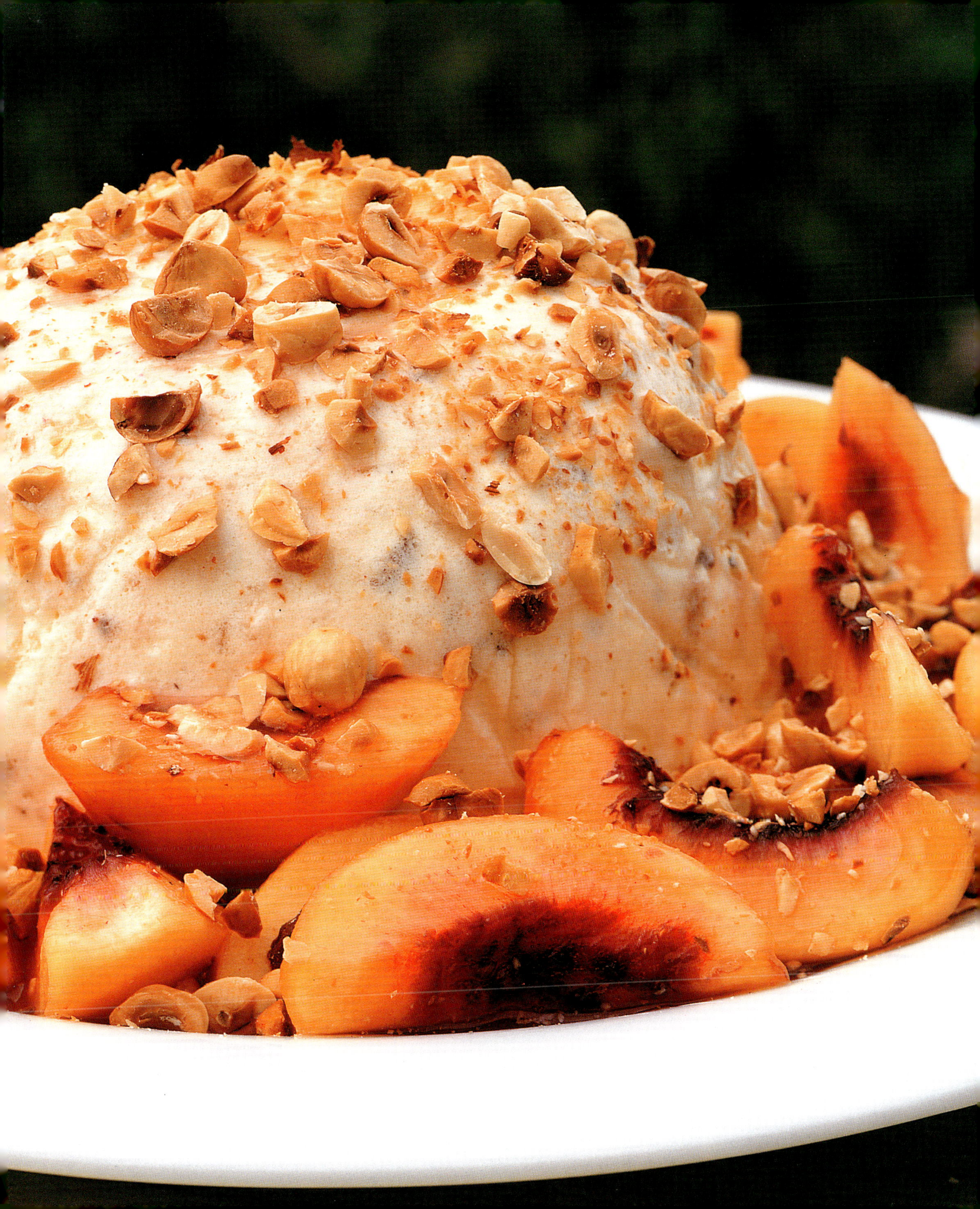

weights and measures

In New Zealand, South Africa, the USA and in England 1 tablespoon equals 15ml. In Australia, 1 tablespoon equals 20ml.

These variations will not adversely affect the end result, as long as the same spoon is used consistently, so the proportions are correct.

Grams to Ounces and vice versa

General

30g	=	1oz
60g	=	2oz
90g	=	3oz
120g	=	4oz
150g	=	5oz
180g	=	6oz
210g	=	7oz
230g	=	8oz
260g	=	9oz
290g	=	10oz
320g	=	11oz
350g	=	12oz
380g	=	13oz
410g	=	14oz
440g	=	15oz
470g	=	16oz

Exact

1oz	=	28.35g
2oz	=	56.70g
3oz	=	85.05g
4oz	=	113.04g
5oz	=	141.08g
6oz	=	170.01g
7oz	=	198.04g
8oz	=	226.08g
9oz	=	255.01g
10oz	=	283.05g
11oz	=	311.08g
12oz	=	340.02g
13oz	=	368.05g
14oz	=	396.09g
15oz	=	425.02g
16oz	=	453.06g

Recipes based on these (International Units) rounded values

Liquid Measurements

25ml (28.4ml)	=	1fl oz		
150ml (142ml)	=	5fl oz	=	$1/4$ pint = 1 gill
275ml (284ml)	=	10fl oz	=	$1/2$ pint
425ml (426ml)	=	15fl oz	=	$3/4$ pint
575ml (568ml)	=	20fl oz	=	1 pint

Spoon Measures

$1/4$ teaspoon	=	1.25ml
$1/2$ teaspoon	=	2.5ml
1 teaspoon	=	5ml
1 tablespoon	=	15ml

In NZ, SA, USA and UK 1 tablespoon = 15ml

In Australia 1 tablespoon = 20ml

1 tablespoon butter equals about 10g

Measurements
cm to approx inches

0.5cm	=	$1/4$"	5cm	=	2"
1.25cm	=	$1/2$"	7.5cm	=	3"
2.5cm	=	1"	10cm	=	4"

Cake Tin Sizes
cm to approx inches

15cm	=	6"	23cm	=	9"
18cm	=	7"	25cm	=	10"
20cm	=	8"			

Alternative names

cake tin	cake/baking pan
capsicum/pepper	sweet bell pepper
coriander	cilantro
cornflour	cornstarch
eggplant	aubergine
essence	extract
frying pan	skillet
grill	broil
hard-boiled egg	hard-cooked egg
icing sugar	confectioner's sugar
king prawns	jumbo shrimps/scampi
kumara	sweet potato
minced meat	ground meat
pawpaw	papaya
radicchio	chicory
rock melon	cantaloupe
seed	pip
silverbeet	Swiss chard
spring onion	scallion/green onion
zucchini	courgette

Oven Temperatures

Celsius	Fahrenheit	Gas	
110ºC	225ºF	1/4	very cool
120ºC	250ºF	1/2	
140ºC	275ºF	1	cool
150ºC	300ºF	2	
170ºC	325ºF	3	moderate
180ºC	350ºF	4	
190ºC	375ºF	5	moderately hot
200ºC	400ºF	6	
220ºC	425ºF	7	hot
230ºC	450ºF	8	
240ºC	475ºF	9	very hot

Abbreviations

g	gram
kg	kilogram
mm	millimetre
cm	centimetre
ml	millilitre
ºC	degrees Celsius
ºF	degrees Fahrenheit

American–Imperial

in	inch
lb	pound
oz	ounce

index

A
almond cake, crumbly 132
amaretti cupola, hazelnut 138
amaretti, peaches stuffed with 122
apricots, in fruit salad 127
Artichoke and Ham Pie 31
asparagus, fried 12
aubergine – *see* eggplant

B
Baby Peas with Sautéed Prosciutto 114
Baby Potatoes on Rosemary Stalks 112
Baked Peaches with Rum 132
Baked Rigatoni with Ricotta 69
Balsamic Dressing 114
Barbecued Eggplant with Balsamic
    Dressing 114
Basic Ferron No-stir Risotto 41
Basic Polenta 42
Basic Risotto 35
basil dressing with steamed mussels 20
beans
    Borlotti and Tuna Salad 17
    Butter Beans and Potatoes 104
    Tuscan Pork and Beans 90
    White Beans Stewed with Rosemary
        and Garlic 105
beef
    Roasted Eye Fillet Wrapped in Bacon 92
    Selvapiana Beef in Chianti 92
berries, glazed 127
bird's eye chillies information 60
Borlotti and Tuna Salad 17
breadcrumbs, dried white 74
Brodetto 18
Butter Beans and Potatoes 104
button mushrooms with conchiglie 62

C
cakes
    Crumbly Almond Cake 132
    Curd Cake with Glazed Berries 137
    Honeymoon Cake 130
caper dressing 116

capsicums – *see* peppers
carrots, glazed 105
Carrots with Gremolada 106
cashew nut and garlic sauce with linguine 61
cauliflower sauce with maccheroni 68
cauliflower, 'suffocated' 109
cheese pie 30
Chick Peas and Tomato 110
chicken
    Chicken Breasts with Browned Butter 82
    Chicken with Lemon and Cream 80
    Spring Chicken 78
    Stuffed Chicken Drumsticks 77
chillies, bird's eye, information 60
Chocolate Sauce 125
Conchiglie with Button Mushrooms 62
courgettes – *see* zucchini
Crab and Lemon Pasta 50
Crêpe Batter 125, 126
crêpes, fruity with chocolate sauce 125
Crispy Veal with Parmesan and Black Olives 88
Crumbly Almond Cake 132
Crunchy Potato Sticks 103
crunchy potatoes 98
Curd Cake with Glazed Berries 137

D
Dried White Breadcrumbs 74

E
Easter Pie 26
eggplant
    Barbecued Eggplant with Balsamic
        Dressing 114
    eggplant and zucchini on pasta 58
    eggplant information 36, 114
    Eggplant Pie 28
    Fusilli with Eggplant and Green Pepper 57
    Oven-baked Eggplant Risotto 36
egg white information 137
eggs fried in chilli oil with ziti 54

F
fennel
    Fennel, Sweet Tomato and Olive Salad 110
    Roasted Fennel 114
    Spring Risotto with Roasted Fennel
        and Scallops 40
Ferron no-stir risotto 41
fettucine
    Fettuccine alla Carbonara 70
    Fettuccine with Gorgonzola Sauce 50
    Fettuccine with Roman-style Meat Sauce 70
    Fettuccine with Zucchini 64
fish
    Borlotti and Tuna Salad 17
    Crab and Lemon Pasta 50
    Fish Rolls with Pine Nuts 77
    fish soup, brodetto 18
    Fish Stock 18
    Spaghettini with Fresh Tomato Sauce, Chilli
        and Saffron Prawns 62
    Spring Risotto with Roasted Fennel
        and Scallops 40
    Steamed Mussels with Basil Dressing 20
    Venetian Fish 74
flan, lemon ricotta 120
Focaccia 34
fresh tomato sauce for pasta 62
Fried Asparagus 12
frittata information 32
frittata, spinach 32
fruit salad, late summer 127
Fruity Crêpes with Chocolate Sauce 125
Fusilli with Eggplant and Green Pepper 57
Fusilli with Tomato and Rosemary Sauce 53

G
Glazed Berries 127
Glazed Carrots 105
gorgonzola sauce with fettucine 50
Gremolada 94, 106
Grilled Panettone with Peaches
    or Nectarines 126
Grilled Parmesan Polenta with Olives, Pine
    Nuts and Rosemary 44

H

ham and artichoke pie 31
Hazelnut and Amaretti Cupola 138
Honeymoon Cake 130
hot buttered noodles 80

I

Isanna's Scaloppine 90
Italian sausage and mushroom ragù
    with lasagnette 67

L

lamb
    Lamb Abruzzi 95
    Leg of Lamb with Parmesan Crust and
        Crunchy Potatoes 98
Lasagnette with Italian Sausage and
    Mushroom Ragù 67
Late Summer Fruit Salad 127
Lattice-topped Rice Puddings 128
Lemon Ricotta Flan 120
Linguine with Cashew Nut and Garlic Sauce 61
Linguine with Zucchini and Marjoram 61

M

Maccheroni with Cauliflower Sauce 68
Macedonia 128
Mascarpone Fruit Nests 122
Milanese risotto 41
Minestra 12
Minestrone 15
Mozzarella and Roasted Red Pepper Salad 22
mushrooms
    Conchiglie with Button Mushrooms 62
    Lasagnette with Italian Sausage and
        Mushroom Ragù 67
    Mushroom Soup 16
    Oven-baked Mushroom Risotto 39
    Polenta and Mushroom Pie 42
    porcini mushroom preparation 16
    Sausage Coil with Hot Polenta and
        Sautéed Mushrooms 96
mussels information 20
mussels, steamed with basil dressing 20

N

No-stir risotto 41

O

Ossobuco 94
oven-baked eggplant 36
Oven-baked Eggplant Risotto 36
Oven-baked Mushroom Risotto 39

P

panettone, grilled with peaches
    or nectarines 126
Parmigiano Wafers 10
Parmigiano with Rocket Leaves 10
pasta
    Baked Rigatoni with Ricotta 69
    Conchiglie with Button Mushrooms 62
    Crab and Lemon Pasta 50
    Fettuccine alla Carbonara 70
    Fettuccine with Gorgonzola Sauce 50
    Fettuccine with Roman-style Meat Sauce 70
    Fettuccine with Zucchini 64
    Fusilli with Eggplant and Green Pepper 57
    Fusilli with Tomato and Rosemary Sauce 53
    Lasagnette with Italian Sausage and
        Mushroom Ragù 67
    Linguine with Cashew Nut and
        Garlic Sauce 61
    Linguine with Zucchini and Marjoram 61
    Maccheroni with Cauliflower Sauce 68
    noodles, hot buttered 80
    pasta information 50, 67, 68, 69
    pasta salads information 67
    Penne with Quick Chillied Tomato Sauce
        and Fried Zucchini 60
    Rigatoni with Tomato Sauce 58
    Spaghetti Puttanesca 54
    Spaghetti Saltati 53
    Spaghetti with Garlic and Oil 69
    Spaghettini with Fresh Tomato Sauce, Chilli
        and Saffron Prawns 62
    Summer Pasta Salad 67
    Tagliatelle with Pesto 56
    Tagliatelle with Prosciutto 68
    Ziti with Eggs Fried in Chilli Oil 54
pastry information 135, 136
pastry, rich shortcrust 135
peaches baked with rum 132
Peaches Stuffed with Amaretti 122
peas wiht sautéed prosciutto 114
pecorino information 56
Penne with Quick Chillied Tomato Sauce and
    Fried Zucchini 60
Peperonata 103

peppers
    Fusilli with Eggplant and Green Pepper 57
    Mozzarella and Roasted Red Pepper Salad 22
    Peperonata 103
    roasting peppers 22
pesto 56
pesto tips 56
pies
    Artichoke and Ham Pie 31
    Easter Pie 26
    Eggplant Pie 28
    Polenta and Mushroom Pie 42
    Polenta Pie with Puttanesca Sauce 43
    Potato Pie 28
    Scacciata 47
    Spinach Torte 32
    Three Cheese Pie 30
Pinolata 135
polenta
    Basic Polenta 42
    Grilled Parmesan Polenta with Olives, Pine
        Nuts and Rosemary 44
    Polenta and Mushroom Pie 42
    polenta information 42, 43
    Polenta Pie with Puttanesca Sauce 43
    Sausage Coil with Hot Polenta and Sautéed
        Mushrooms 96
porcini mushroom preparation 16
pork
    pork crackling information 91
    Roast Pork with Fennel Seeds 91
    Tuscan Pork and Beans 90
potatoes
    Baby Potatoes on Rosemary Stalks 112
    Butter Beans and Potatoes 104
    Crunchy Potato Sticks 103
    Crunchy Potatoes 98
    Potato Pie 28
    Potatoes with Rosemary 106
    Roasted Potato Sticks with White Wine 104
prawns, saffron with spaghettini and fresh
    tomato sauce 62
prosciutto, sautéed with baby peas 114
prosciutto with tagliatelle 68
Puttanesca Sauce 54

Q

Quail Roasted with Vincotto 83
quick chillied tomato sauce 60
Quick Tomato Sauce 30

R

ragù, sausage and mushroom
    with lasagnette 67
Red leaves on the Grill 109
rice puddings, lattice-topped 128
Rich Shortcrust Pastry 135
ricotta cream with strawberries 120
ricotta, lemon flan 120
rigatoni baked with ricotta 69
Rigatoni with Tomato Sauce 58
risotto
    Basic Ferron No-stir Risotto 41
    Basic Risotto 35
    Oven-baked Eggplant Risotto 36
    Oven-baked Mushroom Risotto 39
    risotto information 35, 36
    Risotto Milanese 41
    Spring Risotto with Roasted Fennel
        and Scallops 40
Roast Pork with Fennel Seeds 91
Roasted Eye Fillet Wrapped in Bacon 92
Roasted Fennel 114
Roasted Potato Sticks with White Wine 104
roasting peppers 22
rocket leaves with parmigiano 10
Roman-style meat sauce 70

S

saffron prawns with spaghettini and fresh
    tomato sauce 62
salads
    Borlotti and Tuna Salad 17
    Butter Beans and Potatoes 104
    Chick Peas and Tomato 110
    Fennel, Sweet Tomato and Olive Salad 110
    Mozzarella and Roasted Red
        Pepper Salad 22
    Salad of Red Leaves with Caper
        Dressing 116
    Summer Pasta Salad 67
    Zucchini, Basil and Black Olive Salad 116
sauces
    carbonara 70
    cashew nut and garlic sauce 61
    cauliflower sauce 68
    Chocolate Sauce 125
    creamy sauce information 50
    fresh tomato sauce 62
    garlic and oil 69
    gorgonzola sauce 50
    Italian sausage and mushroom ragù 67

meat sauce, Roman-style 70
pesto 56
Puttanesca Sauce 54
quick chillied tomato sauce 60
quick tomato sauce 30
tomato and rosemary sauce 53
tomato sauce 58
sausage and mushroom ragù 67
Sausage Coil with Hot Polenta and
    Sautéed Mushrooms 96
Scacciata 47
scallops with spring risotto and
    roasted fennel 40
scaloppine – *see under* veal
Selvapiana Beef in Chianti 92
soups
    Brodetto 18
    Minestra 12
    Minestrone 15
    Mushroom Soup 16
spaghetti
    Spaghetti Puttanesca 54
    Spaghetti Saltati 53
    Spaghetti with Garlic and Oil 69
Spaghettini with Fresh Tomato Sauce, Chilli
    and Saffron Prawns 62
Spinach Frittata 32
Spinach Torte 32
Spring Chicken 78
Spring Risotto with Roasted Fennel
    and Scallops 40
Steamed Mussels with Basil Dressing 20
Strawberries with Ricotta Cream 120
Stuffed Baby Zucchini 112
Stuffed Chicken Drumsticks 77
'Suffocated' Cauliflower 109
summer fruit salad 127
Summer Pasta Salad 67
sweet tomato, fennel and olive salad 110

T

Tagliatelle with Pesto 56
Tagliatelle with Prosciutto 68
teflon baking sheets 10
Three Cheese Pie 30
tomatoes
    Chick Peas and Tomato 110
    Fennel, Sweet Tomato and Olive Salad 110
    fresh tomato sauce 62
    Fusilli with Tomato and Rosemary Sauce 53
    quick chillied tomato sauce 60

Quick Tomato Sauce 30
    tomato sauce tips 58, 60
Torta Pasqualina 26
torte, spinach 32
tuna and borlotti salad 17
Turkey Tenderloins with Lemon
    and Rosemary 82
Tuscan Pork and Beans 90

V

veal
    Crispy Veal with Parmesan and
        Black Olives 88
    Isanna's Scaloppine 90
    Ossobuco 94
    Scaloppine Colosseo 86
    scaloppine information 86, 88
    Scaloppine with Lemon 86
    Scaloppine with Melting Mozzarella 87
    Veal Fillet with Green Olives and
        Fresh Bay Leaves 85
Venetian Fish 74
vincotto information 83
vincotto with roasted quail 83
Vin Santo 132

W

White Beans Stewed with Rosemary
    and Garlic 105

Z

Ziti with Eggs Fried in Chilli Oil 54
zucchini
    Fettuccine with Zucchini 64
    Linguine with Zucchini and Marjoram 61
    Penne with Quick Chillied Tomato Sauce
        and Fried Zucchini 60
    Stuffed Baby Zucchini 112
    zucchini and eggplant on pasta 58
    Zucchini, Basil and Black Olive Salad 116